My Wild Hockey Life

My Wild Hockey Life

Defection, 1980s with the Maple Leafs and Surviving a Liver Transplant

MIRO
FRYCER

WITH LUBOS BRABEC

Translated by Andrew Oakland

Cover image by Steve Babineau/NHLI via Getty Images
Cover and interior layout by Pavla Vesela

Published by
Lubos Brabec
Pod Haltyrem 1497/7
Praha 4, Czech Republic

First published in 2017 under the title *Můj divoký hokejový život*

ISBN 978-80-270-3855-8

I dedicate this book to my parents, children, and my wife Lenka, who have always stood by me. I dedicate it, too, to my former teammates and coaches, without whom my life in hockey would have been less successful and far less interesting.

M. F.

Contents

1

Overtime

SNOW IS POURING from the sky. By the ton. It's the day after Christmas 1999, and in Merano, as in the whole of South Tyrol, the snowfall is heavy. We're supposed to be playing a league match against HC Varese, but their bus is two hours late. The guys are sitting in the dressing room, waiting.

I'm pacing in the corridor. My cellphone rings, unknown number, and stops almost straightaway. Then it rings again and keeps ringing. This time it's my wife, Andrea. "Why aren't you picking up? They just called me from the hospital to tell me they can't get a hold of you!"

It's the call I've been waiting for for three months, the reason I've always got my cell on me, even during practice on the ice. The call that could save my life.

At last. They've found a donor, as it's so loftily termed. What's actually happened is that a man has just died—six feet tall, blood group B, with a healthy liver. Details that offer my only chance of accepting a new organ.

My heart skips a beat and then starts pounding. I've told myself a hundred times that I'm prepared for this news. But I'm not.

The moment I disconnect, my phone rings again. This time the voice on the line belongs to a doctor at the clinic in Innsbruck. "Take the pills we gave you and we'll need you on the operating table within six hours," he tells me. I first heard these instructions in the fall, after a series of examinations established that I needed a transplant as soon as possible. If I didn't get one, well …

Before anything else, I go to the players, who by now are circling around on the ice. I call over the captain Markus Brunner and

Karel Metelka, the only Czech I have with me here in Italy. My time has come, I tell them. They've known since September what my situation is and what awaits me. Having seen us talking, the others come over to the bench, heads down, somber. "Good luck, coach," they mumble.

It's an emotional moment for us. Just the spring before, we celebrated winning the championship together, and now who knows if we'll ever see each other again? It's not the first time I've been in this place: in 1981, when I left my homeland for Canada, with the heaviest of hearts I said goodbye to grandma, grandpa and friends. The difference between then and now is, this goodbye may be once and for all. I will find out later that the players don't want the game with Varese to go ahead. With their coach fighting for his life, they have no desire to charge about the ice after a puck. But the club president will talk them into playing, telling them they must do it for me. So they do—with the initials *MF* on their helmets.

I live pretty close to the stadium. Back home, I pack a few things and take my pills. Then my wife, my son Mike, the team manager Giulio Pallaver and I get into the car, ready to go.

Everything is white. It's still snowing heavily, and the roads are slippery. Usually, it takes two hours to get from Merano to Innsbruck, but there's so much snow in the Brenner Pass that this trip takes us twice as long. It's quiet in the car. I'm sitting in the back, Mike lying in my lap. He's six years old, and as the rest of us are sad and tearful, surely he knows there's something serious going on.

There's a lot he doesn't know, though. He doesn't know that there's only a 20 percent chance that we'll ever play soccer together again, for that's how likely it is that the operation will be a success. Or so the doctor told me.

Twenty. A terrible number. In hockey, if power play efficiency is 20 percent, you can be pleased with your work. But if your chances of waking up tomorrow, the next day and the day after that is 20 percent, you have good reason to be nervous.

But I'm not moaning about it, either openly or inwardly. Ever since I found out my liver was a goner, I've been resigned to my fate. Either it'll work out or it won't. It's in God's hands. Like everyone who waits for a transplant, I've had compulsory sessions with a psychologist, to prepare me for the possibility of my story ending unhappily. These were unnecessary: comfort is the last thing I need. "You could help me out with my other patients," she told me after 10 minutes. "You're the only one who's taking this in stride."

I don't see my fate as an injustice. Unlike some others, I don't keep asking myself, *Why me?* I'm well aware of the paths I've taken to bring me to this crossroads.

I spent eight seasons as a player in the National Hockey League, and in the 1980s that meant "play hard, party hard." I'm not the first those wild years have left their mark on, and I won't be the last.

I played a lot of matches, in Canada and in Europe, despite what my body was telling me. I swallowed painkillers like candy, while the doctors gave me one shot after another, just to get me out on the ice. This way of treating lingering injuries can't have been good for my liver either.

To make matters worse, I developed a taste for alcohol, which finally got out of hand in Italy, a beautiful country with excellent wine. For a long time, I was unwilling to admit that I had a problem. I went on the wagon 107 days ago. But that was too late. I'm no longer able to save my liver by willpower and a change in lifestyle. I'm well beyond the one-minute-to-midnight scenario.

I lived the life I chose, and when I was 40 I was presented with the bill. I have no one to blame but myself. I've known this from the beginning, and it's all I think about in the car.

We reach Innsbruck at last. The glass door into the Department of Transplant Surgery admits patients only. The toughest moment arrives—saying goodbye to Mike. I put my chain around his neck and fasten my watch around his wrist. "You're the man of the family now," I tell him before giving him a last wave.

Is it truly the last?

In my room, I fill out and sign some forms; then I go for my ECG. After that, I'm given a shave and injected with some kind of tranquillizer. "Seems to me you're calm as it is," says the nurse, smiling. It's true—as soon as I said goodbye to my nearest and dearest, calm washed over me. Absolute inner calm. I feel OK. I'm resigned to whatever will happen to me.

The nurse takes me in the elevator, up to the operating room. As the door opens, I catch sight of the doctors who are going to operate on me. Now it's up to them.

They lay me on the table and put the anesthesia mask on my face. The last thing I remember is light. Huge bright lights on the ceiling.

I black out.

———

Eight hours later, I wake up. Standing over me are a doctor and two of his assistants. I'm still a bit woozy, so at first I don't understand what they are trying to tell me. "The new liver has a leak, so you need to have another operation," they whisper.

This is the end, I tell myself. *This is a bridge too far.*

They work on me again for almost six hours. When I wake up in the ICU, I'm wired up like a Christmas tree, and a cannula has been inserted into one of my veins. I'm surrounded by beeping equipment. Doctors are watching me from their coop, checking that I'm alive.

Yes, I really am alive. I've been reborn.

Even the consultant calls it a miracle. "You're lucky that you were a top athlete. If you hadn't been, your heart might not have withstood two long operations in quick succession. The first was tough enough, but the chance of you surviving the second was slim indeed." He certainly doesn't pull his punches. "But you're not out of the woods yet. The first three days will be critical. Then, if no complications set in, we can start to hope."

I take all this in.

I imagine myself lying undisturbed for a few days before they take me to a normal room. Nothing of the sort! Before long, a nurse comes and detaches the wires. Then she tells me to stand up and walk a few steps. "We need to get the blood to the liver," she explains.

I'm so weak, the shuffle over to the window is an arduous one. The window has a magnificent Alpine view. Then I look down—on a cemetery. I can't help but laugh.

How glad I am to be up here instead!

As soon as I wake up after the second operation, I start to live my "overtime." The man upstairs has given me a second chance, for which I'm eternally grateful. And I intend to make the most of it. I'll take every day as a gift and live it to the fullest. It's crystal clear to me that I'll avoid all the pointless and trivial things in life, and that I won't waste time on people who aren't worth it.

Since that time, I celebrate December 26 as a birthday just as important as the one recorded on my birth certificate. On this day, I've now drunk (mineral water) to my own health 18 times.

2

Paradise in Zagreb

I WAS BORN for the first time on September 27, 1959. I was given the name Miroslav after my grandfather on my dad's side. I never actually met my grandpa—during World War II, he was arrested by the Gestapo and sent to Auschwitz, and he never came back. I was a longed-for child. My parents tried for a baby for a long time without any luck; they may even have lost all hope of ever having children. Nor did I make it easy for them. It was a high-risk pregnancy, and my mother and I had to stay in the hospital for several weeks after I was born.

So I grew up an only child. Although my parents had good reason to wrap me in cotton wool and fret over my every need, they never treated me that way. I could never complain that they spoiled me and tiptoed around me. I thank God that they didn't.

My parents were lifelong athletes, having started in pre-war Czechoslovakia as keen members of the Sokol gymnastics movement. My mom, Otilie, a track and field athlete, was the sister of Rudolf Otava, several times a national sprint champion. My dad, Jaromir, turned from gymnastics to hockey, having played handball (briefly) and soccer in between. As a hockey player, he represented several clubs in Ostrava, an industrial and mining city in the borderlands of northern Moravia and Silesia, working his way up to the second league before he left for nearby Opava, where he played hockey and worked in an office. Years after the fact, he would explain why he had been glad to sign a contract with the Slezan sports club—his reward had been the deeds of an apartment and a small black-and-white TV.

This explains why hockey cards and yearbooks give my place of birth as Opava, even though I barely know that city and have no special feelings for it. It's no more than an entry on my birth certificate and my ID. I lived in Opava until I was three, when we moved to Zagreb, before I'd begun to take much notice of the world around me.

Yugoslavia (as it was then) would be my home for the next three years. Or I might say three seasons, as we moved there because of hockey.

In the early '60s, officials in communist countries began to look for experts in friendly states who could take their hockey to the next level. This presented my dad, who by now had risen from player to coach in Opava, with an unlooked-for opportunity. Through the hockey association, he received an offer from Medvescak Zagreb. These days, Medvescak is a well-known team with a large, boisterous fan base—not so long ago, Jonathan Cheechoo and Steve Montador wore its colors— but at that time it was taking its first tentative steps. My dad was only the second coach in its history. His main jobs were to teach the local enthusiasts a few lessons from the hockey school of Czechoslovakia and to provide them with a direction and a system.

So in the summer of 1962 we packed our suitcases, boarded a train and traveled south—to the country where I would spend a few magical childhood years and where I learned to skate. That's right: my long journey in hockey began in Yugoslavia. Or, if you will, Croatia, as it is today.

The club fixed us up with an apartment in Zagreb's Salata sports complex, right under the stands at the outdoor rink, where Medvescak trained and played. Nearby, there were tennis courts, soccer and handball fields, and a swimming pool. As my parents didn't send me to a Yugoslavian kindergarten, I spent my days in Salata. I roamed the neighborhood to my heart's content, but there was no need for my parents to worry about my whereabouts: Mom knew very well that if I wasn't at the outdoor rink, I'd be by the tennis courts, and if for some reason I wasn't, I'd be in the sports hall.

Thus I began to discover the magic of sport without fuss or fanfare. Before long, I could catch a handball and a soccer ball, and I was learning to handle a tennis racket. But it was hockey I liked most of all. I liked to go to practice with Dad, where I'd hand out the pucks and keenly follow everything that went on.

The dressing room was my kindergarten.

It amused the players to treat me like one of them. They made me a little stick, the heel of which they would solemnly shave before each training session, before taping up the blade. As they went about their business, I would stand by the boards, nudging a puck about. It was hard work: with each new layer of tape, the stick became fractionally heavier, until I struggled to hold it.

When I was at last old enough to exchange my child's skates with their straps and two blades for some proper skates, my blades were sharpened in the dressing room, as if I were a real player.

A big advantage of these new skates was their reinforced ankles. With them on, I no longer stumbled about the ice; indeed, I could skate from morning till evening at full speed and with full stability. I enjoyed myself so much that they practically had to drag me from the ice. By evening, I would be dog-tired, asleep as soon as my head touched the pillow.

On weekends, I would even use the rink when it was open to the public, getting under people's feet but annoying no one—they all knew me and greeted me. I became a mascot for Salata at large.

The opportunity to go skating whenever I felt like it was a training opportunity second to none. No team in the world will give you that. In later years, whenever I was complimented on my excellent skating skills, I knew it was thanks to the many hours I spent on the ice in Zagreb.

I know from my dad that the level of the Yugoslav Ice Hockey League was pretty low. All Medvescak's players were amateurs who went to work. And not just once a month to pick up their wages, as was the rule in the years of pseudo-amateurism in communist Czechoslovakia.

A few of them worked for the club as rink maintenance men or machine operators, the rest in various factories and offices. Whenever there was a tournament or a game halfway across the country, they had to take leave. But they loved their hockey all the more for it. The fans loved it, too. Although it wasn't as popular in Zagreb as soccer, handball or water polo, hockey games were regularly attended by five thousand people.

Medvescak trained three times a week and there were only 14 games in the league season—hardly an unremitting, exhausting schedule. As a result, Dad was with us most of the time. Sometimes we'd travel to away games—in Ljubljana, Kranjska Gora, Jesenice and Belgrade, for instance—as a family. By train, of course. For a boy of my age, this was an unforgettable experience. As were our trips to the Adriatic, where we fell in love with the island of Losinj.

We might have stayed in Yugoslavia longer than three years—Medvescak offered to extend Dad's contract—but I was due to start school at age six, so we went home. My parents didn't want me to fall behind in the first grade.

Even so, I found school pretty tough at first.

I'd come back from Yugoslavia with a fascination for sport and speaking fluent, Zagreb-accented Croatian. I'd discovered something else there, too—a taste for freedom and free thinking. This taste has never left me. I bridle when someone tells me what I should or shouldn't do, tries to force their opinions and ideas on me or to control my movements.

For those three years in Zagreb, I'd done what I wanted. Having never been part of a collective, in Opava I suddenly found myself behind a school desk. I just couldn't understand why I had to spend half the day sitting there, listening to a lady who was a stranger to me. I was forever itching to get outside. One day, to my parents' great surprise, I rang the doorbell and declared myself back home about an hour after they'd dropped me off at school.

For a few weeks after that, until I'd gotten used to my new circumstances, Mom went to school with me and sat at the back of the class.

And after that, the teacher would lock the classroom during lessons to keep me in there.

It wasn't until we were living in Karvina, where we moved midway through first grade, that I got back on an even keel. The school was only about 300 feet from home. I was okay after that.

———

In the late '60s and early '70s, Karvina was an affluent, colorful, somewhat wild town. The coal mines were working at full capacity, providing well-paid work that attracted people from all over the country. Lots of Poles lived there, and there were still bilingual signs on some of the stores. The Slovaks had their own elementary school. The mosaic of ethnicities was completed by Romanies and remnants of the original German-speaking population, most of whom had been expelled and forced to move to western Germany after the war.

This was Silesia in all its rawness.

Whereas Ostrava, the heart of the coalfield in those days, had big-city aspirations, with theaters, colleges, public offices, monuments and national ambitions, the strongest unifying element for most people in Karvina was the pub. Most streets had one, and on some the pubs even stood side by side.

They were open from early morning, giving the miners somewhere to grab a beer as soon as they came up from the pit. The miners would sit down at the tables with the dust still on them, streaks of soot on their faces, white circles around their eyes from where protective goggles had sat. They must have worked up a real thirst underground, as they were able to down 10 beers and then start a fight over something stupid.

Pint glasses flew, and we thought nothing of it, because we'd grown up with it. Boys would adapt quickly to the mentality and laws of the Karvina jungle, understanding that if they didn't make their own elbow room, no one would make it for them. This lesson has been very useful to me in my career as an athlete and in my life in general.

My family didn't move to Karvina to work down in the pit, of course, but for the hockey. Had I known then that his would be the pattern of my whole life …

Dad's new employer was the Banik Czechoslovak Army team, which was then in the second league. In our first years there, games were still played outdoors; in our region, only Ostrava, Opava and Havirov had indoor rinks. One of my first hockey-related memories of Karvina is of me wielding a shovel to help get the snow off the ice, or, if the sun was shining, giving a hand with the tarpaulin that kept the ice from thawing.

Thanks to my dad and our three years in Zagreb, hockey was now the sport I was closest to. Still, it took me a while to decide to drop everything else. I enjoyed all sports, particularly soccer and tennis. I represented the school in athletics, and I even tried handball.

I knew no more meaningful way of spending my free time. And I wasn't the only one. We'd get home from school, drop off our bags and run straight back out again. To the playground, to the swimming pool, for a bike ride. What about TV? In those days, there were only two channels in Czech, although we caught a signal from neighboring Poland, too. In any case, apart from sports broadcasts, we did without TV without a second thought.

We could have much more fun outdoors.

The parking lot was ours: in the late '60s, hardly anyone in Karvina had their own car. Having set up goals in some deserted spot, we'd thrash a tennis ball about with our hockey sticks. No grown-up took offense when the ball ended up on the hood of someone's car, at least not in our presence. In subzero winter temperatures, our dads would spray water on the parking lot, making an improvised skating rink at our doorstep. Hockey would keep us amused all day; in fact, we couldn't get enough of it. Soon we were with the novices, playing Sunday games that would start at nine in the morning so that we were home by lunchtime. And as we still had plenty of steam to let off, we would get together in front of our building and keep playing into the evening. We never had any trouble staying in shape.

After a few months, it was clear that if I wanted to do all these sports well, I couldn't do them all at the same time. I was keenest on hockey, so I gave up handball. But I still like handball. It's fast and aggressive, and there are lots of goals; when I have time, I like to watch it on TV. But for me, there's nothing quite like skates and a hockey stick.

My first childhood dream was to become a hockey player. Practice for novices started at six in the morning, so we had to get up brutally early, at five. But we never moaned about it because we looked forward to getting to the rink. The caretaker would have the heaters going in the dressing room so that we didn't freeze as we were changing. And how great it was to be out on the ice! After practice, there was no time for us to take a shower. In fact, we had to rush to school with our kit bags to get there before the bell rang.

As one of the tallest kids in the class, I sat right at the back, by the window. Every morning, I'd look out for Jaroslav Motycka, a hockey legend in Karvina, as he moved slowly along the sidewalk reading his newspaper, on his way to practice with Dad. This sight never failed to captivate me. How I envied Mr. Motycka! I imagined myself leaving school behind, playing hockey for the first team and studying a newspaper on the way to the stadium.

In those days, that was all I wanted from life.

3

Frigo

I WAS ALWAYS THE MOST cheerful member of the group. I never let things get me down, and I could turn every situation into a joke or a gag. The boys called me a comedian. And as *The General*, a slapstick silent movie starring Buster Keaton, known in Czechoslovakia for some reason as "Frigo," had made some kind of comeback, that nickname was inevitable.

Keaton may have been known for his deadpan expression, whereas I'm known for my broad grin, but the name Frigo has stuck with me all through my hockey career. The main thing is, it shares a first syllable with Frycer. Before long, teammates and opponents as well as friends were calling me Frigo. Many years after I started out, this is what Borje Salming and Wendel Clark called me in the Toronto Maple Leafs dressing room.

One other name was important to me in the early days. Ota Parik. Ota was a kid from Karvina who had given up hockey but whose registration hadn't been canceled. I took advantage of this when I represented the peewees, for whom I was ineligible to play. (This was before players could officially be bumped up an age category.) I nearly always played in a higher age group than the one the tables placed me in, which meant regular trips to the doctor's office in Ostrava for the stamp I needed. Once I had the stamp, the goals I scored could be credited to Frycer.

We peewees were brought along by Messrs. Badal and Brudny, my very first coaches, who took us forward by creating some order to our race for the puck, which they did in a simple, clever and entertaining way. Mostly we played end to end, trying out dekes and other fancy stuff. Sometimes we worked on our shooting, and we did a lot of skating. Because the coaches didn't burden us with too many tactics, our creative enthusiasm wasn't dented—the worst thing that can happen to a young hockey player. A player will never amount to anything if the coach puts him on defense just because he's the tallest, or if he's forced to spend all season out by the boards.

Our equipment was every bit as unpretentious as the coaching methods of that time. Our helmets had a hole at the top to allow us to wear a bobble hat under them. We were given shin pads and elbow pads backed with yellow felt, gloves that a motorcyclist of today would sniff at, vests that were stitched together this way or that and were often very itchy, and pants with a pocket at the back to keep a puck in. Everyone had his own puck, into which he etched his number with a nail. As soon as the coach announced the end of practice, we'd slip the puck into the pocket and go off to play. Anyone who fell on his backside got quite a bruise, I can tell you!

The sticks and skates we used were the only ones available. We were grateful for anything we could get. We'd draw on the sticks with markers to make them look better. If our parents managed to get us the same skates that Vladimir Martinec wore for the national team, it was like a second Christmas.

From the very beginning, I fancied myself a forward, and it never crossed my mind to play anywhere but center. I loved scoring goals, and I scored a lot of them. That's what hockey's all about, after all. I knew no better feeling than to poke-check an opponent, break away on goal, round the goaltender, and stick the puck under the crossbar. When I was starting out, my grandpa, who worked at a news and tobacco stand, attempted to motivate me by promising me 10 crowns for every goal I scored. Before long, however, I was scoring, say, 10 per game, and I asked him to cancel this arrangement; I didn't want to lead him into penury. "Why not give me a cigarette for each goal I score?" I suggested. I started smoking at 12, and I haven't quit yet.

Soon there were whispers in the Karvina hockey community that young Frycer was a special talent. Maybe my athletic genes were coming to the fore, and certainly the start on skates I'd had in Zagreb worked to my advantage. But I didn't waste time thinking about this. I was playing in the top peewee league, and sometimes I was called up to represent the county, but I didn't give much thought to how far I might go. I may have scored five goals against Havirov, and eight against someone else, but I celebrated every goal for its own sake, because I lived in the moment. It's always been important to me to celebrate a goal properly. When I'm out there, I like to give my emotions free rein. For me, the behavior of Russians like Valeri Kharlamov, who often didn't even bother to raise his arm after scoring, really went against the grain.

In those days, my only interest was hockey and the pleasure it could give me. Perhaps that explains why I never got stage fright. I wasn't one of those players whose hands tremble so much before a game that they can't hold a mug of tea. Whether I was playing minor hockey against Koprivnice or, 15 years later, in the Maple Leafs/Red Wings rivalry in the NHL, I took everything in my stride.

Because each time I went out on the ice, I intended to have fun. Nothing more, nothing less.

———

At first, my father followed my progress from a distance and didn't have much to say about it. Luckily for me, he wasn't one of those parents who wish to live out their unrealized dreams in sport through their children. But when he saw how much I enjoyed hockey, how much it meant to me, and how serious I was about it, he decided to take a hand in it. By giving me ever more advice.

Because he was able to put this to me gently, I was grateful for it. He was well aware of my stubborn nature. He knew that if he tried to force me into something, I was likely to do the opposite. He presented and explained things to me in such a way that I could see for myself that what we were about to do made sense and was right.

In those days, it was a commonly held belief that 90 percent of an athlete's success came down to talent. In insisting that what you are born with isn't enough, my dad was ahead of his time. He made sure I worked on myself every day so as not to waste my talent.

His earlier involvement with gymnastics and athletics gave him a broader perspective on how to train; he didn't see everything through the prism of hockey. Some of the ideas he instilled in me—like dynamic play in short, sharp bursts—became commonly accepted only several years later. Every time I went off to practice, he would tell me, "No matter how stupid or boring the exercise, always try to take the first three steps at speed. If this becomes second nature, you'll do it automatically in games. You get the puck and away you go—you've got a head start already."

Dad came up with the idea that I should devote my summer vacation to shooting practice. I had a board piled high with pucks that I flicked at the net, one wrist shot after another. I did this for two months, several times a week for the whole afternoon. The next season, suddenly I knew how to shoot at the net without the goaltender knowing two seconds in advance what I had in mind and before the defensemen had time to get a stick in the way. The puck flew right where I intended it to go. I scored 80 goals. It became obvious that Dad knew what he was talking about.

Another time, he mentioned, as if in passing, that if I wanted to play hockey at a high level, I should build up my strength. The push-ups and pull-ups we did at the end of a training session weren't enough. He was right. Even though I ate my fill at home, I was quite the spider, all skin and bones; I just didn't seem able to gain weight.

"I could give it a try, I suppose," I said, shrugging. A few days later, he brought home a large black barbell with a ball welded to each end. Goodness knows where he'd gotten it. It looked like the kind of thing a circus strongman would do battle with. It might have weighed 90 pounds. The first time I tried to lift it, its weight almost snapped me in two. Dad told me to have patience and take it slow—I wouldn't get stronger overnight, he said.

As well as working on my biceps, I started doing thrusts and squats to strengthen my lower body. This had an obvious effect on my game.

Again, I had to admit that Dad's ideas were good ones. Indeed, I can still remember much of his advice and many of his remarks, almost 50 years later. It's as if he were still standing next to me.

Keep your stick in front of you, not too close to your body. It's your weapon. The longer its reach, the better for you.

Don't lean forward. If you stand straight, your legs will work better, giving you an altogether different glide.

Keep your head up and watch the game, watch the puck. When you don't have it, try to move so that you force the pass. If you spend three shifts just skating, with no puck possession, what's the point of being out there?

If you lose the puck, don't just stand there watching four against one. Stop, then step on it to get back.

Don't talk back to the officials. If you get a 10-minute penalty, you're harming no one but yourself by missing the game. Practice is preparation to be out there, not to sit in the penalty box.

He was especially keen on making the last point. Now that I was getting myself noticed and scoring goals, opponents paid more attention to me than was good for me. Sometimes I'd strike someone who'd struck me first, or I'd complain to the referee. And I wasn't above using my stick to poke an opponent in the belly. Or lower.

If someone tried to wind me up, I was capable of all kinds of crap. "Listen, Mirek," my father would explain patiently. "If you're seeing red, you can't play hockey. And if you lose your focus, you weaken yourself and the team. They may be lashing out at you left, right and center, but if you want to score, you've got to keep your concentration."

My mother's behavior was less diplomatic. She was impulsive and quickly on the offensive, whether the matter was my threatened suspension from school or mischief on the ice. Once, when I was about 12 and an opponent was laying into me, I hit him with my stick and had words with the referee, getting a minor penalty for my trouble.

Hardly had I taken my seat in the penalty box than I caught sight of my mother hurrying from the stands in my direction, obviously seething with rage. When she reached me, she set about me with her umbrella and told me loudly that I should be ashamed of myself. Then she told me to go home. The whole scene was great entertainment for everyone at the rink. Fortunately, a polite usher led my mother away, and I finished the game in peace.

When Dad became coach at Trinec, sometimes I'd go there with him. We'd have long discussions in the car. As well as hockey, we talked about life. Dad knew I had a mean streak, but he understood that I needed it to get ahead. Hockey isn't the kind of game where you turn the other cheek when you get hit. No, you must return the blow. My dad impressed on me how important it is to keep things in balance— he wanted me to know where the boundaries lie, the point at which my standing up for myself gives way to arrogance.

According to my dad, there was nothing more important than behaving well off the ice. He kept my feet on the ground by telling me repeatedly that life doesn't always go the way you plan it. A favorite maxim of his was: "Be good to others when you're on the way up. You never know who you're going to meet on the way down."

I didn't make things easy for him. I dealt impulsively with whatever came my way, as an athlete and otherwise. I saw things in black and white, with nothing in between. But as time passed, I came to see how right he was. About most things.

Later in my career, I encountered other coaches who had a great influence on me. I didn't get on with some of them, although I always respected their knowledge and achievements. Others I admired and enjoyed playing for. But none of them gave me as much as my father.

4

Messrs. Hlinka, Dzurilla and Co.

MY FIRST REALIZATION that my hockey-playing days wouldn't necessarily end in Karvina came with a ring on our home doorbell. I was 15 years old. The visitors were the manager and the coach of the Litvinov youth teams. Litvinov was a small industrial town in northern Bohemia, where hockey had and still has a strong tradition. At the time of writing, its team has given a start to 21 players who have gone on to play in the NHL, most notably Petr Klima, Petr Svoboda and Petr Nedved. The manager and the coach had come with the intention of convincing me, and most importantly my parents, to sign myself over to them.

They sat with us for a long time. The signature of this ninth-grader must have meant a lot to them if they had driven all the way to Karvina for it. It was a full-day trip. If I agreed to come, they told me, they would make every arrangement for me—they would even get me a place at a high school that specialized in chemistry. I didn't know what to think about this offer. I sat there in silence and waited for what my father had to say. But I could tell that this was a big deal.

The attempt to persuade reached its climax with the following statement: "The boy would get to play with Ivan Hlinka."

The tip may have come from a brother of the Litvinov manager, who had played under my father in Karvina. How else would they have known the identity of my favorite player? The boys I played with would pore over newspaper articles and devour radio broadcasts about the older generation of greats; their (and my) idols were Jan Suchy and Josef Cerny. For me, though, the unchallenged number one was Ivan Hlinka, a forward with the Czechoslovakian national team. And I made no secret of the fact. The first time I saw him play, he pretty much bowled me over. Like me, this amazing player was a center. And he was incredibly charismatic. And now I was being given the chance to play with him. It was almost too good to be true!

"You know what?" I said. "I think I *would* like to go to Litvinov."

But my father was against the idea. He didn't change his mind even after a second visit and much coaxing from Litvinov. Sparta Prague expressed an interest, too, also to no avail.

"You're not going anywhere yet. It's too early," Dad told me flatly. "You'd just run wild."

The idea of 15-year-old me living in a dorm 300 miles away didn't appeal to Dad. He wasn't yet prepared to grant me so much freedom. No surprises there. He knew I was game for any amusement on offer, to put it mildly. Not long before, when the rink had been open to the public, my friends had plied me with beer and brought me home as drunk as a skunk, propped me against the door of the apartment, rang the doorbell, and scarpered. The swine. This was all the justification my parents needed.

But I wouldn't be staying in Karvina much longer. One year later, I made the move to the big league—to Vitkovice, the first-division club in Ostrava. This was acceptable to my father, as it was nearby and he'd be able to keep an eye on me. As a minor whose every move needed to be sanctioned by his parents, I had to go along with it.

If you were thinking that my knees gave way when I got the offer, you'd be wrong. I didn't want to go there. My friends and I were no fans of Vitkovice types. In fact, we thought they were pretty weird. We listened to Deep Purple and Led Zeppelin and wore our hair long, while they all looked the same, with their hair cut above the collar. They were townies, which we found off-putting.

Games against Vitkovice were our most prestigious and hyped. In those days, we weren't involved in any memorable tournaments, our travels farther afield being limited to a few friendly games in Poland. So scoring a goal against Vitkovice was something truly special, regardless of age category. They were better than us, of course—they had 15 good players on their team to our four. But because we were a close-knit, properly psyched-up group, sometimes we managed to beat them. We would fall on them like a hungry pack.

In spring 1976, Dad and I were in Katowice to see a world championship game. While we were there, we came across the Vitkovice team bus in the parking lot. Dad introduced me to Ladislav Stemprok, the coach. I knew already that a few weeks later I'd be reporting to him for summer training. We shook hands and exchanged a word or two. All that remained to arrange was my transfer to the high school for economics in Ostrava. After that, I'd take a few things to my grandparents' in Hrusov, where I'd be living to begin with, and the move would be complete.

There are few things in life one can truly plan. Who knows what would have become of me if I'd made that move to Litvinov. Maybe I'd have gotten to play with Ivan Hlinka, or maybe not. Maybe I'd have managed the change of environment without problems; maybe my nature would have messed things up for me. I'll never know. But I'm grateful to my father for making the big decision for me, even if it went against my inclinations at the time.

The choice was the right one. At Vitkovice, a new world opened for me. Step by step, I set about realizing a whole new batch of hockey-related dreams.

———

The first half of the '70s wasn't exactly a great period for TJ VZKG Ostrava, the club's official name until 1979. The team spent a few seasons in the second division, and even after it gained promotion, it struggled to stay among the elite. Attendance at games was low. No one beyond Ostrava took much interest in this bridesmaid of the league.

Returning coach Stemprok was determined to improve the club's fortunes by making radical changes. A few of the older players were shown the exit and replaced by fresh, young blood. As well as myself, the five newcomers included Lada Svozil, who was a year older than me; before long, Lada and I were inseparable. We were to form the backbone of a new team that would play a more respectable role in the league.

Although I never fretted about my game and was on the self-confident side, my move to Vitkovice was a big deal for me. For one thing, this was the first division; for another, I was playing for the seniors. Until then, I'd played for the midgets, albeit often against older opponents, who were juniors nevertheless.

I wondered how the dressing room would receive me. Some of the players were getting on in years; they had things to contend with in their private lives of which a snotty-nosed kid from Karvina could have no notion. Anyway, they took to me just fine.

There was a traditional initiation procedure for young players. To become accepted members of the team, we went out with our teammates for a few beers and picked up the tab. Our duties to our elders included carrying their hockey sticks, bags and skate sharpeners. Lada and I didn't shed this burden until we'd been there for about three years. New players would join, but still we would be the youngest. We were already playing for the national team, but our status at Vitkovice was unchanged. We'd return from competing at the world U20 championship or the Izvestia tournament to find that we were still expected to collect pucks and carry bags.

The first summer training under Coach Stemprok was pretty hard work. As was the next. The way he led it, it was pure drudgery. We lifted weights by brute force—there were no strength and conditioning coaches with the team to present us with a meaningful fitness plan, and there was no gym. We used the same weight room as Vitkovice's top athletes—while future world champion shot-putter Helena Fibingerova lifted her crazy weights, we went about our business. Our training sessions were pointless; the only thing they were good for was doing your back in. But since Soviet hockey players lifted tons of iron over their heads, so should we. Plus, we were forever running—400 meters with weights in our hands or at well-timed intervals.

Stemprok was a strange coach. He was a former pro, though I never saw him skate. At practice, he would stand by the boards in his fur coat as his assistant led the session. He would occasionally interrupt us to call us over and give out some instruction.

An elderly gentleman, his sight was poor without glasses, which was particularly problematic when he was timing our board-to-board sprints. When we approached Stemprok for his assessment, he would squint at his stopwatch as we struggled to catch our breath. If he saw that the player in question was getting on in years, he would nod and say benevolently, "Good. That's enough for now." If the subject was one of us youngsters, his answer was pretty much automatic: "No good. Too slow. Go again." So it was, over and over again. Though our legs were aching, he kept sending us back to the ice. Sprint, stop, sprint, stop.

One day after practice, he took Lada and me aside to inform us of his intention to put us on the third line with team captain Vladimir Vujtek. We were less than happy, believing it couldn't work. All three of us were centers—we just wouldn't click. But it was a masterstroke on Stemprok's part. Indeed, it was the best thing he could have done for us.

Vladimir took us under his wing and told us everything a newcomer to the league needed to know. A great teacher, it was no fluke that he became a successful coach; he was a two-time winner in the Russian Superleague before going on to manage the national teams of both the Czech Republic and Slovakia.

He would sit with us, over a beer or in the dressing room, giving us directions, calming us down, telling us what to expect. He did the same out on the ice. Vladimir was never one of the quicker skaters, and anyway he was pushing 30, while Lada and I were forever dashing this way and that. Both of us were quick, energetic and capable of scoring. As the boss, Vladimir dictated the play and sent the puck out to the boards, where we were bombing along—I on the right wing, Lada on the left. Two years later, Lada would return to center. I was out on the right for good.

Stemprok's idea worked to everyone's benefit—Lada and I had the perfect mentor, Vladimir's first-team career was extended by two years, and Vitkovice got itself an interesting third line.

I'll always be grateful to Vladimir for the way he treated us. If I hadn't gotten to know this great player and smart man right at the beginning of my career, it might have turned out very differently. He's been one of the most important people in my life in hockey, that's for sure.

———

My wait for my first senior league game ended on September 21, 1976. The opening game of the season was filled with pomp and ceremony. We were playing against Tesla Pardubice, whose forwards Vladimir Martinec and Bohuslav Stastny received carnations for their part in the recent Canada Cup, in which Czechoslovakia had sensationally defeated home-grown Canadian pros from the NHL 1-0 on their way to the final.

We won the game against Tesla. Lada and I felt good even though neither of us scored any points. Out there on the ice, we would wink at each other and say, "Piece of cake, the seniors."

For our next match, we traveled to Zlin, then called Gottwaldov. It was three days before my 17th birthday, and I got my celebration in early—we won 4-1, and I scored a hat trick. This is still a league record.

But no one made much fuss about it. Stemprok tended to be sparing with his praise, and this occasion was no exception. My teammates were a little more appreciative. Back in the dressing room, goaltender Ludek Broz told me with a grin, "You might make a player, kid." Other old pros reminded me that I would be buying the beer that night.

Today, it is considered remarkable for a youngster to be playing regularly at the highest level. No one said much about it in our day, although it was much more difficult to break into the seniors than it is now; there were only 12 teams in the league, and three of those were in Slovakia (today there are 14, from the Czech Republic only), play was in three five-men units, and it wasn't yet the case that our hundred best players were abroad. If someone short of his 17th birthday were to achieve the same feat today, it would be celebrated as something extraordinary. It would be one of the main items on the evening news, and there would be a two-page interview with the young hopeful in the newspaper the very next day.

This early achievement of mine was barely mentioned. One newspaper reported the game under the striking headline "Second win for TJ VZKG"; another put out the confusing message that Milan Frycer was a burgeoning talent. There was little interest in cultivating star status. Which I consider a good thing. If my hat trick had been presented as a thing of wonder, the attention might have turned my head. As it happened, my delight in my first goal and at the realization that Lada and I weren't in this league just to fill out the roster was nothing out of the ordinary. Life went on with a minimum of fuss.

In those days, for me every game was a small cause for celebration. Every game taught me something, as I was playing against some great players—those of the golden generation of the '70s. I never gave an inch out on the ice—of course I didn't—but I had enormous respect for my opponents. I'd been brought up to esteem all those who had achieved something in life. For me, every face-off with Mr. Hlinka and every battle along the boards with Mr. Martinec was something special. I wanted to be a match for them, and I hoped that if I performed well against them, they would take notice of me and reckon that Vitkovice's young number 16 had something about him.

For the third game of the season, we hosted Zetor Brno and their legendary goaltender Vladimir Dzurilla. In the first period, Brno lost possession of the puck at our blue line, it came to me, and suddenly I was in on goal. The stadium erupted. There in front of me stood a goaltender 17 years my senior, whom just a few weeks earlier I'd watched on TV making brilliant saves against Phil Esposito and Bobby Hull in the Canada Cup. He was more than ready for me. Craftily, he left a space for me to move into, and like a fool, I took my shot, which Dzurilla succeeded in blocking. My decision making had been poor, and I'd played right into his hands. I should have shaken things up a bit, tried a deke—Dzurilla didn't like to go down, as his belly made it difficult for him to get up again.

A few minutes later, I was given another lesson. Out by the boards, I believed myself to be comfortably past defenseman Oldrich Machac when he thrust out his behind, sending me flying. I found myself staring up at the lights under the roof of the stadium. An exquisite hip check. He was the best at it in Europe. It was as though he was telling me, "Welcome to the big league, kid."

I respected players younger than Machac and Dzurilla, too. I remember the first time we played against Slovan Bratislava—in particular, making my way to the game. It was my afternoon ritual to stop off at a bar for a cola before sauntering over the bridge to the stadium. As our opponents mostly stayed at the Hotel Imperial, they would be going the same way. So I'm walking along and I see Peter Stastny 30 feet ahead. Wow! He may have been the 20-year-old brother of my friend Anton, but he was also a world champion from Katowice 1976 and a star of the league. Afraid to overtake him, I hung back and watched him with reverence.

This boyish wonderment accompanied me all the way through my first season. Then I got used to things and knew myself to belong in the top league.

5

Scenes from the Life of a Hockey Pro

THE MOMENT I SIGNED my contract at Vitkovice, hockey became my job. There was no longer any need for me to envy Mr. Motycka. Instead of school, I went to morning practice, and I was given money for indulging in my hobby. Quite a lot of money. Certainly I had no cause for complaint—compared with other livings made in Czechoslovakia, the standard of ours was high. I kept a few hundred crowns back for my beer and gave the rest to my parents to put in the bank for me. It was more money than a 17-year-old could know what to do with in Ostrava.

The precise amount I was paid depended on the level of the win bonus. Or the extent of the fine I'd just been issued. When things weren't going our way and we were on a run of poor performances, the management came up with a punishment worse than the toughest skating drill: we were forced to go to the Vitkovice Ironworks, where we were officially employed. As we stood at the little window waiting for our pay slips, the men alongside us gave us far-from-pleasant looks that contained all this: you don't have to work grueling shifts, you play a game for your living, you earn twice as much as we do—and still you're playing badly.

Fortunately, this didn't happen often. In the 1976-77 season, our rejuvenated team achieved seventh place, which was regarded as a promising start. We played entertaining hockey, and many important things began to come together, on the ice and in the dressing room. These first steps seemed set to move us up the league in the next few years.

And at last the fans were turning out in greater numbers. Officially called the Josef Kotas Ice Stadium (after a postwar communist may-

or), no one called our home anything but Kotas. It was the first in Czechoslovakia to have a roof. From outside, it looked like a factory. It had the capacity for 10,000 spectators, but I'm pretty sure that for our biggest games a thousand more were squeezed into the stands. From time to time, on the way to our morning skate we'd see men who had just come up from the pit standing in front of the ticket windows. Sometimes there were so many fans hanging around that we players had to force our way into the stadium an hour and a half before a match.

Kotas may have been an old barn, but when games were in progress the atmosphere was amazing. I've never known a facility like it anywhere else. The place smelled of wood, old age, hotdogs and tobacco. These were the days before Plexiglas behind the goals. The only protection was dusty netting marked with puck streaks—after every close-fought duel, you would end up with a black grid on your face. A canny shove from an opponent would sometimes send you over the boards before the net pulled you back in. Duels by the side boards might result in players falling into the front row of spectators.

Other teams weren't keen on visiting Vitkovice's "cauldron." The stands at Kotas were steep, and when chanting fans jumped up and down on the wooden steps, the atmosphere was thunderous, which was positively awe-inspiring but more than a little frightening. High up, the gondola seating provided a great view of the game. The ice was illuminated by old floodlights, but the space under the roof was in darkness. All this was supplemented with the rumble of trains passing by the east stand. Fantastic. In such surroundings, full-blooded commitment from the players was a given. In any case, our fans wouldn't have stood for anything less.

I loved stadiums like this. The one in Bratislava was similar, before it was redeveloped; the choral singing of its fans really got us going because we felt as though we were back in Ostrava. I liked the Sports Hall in Prague, too. Later in the NHL, I most enjoyed playing at the old Chicago Stadium—stands on four levels, Kotas-like floodlights, a glorious past breathing from every pore. In fact, I felt good in every arena with tradition, from Quebec to Los Angeles. The modern arenas of today may be luxurious, well lit, multifunctional and comfortable, but they are also cold and impersonal, one much like another. It's not the same, and it just doesn't do it for me. When I'm up in their stands, I ask myself what all this progress is good for.

I'm one of those who regret the fact that Kotas was demolished some years ago.

Our dreary dressing room was nice and old-fashioned. There was a corner table in the lobby, where we would sit after practice, preparing and consuming tea or sausages. We celebrated birthdays at that table, too. At the back, there was a massage table and a communal bath. Mr. Krpela, the caretaker, had his closet next door, and there was a store-room for our skates and sticks. A chance visitor would probably have been taken aback by the stink. For a stink it was—to outsiders. To us, the characteristic dressing-room smell had a special charm; it was part of the hockey world. Underwear was washed once a week, and besides, it took a while for leather goalie pads and sweaty gloves to dry.

Our equipment was taken care of by Mr. Netolicka, club secretary and purchasing officer. The sticks he got us were mostly the home brands Artis and Vitez. Each team had these made in a different color: ours were light blue, Kosice's orange, Ceske Budejovice's yellow and so on. Players who represented the national team were naturally given better ones, most commonly Koho or Titan, made to measure in Finland.

Sometimes, you could tell a national-team player by his skates. Bauer and Graf were for the select few; the rest had to make do with ordinary red-and-black skates that were made in Czechoslovakia. The gloves were different from today's; they were stitched together, with tough, inflexible palms. Often when I was breaking in a new pair, I couldn't even bring my fingers together. Solid as concrete, they were more suitable for weight training than a competitive game. We tried various tricks to get them to give a little, like leaving them to stand in water, or rubbing lard or shoe polish into them.

In the '70s, a league hockey player's work week was seven days long. Although games were on Tuesdays and Fridays only, a day off was practically unheard of. The longest training session, usually lasting an hour and a half, was on Mondays. On Wednesdays, we were required to work on rehabilitation, which meant a sauna and a massage. There were further training sessions on Thursdays and Saturdays. On Sundays, we were out on the ice in the morning before heading *en masse* to a bar for a beer or two before going our separate ways for lunch.

No wonder, then, that my school attendance was so patchy. Practices, games, traveling, training camps *ad infinitum*. I just didn't have time for school. I struggled with it for half a year, then I transferred to evening classes; in the end, by making a supreme effort, I completed my studies at the school of economics by correspondence. I confess that my matriculation exam—my final high school exam before receiving my certificate—wouldn't have won any prizes.

But we always found time for fun. We were young, and we were no saints. We needed to let off steam. Life is about more than goals, games and practicing power plays.

After practice, it was customary to go for coffee at the Hotel Imperial. In the evenings, we'd sometimes go out for a beer or to see some live music. It goes without saying that Coach Stemprok didn't have much understanding for this kind of relaxation. Dogged in his determination to stop it, he set strict rules. There was an absolute ban on smoking, enforced through fines. Although the law stated it was legal to drink alcohol from the age of 18, we were permitted to do so only after we turned 21. The restrictions occasionally produced the absurd situation where men just shy of 21 were forced to drink soda at a team lunch, even though they had done their military service and perhaps even started a family.

Stemprok really made us youngsters pay. For the slightest misdemeanor, he was capable of working us so hard in practice, we'd end up on all fours. There was no negotiation. If it reached his ears that we'd been partying, all hell would break loose. No proof was needed—he knew what he knew.

We thought up all kinds of tricks to outsmart him. In those days, all the best bars were in downtown Ostrava. If ever anyone needed to find one of the players, they knew exactly which three bars to look in. So we took to holing up in train station bars and smoky dens, where we'd sit in a corner to be out of sight. In some of these places, we'd agree with the waiter that if a coach appeared in the doorway, he'd give us a sign, allowing us to make a preplanned escape. It was safest of all to do our boozing out of town.

As you see, for Czech hockey players, creativity, an ability to improvise, and combination skills came in handy off the ice as well as on it.

———

In our second season under Stemprok (1977-78), we finished fourth, the club's best performance in 20 years. We were a force to be reckoned with again.

We showed our ambition and hunger for success in the very first home game, in which we demolished a celebrated Dukla Jihlava side 8-1, the young line with me on it scoring four times. An incredible game with an incredible result. Dukla may not have been the powerhouse of a few years earlier, but it was still a top team stoked with experienced internationals; plus, as it was an army club, talented youngsters could do their mandatory two-year military service in its ranks. After the game against us, coach Jaroslav Pitner fumed that this was the heaviest defeat he had suffered in his many years with the team.

Games against Jihlava were always prestigious affairs, but as far as we were concerned, every league game had something special about it. Every club had at least one interesting player, usually an international, against whom we looked forward to pitting ourselves.

In the '70s, club rosters changed very little. Most players ended their careers where they started them. Once they passed 30, the long goodbye began, and a player from the juniors would be promoted to take their place. Those who had represented the national team were given a couple of keepsakes (a jersey and a watch), after which they were granted permission to take their aging bones to the Austrian or West German league, where they could earn some hard currency. Others dropped down a league, or else they quickly prepared themselves for the matriculation exam so they wouldn't end up on a factory assembly line.

Clubs never traded players, and it was exceptional for an international player at the best age to be given permission to change team. So it was that year after year, teams would play each other four times a season with practically the same lineups. We knew each other so well that surprises were few and far between. As for tactics, all teams played with a left-wing lock, in accordance with a pattern of play devised some years earlier by a professor called Vladimir Kostka. This meant our coaches had no need for complex analyses and instructions before games. We always knew what to expect.

It's safe to say, though, that the pattern of play practiced at Vitkovice was a little more chaotic. We were forever on the move, taking risks with our defense, losing the puck and relying on goaltender Jaromir Sindel to save us. Our despairing defensemen would shout at us, "At least get back to the red line, for God's sake!"

Because we were difficult to read, opponents would sometimes struggle against us. And after Vladimir Vujtek left and was replaced by Jaroslav Vlk, teamwork on our line went up a level. I stayed out on the right, Lada Svozil moved into the center, where his strength and speed could be put to best use, while Vlk, who could skate facing forward or backward, skated on the left. It worked so well, before long we were playing practically blindfolded. I'd drive up the wing and automatically switch the puck to the left, trusting that one of the others would be onto it.

Over parts of the season, the super-productive Frycer-Svozil-Vlk line would be responsible for half the goals Vitkovice scored. Fans from the old Kotas days still look back on it. It was great to watch, they say.

All these years later, that's nice to hear.

6

A Lion on My Breast

AUGUST 21, 1968—a day that changed the life of my generation forever. On that day, Czechoslovakia was invaded by countries of the Warsaw Pact, led by the Soviet Union, suffocating our hope of a life in greater freedom. The consequences were devastating. Before the borders were closed, tens of thousands of smart and educated people had fled to the West. Many others were fired from their jobs for disagreeing with the occupation. Books by authors with inconvenient views were removed from libraries, dozens of films were locked away in the vaults, and rock bands were forced to change English names for Czech ones and apply to the authorities for permission to perform in public. It was as sad as it was bizarre.

In the 1970s, Czechoslovakia was in a state of stagnation. The future looked hopeless, and there were very few things we could take pride in. But one of these was sport—and hockey in particular. In hockey, we were among the best in the world. When those 16 players went out on the ice with a lion on their breast, they weren't playing for the glory of the communist regime. They were playing for Czechoslovakia. For us. For the land founded by our grandfathers.

So it's hardly surprising that practically every second family would gather around the flickering black-and-white screen for every international game, regardless of whether it was an exhibition or a prestigious tournament encounter, and live through it with great intensity. Internationals were the hub of our hockey world, trumping everything else. Yes, we knew that Canadian professionals had their NHL, but that was so far away, it might have been in another galaxy.

Even as a boy, I'd imagined playing for the national team one day. At least once, if only for a few shifts.

In those days, I'd believed this ambition to be way beyond my reach. But my dream came true in 1976, when I was called up to represent the under-17s in three games against a team from Montreal's Concordia University. Although these games were not official internationals, we wore the genuine national-team jersey. The same one our famous idols wore.

The first time I pulled it over my head in the dressing room, the feeling was indescribable. Though it might sound childish and dramatic, elation and pride at having realized my childhood dream were only part of it. All of us thought it a great honor to represent our country. We never took it for granted, even when we played basically pointless games against East Germany and Bulgaria, or we traveled to Romania to provide a sparring partner for their senior side. The chance to play for our country was always a big deal.

We played against the Canadians in sold-out stadiums. It was the first time Anton Stastny and I were on the same team; we've been friends ever since. In the last of the three games, I was captain and scored two goals, one of which clinched our victory just before the end.

Back in the dressing room, I found some scissors and carefully cut the tricolor from the sleeve of the jersey. A memento. What if this was the last time I'd ever represent my country?

I needn't have worried. Over the next six months, I represented the under-18s, too, and I did well enough to get selected for the European championship in Bremerhaven, West Germany, where we finished second to Sweden. What I remember most about this tournament is almost losing my teeth, a first for me in hockey. It happened unexpectedly. We were playing against Poland. I went for the puck in the company of one of their defensemen, who lost his balance and hit me right in the mouth with his stick as he fell.

My blood was all over the ice. I was taken to hospital, and I ended up needing several root canals. Horrible.

Up till then, I'd avoided injury, apart from a few scratches. To make matters worse, for a long time I'd worn a plastic mouth guard, which I'd stopped using just before the championship, in honor of its importance. A poor decision I paid for in spades. Murphy's Law, you might call it.

My father saw the funny side of my broken smile. "At last you look like a real hockey player!" he declared, as he welcomed me home.

Our victories in Bremerhaven included one over the Soviet Union, which always went over well. They were the occupying force. National enemy number one. Even as juniors, we'd taken games against the Soviets extremely seriously. Having grown up with an aversion to everything Russian, we were motivated to the point of fanaticism. I was nine when Brezhnev's tanks rolled in, and before every match I remembered Dad and I painting the words "GO HOME, IVAN" on banners, and how our whole school attended the funeral of a boy from a higher grade who had been shot by a Soviet soldier.

In our games against the Russians, we played every minute to the maximum, to the very end. This was about more than hockey, in our eyes at least. We didn't care if it meant losing against Romania the next day—against the Russians, we expended every last drop of sweat.

After the game, we tended to ignore the Russian athletes. Some players—I was one—refused to shake hands with them. At evening functions and official banquets, we made it very plain that we were keeping our distance from them.

I realize now that this attitude was unwise. Those boys weren't to blame. Their lives were far from easy; in fact, ours were wonderful in comparison. Unlike them, we weren't kept at base 11 months of the year, training like crazy, living for nothing but hockey; the pressure must have been enormous. They were well-paid serfs. The communist regime granted them great material advantages in return for top performances and absolute loyalty. Which explains why no Russian attempted to escape to the NHL before 1989.

If they toed the line, they did just fine. A few years later, again in Sweden, we went to a discotheque with players from other teams, and we looked on open-mouthed as Valeri Kharlamov pulled a wad of hundred-dollar bills from his pocket as he ordered some drinks. All we had in our pockets were a few hard-won West German marks.

The next day at the airport, the Russians made us feel like losers again. They had arrived there in two buses, one for the players, the other for all the goods they had bought—televisions, washing machines, radios, even a model of a Volvo a child could ride about in. We, on the other hand, congratulated ourselves on taking home T-shirts, jeans, and shampoo.

Smuggling purchases home was a popular pastime. When we were abroad, we hunted for all kinds of treasures that either weren't available in Czechoslovakia or produced only in low quality by the communist economy. Older players would ply younger ones with advice on what, where and how to buy, and what and where to sell.

Trips to Moscow naturally scored very low on the popularity scales. We disliked them because we knew in advance just how boring the program would be. We knew we'd have to go to the mausoleum to see the shriveled, embalmed body of Lenin; we knew we'd be hungry all week long and lose weight, and that we'd have to get through lots of vodka, as well as a game against the Russians. There wasn't much we could take home—just caviar, vodka, Soviet champagne and Armenian cognac. We didn't cast the net very wide, because the *dezhurnaya*—or floor attendant—would always collar us to see what she could get out of us.

The commonest currency was Bohemian crystal, which we also took to the West. The equipment managers joined us in the smuggling. Goods were packed in our kit bags; marks and dollars we'd bought on the black market were sewn into the goaltender's leg pads.

Before our journey home, we would take the same care with hiding the things we'd bought. But we didn't really need to—when customs officers saw that the bus was carrying the hockey team, they turned a blind eye. If we'd won.

In 1977, just before the Christmas holidays, something happened to change my ideas about hockey, and consequently about my life in general. I went to Canada for the first time. To the world junior ice hockey championship, held in Montreal, Quebec City and Hull.

This wasn't my first trip to a Western country—I'd been to Italy, Germany and Sweden—but Canada was a completely new experience for me. It was a different world. For the vast majority of people in communist Czechoslovakia, it was an altogether inaccessible land.

For the whole of our first day in Montreal, we were in a state of culture shock. Our astonishment began on our way from the airport, after which it became stronger by the day. Everything was big—enormous, in fact. Buildings, streets, steaks, cars, you name it. As I looked at the skyscrapers in the downtown, I could scarcely believe that people actually lived in them. One evening, we wanted to see a movie, so we asked at the hotel reception for directions to the theater. No problem, it's just a little way down Sainte-Catherine Street, we were told. It took us almost an hour to walk there.

Some things we got used to quickly, like people's smiles, sales assistants' willingness to help, and the buildings adorned with lights for Christmas. The blue sky and the clean white snow, the likes of which I had never seen in gray and gloomy Ostrava.

The TV at the hotel had about a hundred channels, so we could watch hockey whenever we felt like it. We were taken to see an NHL game at the Forum, sanctuary of the Canadiens, and were suitably overwhelmed. Eighteen thousand people, all of them fired up. At every break in the play, the arena resounded with the playing of an organ, to spellbinding effect. The Canadian obsession with hockey was apparent wherever you looked.

The visit to the Forum was a moment of revelation for me. *One day, I want to play here and experience this week after week,* I told myself.

I'd no idea how I would achieve this. The NHL was a forbidden land to players from Czechoslovakia; the only one playing there was the defector Vaclav Nedomansky. But I knew myself to be prepared to make any sacrifice to realize my new dream.

For the time being, I would need to make do with appearing at the Forum for Czechoslovakia's under-20s, on December 25, 1977. We were to face Canada, whom we had little hope of beating. The host nation was taking this tournament very seriously; for the first time, its team at these championships was composed not from a single club but from the best juniors from the whole country. As is their way, the Canadians were expecting nothing less than the gold.

We'd played a warm-up game against them before the tournament, at which they had given us a pasting. We'd been most impressed by the skinny, pimply center wearing the number 9, who seemed to do what he wanted with us. Although he was yet to turn 17, the newspapers were full of him. A truly fantastic player. The only player of his age I've ever seen dominate athletes three years older than himself. And such a lightweight, too. Back in the dressing room, we swore to remember his name—there was no doubt we'd be hearing much more from him.

His name? Wayne Gretzky.

In Montreal, he got a hat trick and three assists against us; largely thanks to him, Canada beat us 9-3. Gretzky scored another goal against us in the championship round, and again Canada won. The youngest in the tournament, he led all players in scoring and was declared the best forward. The only prize he didn't get was the gold medal the Canadians had promised themselves.

Gretzky wasn't the only great player on that Canadian team, but none of the others stuck in my memory. Years later, I read through the roster and saw the names Rick Vaive, Mike Gartner, Craig Hartsburg, Rob Ramage and Bobby Smith. One star after another. That time, all of them had played in Gretzky's shadow.

I was lucky to come up against such fine players at junior tournaments. The generation born between 1958 and 1960 was a very strong one, its great players of the future standing out as youngsters.

In our games with the Soviets, we came to know all the members of what would become Viktor Tikhonov's Russian Five from CSKA Moscow; we also pitted ourselves against Sweden's Pelle Lindbergh, Mats Naslund, Tomas Jonsson, Hakan Loob and Thomas Steen, and Finland's Jari Kurri.

Ours wasn't a bad team either. As many of us were league regulars, we were experienced, and in Pavel Wohl we had one of the best coaches I've ever met. A terrific guy who treated his players like the human beings they were. He was also a fine motivator, and he knew practically everything there was to know about hockey. It was a pleasure to play for him.

We ended up in fourth place, although I don't believe we were so far behind the others. I think what did us in was the whole atmosphere of playing hockey in Canada. It made us incapable of playing to the best of our abilities. It was as though we couldn't quite get over the fact that we were playing in Montreal and Quebec City.

———

When I got my first call-up to the senior national team, things happened so fast that I barely had time to wonder whether I was surprised or to contemplate the scale of the honor.

I arrived home from a summer tournament for the under-20s to find a message from coach Karel Gut. I was to report to the squad for the Rude Pravo Cup. I changed the underwear in my bag and headed straight for the train.

This tournament had been introduced only the previous year. Although it was the first international event of the season, because it was played to mark the propagandistic Day of the Press, Radio and Television, the house seats were filled with comrades of the highest rank, and the games had to be taken seriously. The structure of the tournament varied from year to year. In the first, Czechoslovakia had competed against the Soviets and the Cincinnati Stingers from the WHA; this time out, all three games would be against the USSR national team.

I wasn't the only player the coaches promoted from the under-20s—Anton Stastny was there, too. Otherwise, the squad comprised experienced players who were world champions. As I'd faced these players for two years in the league, I wasn't shy to show off what I could do. But I kept an admiring distance from them rather than engaging in conversation. When I first walked into the national team's dressing room, I was so excited I could hardly breathe. And I had the feeling I was about five foot five rather than six feet tall.

It was a few minutes before the first practice, and I was in a hurry to tape my stick. I could see the tape, on a bench in the corner, right where a group of veterans was sitting, with Ivan Hlinka at its center. I wondered what to do. It didn't feel right to reach for the tape without saying anything. For a few moments, I stood there feeling embarrassed. Then I blurted, "Mister Hlinka, would you be so kind as to pass me the tape?"

Ivan gave me a look I'll never forget. Half-amused, half-aggrieved, he replied, "Holy shit, Frigo! This is the national team, and we're in this together. Call me Ivan. Here's the tape." Then he muttered something about youngsters treating him as if he were an old man.

At last, it had come to this! I'd gotten what those officials had tried to tempt me to Litvinov with; I was on the same team as my idol. What's more, we were fellow internationals.

I was expecting to have plenty of opportunity to watch Ivan's game—no one was expecting me to be actively involved in the tournament. I was there as a reserve, a substitute. But during the second match, Vincent Lukac got injured. Coach Gut slapped me on the shoulder and told me to get ready to go on.

My career as a senior international began in the 46th minute of that game. I'd never played this kind of hockey before. The Soviets were all over us. We might have stopped Helmuts Balderis with a lasso, but as it was ... What a step up from the league!

I got on in the third game, too—after a collision with Valeri Vasiliev, Jaroslav Pouzar had to go off. A couple of minutes later, I received a pass between the red line and the blue, and found myself with no one to beat but celebrated goaltender Vladislav Tretiak. Before I could control the puck and look up, he was out in the face-off circle; rashly, I drove the puck straight at him. Like a deer in the headlights, this newcomer. Had I tried to lift the puck over Tretiak or ventured a deke, I might have had an empty net to shoot into …

It was too soon for my first international goal. But I didn't have long to wait.

In April 1979, we played our last warm-up game before the world championship, against Sweden. We beat them 6-0, and I scored past Pelle Lindbergh. This goal had an extra significance for me, as I came up against Pelle as often as anyone in my career. We had already faced each other as under-18s and under-20s. Later, we would be opponents in the AHL and, on a regular basis, in the NHL. He was a fantastic goaltender and a great guy. In November 1985, he was killed in a car accident. A long time passed before I came to terms with that tragedy.

It was maybe thanks to this goal that I forced my way into the final selection for the world championship in Moscow. I hadn't counted on being picked. This time, too, I started out as a reserve. I had to wait until the third game for my chance, when it was already clear that we would advance from the group.

We played against the USA, and we played badly. All of us. But my blunder really stood out. I sent a cross-ice pass through the neutral zone, straight to one of the Americans, who mounted a breakaway. Fortunately, he didn't get past our goaltender, Marcel Sakac, and the game ended 2-2. Even so, that was my last appearance at the tournament. And no wonder—I'd committed the kind of blunder a novice gets bawled out for.

I spent the rest of the tournament standing by the boards, opening the gate to the ice as my teammates came and went. I didn't get a second chance from Gut.

I have to say that Gut wasn't my cup of tea as a coach. He and my dad were pretty close—during their military service, they had shared a room for two years. But Gut and I just didn't see eye to eye, and I couldn't relax around him. He was uptight and his expression was gloomy. He never smiled. He made it clear that he was the boss, and he liked to hand out fines. The one-hundred-crown charge for smoking in our rooms was especially unpopular. Tired of the constant expense and the games of hide-and-seek that went along with it, Ivan Hlinka went to Gut and said to him, "Take this five hundred, Coach, and save yourself the bother of checking up on us."

Despite all my reservations about Gut, however, I fully understood why he kept me out of the rest of the games. I'd played badly and done something stupid.

While the tournament was in progress, in Ostrava my benching was a topic of discussion. Miroslav Vlach, a great forward in his day, wrote in the local press that there was no point in having me in Moscow if all I did was open the gate; they could have taken another executive instead. I don't think he was right.

I had to take a realist's view of the situation. I was 19 years old—I was happy just to be rubbing shoulders with such great teammates at the world championship. It was a huge part of my education. Others might have seen my position by the boards as a demotion, but I knew I had the best seat in the house at the Luzhniki Palace. I got to see the stars of all the teams up close and to learn from them. And how much there was to learn!

The Soviets were the best, of course. Their motivation was sky-high, plus this was the first big event in front of the Moscow public for coach Viktor Tikhonov. They were a class above the rest, beating the Canadians and the Swedes 9-2 and 11-3, respectively; they put 11 past us, too. They were like guerillas who took no prisoners and showed no mercy. It was as though they delighted in paying us back for all the defeats we'd inflicted on them in earlier championships.

One game against them in the final round was reminiscent of an execution. I actually felt sorry for our boys on the ice. They were turned this way and that as the Russians kept hold of the puck and had a wonderful time with it. The Soviets had just been on a power play and were up 8-1. Our defenders were bumbling around our zone in confusion, practically on all fours with their tongues hanging out. I looked on from close quarters as an amused Boris Mikhailov leaned on his stick and called over to Valeri Kharlamov, "They're jumping about like frogs!"

These guys hardly ever showed their emotions, but now it was plain that they were having fun.

It was nice to be given silver medals at the end of the tournament, but we didn't feel much like runners-up in a world championship. And my contribution had been a very modest one. Still, it was an honor for me to be invited to join Ivan Hlinka and Vladimir Martinec for a beer and a smoke.

We would go to a snack bar behind the stadium, where a *babushka* served Pilsner beer at the counter. Sometimes we'd run into Mikhailov, Kharlamov and Tsygankov in their red tracksuit tops with CCCP on the back; they would be drinking one shot of vodka after another. They would wave to Vladimir and Ivan, ignore me, then go back to what they were doing. This, too, was an amazing experience for me.

Although a silver at the world championship was usually considered a success, this wasn't the case in 1979. We had twice beaten a Canadian team that included Marcel Dionne, Garry Unger and other NHL players, and we'd finished above the combative Swedes. But no one at home would forgive us those two debacles against the Soviets. A score of 11-1 against the Soviets was as bad as losing to Poland.

The reception to mark our homecoming at the headquarters of the Czechoslovak Association of Physical Education was an awkward occasion. As runners-up in previous years, Ivan Hlinka and co. had been given cars; this time, each of us received a mere five thousand crowns. Some older players grumbled about their reward, but I was happy with mine. To me, it was a lot of money. And I was looking forward to all the fun I'd be able to have with it in Ostrava.

Our so-so performance at the world championship in Moscow had an unpleasant consequence for me: I was dropped from the national team.

Fortunately, things were going well for me in the league, as they were for Vitkovice as a whole. I put four goals past leaders Dukla Trencin, and coach Karel Gut was at the stadium to see us play Slovan Bratislava. We thrashed them 7-3, and I scored a hat trick. After the game, Ostrava journalists flocked to the coach to ask his opinion of our performances. "As for Frycer, I believe that his removal from the national team after the world championship in Moscow was the best kind of doping," he told the press. "He has taken it the right way and shown a great deal of ambition. His performances show that he's on the way back."

I returned to the national team in December, plus I was the youngest member of the squad named for the Olympic Games in Lake Placid, USA.

The standard at that tournament wasn't then as high as it would be at Nagano and in subsequent years—it didn't yet include professionals from the NHL—but it was the Olympics nevertheless. It was every athlete's dream and a great event for fans. And it was definitely the high point of my career up to that point.

As a child watching TV, I had imagined and dreamed that everything would look just as it did at Lake Placid. I was greatly impressed by the opening ceremony, with its parade of participating nations, an event at which, fortunately, the dreadful cold bothered us very little: in our coats and fur hats, we looked ready for the Eastern Front. The pair of Cypriot skiers marching next to us had a much worse time of things—the guy was wearing a blazer, the girl a short skirt.

After the lighting of the Olympic flame, there was a rather morbid scene as the doves of peace were released. The organizers had had them ready in their cages for too long: the cold had been too much for some of them. They flapped their wings, then fell down dead …

The Olympic Village was anything but fancy. It came as no surprise to me that after the Games it became a youth detention center. Two to a room, we had to move about carefully in our 65 square feet; so tight was the space, we had to approach the window in turns. We had our own toilet, but the showers were communal. But we didn't grumble. We were no pampered kids from Manhattan—we could manage the spartan conditions for two weeks.

I went out to watch some of the other events. When five-time Olympic champion speed skater Eric Heiden sat down next to me, I could hardly believe my luck. He was obviously in great shape—what I would have given for thighs as powerful as his!

There was just one blot on the lovely, tranquil landscape of Lake Placid. But it was a pretty big one. Our performances were woeful and we finished fifth.

We really blew it in our second game. We had been very confident of beating the USA. Even after the first period, with the score at 2-2, we told ourselves in the dressing room that we were sure to get the better of these college kids. Well, they put seven past us. Who could have guessed that we'd just been beaten by the soon-to-be Olympic champions, whose achievement would go down in sporting history as the Miracle on Ice?

To advance from our division, we needed to beat the Swedes in the last game. We messed up. By the time we got going, the game was almost over and we were losing 3-0. All that remained for us then was a game against Canada to decide fifth place. This we won 6-1, and I scored a goal, but it did little to make up for the overall disappointment.

Something wasn't right from the very beginning. Twenty-five of us had flown over knowing we would be playing a couple of exhibitions against Canada, in Calgary and Montreal, after which the coaches would make the final cut. Twenty of us would go to the Olympics; the five who didn't make it would join up with the B team. This unusual selection process created anxiety within the camp. We spent a whole week not knowing who would make the cut and who wouldn't.

Once the coaches announced the final roster, I expected things to settle down. We were told that the players who hadn't made the cut would be bused out at six the next morning. So you can imagine my surprise at breakfast when I encountered players who were supposed to be gone, while others who had been selected to go to Lake Placid were no longer with us.

I had no idea what was going on or why the roster had changed overnight. Only years later did I discover that some older players had ganged up on the coach to demand that Slava Duris be retained on defense instead of Jan Zajicek. The official reason for Jaromir Sindel's being dropped from the roster was concussion, sustained by a knee to the head during the game in Calgary. This was nonsense—he was perfectly fit to tend goal, but plainly someone wanted Karel Lang in his place.

Things like this can destroy the strongest groups. And we weren't that strong to begin with. The atmosphere in the dressing room was strange. Cliques were formed, which is never a good thing. I got wind of tensions between nations—apparently some people were bothered by the fact that there were four Slovaks on the team, maintaining that things had been better four years earlier in Innsbruck, when the group had included Czechs only. This confused me. I'd never made a distinction between Czechs and Slovaks, and I tried to get along with everyone.

What bothered me most was that Ivan Hlinka didn't take part in the Olympics. I've never found out why. Although he had a knee problem, he played two matches in West Germany that January with no apparent ill effects. We certainly missed a leader of his stature, the kind of character who could reduce a dressing room to silence just by walking in. We had Vladimir Martinec, also a big personality, but Vladimir lacked Ivan's authority. Anyway, he broke his arm in our second game and spent the rest of the Olympics as a tourist, dressed in the national team's uniform.

It wasn't uncommon for conversations in the dressing room to be about nonhockey matters, such as who got $200 for playing with a

Koho stick or $500 for wearing Adidas instead of Graf skates. Some of the guys wore new boots that gave them blisters. They couldn't skate properly, but at least they were making money. Ridiculous.

It was as though team success was secondary. For some people, the most important thing was to enjoy the Olympics—if things went wrong on the ice, whatever, no reason to spoil the mood. At least that's the impression I had. A real shame. I think we were good enough hockey players to get at least the bronze, but other things got in the way.

Our fifth-place finish caused consternation at home. One year earlier, people had turned up their noses at a silver medal from Moscow. Compared with that, this was a fiasco. After 12 years of top-three-finishes, the national team had returned from a major tournament without a medal. That no one would be applauding our efforts was clear to us as soon as we touched down at Prague's Ruzyne Airport. Skier Kveta Jeriova, Czechoslovakia's only medal-winner, was the first to emerge with her trolley. She passed through customs without being stopped. The customs officers had a good rummage in our luggage.

———

After the failure in Lake Placid, Ludek Bukac was appointed head coach of the national team. Many players were dropped in favor of younger ones. Fortunately, I kept my place. And in late 1980, I gave my best performance on the international stage.

We were playing an exhibition match against the Soviet Union, and maybe Prague's Sports Hall worked its magic on me again. We were only in the sixth minute when I deflected a pass from Ivan Hlinka behind Vladimir Myshkin. 1-0 for us. Although Valeri Kharlamov tied it up in the second period, the next key moment would be mine. Ivan played the puck and no one went after it, believing the play would be stopped for icing. Experienced defenseman Vladimir Lutchenko casually corralled the puck. I don't know what got into me, but I launched myself in Lutchenko's direction, cheekily lifted his stick, robbed him of the puck, and scored my second goal. The best move of the match, it would be shown often on TV.

We didn't win, unfortunately. Vladimir Krutov had the last word on a power play; the game ended 2-2. Still, I was delighted with my performance. At last I'd played the kind of game for the national team I'd always dreamed of.

There wouldn't be many such moments, which is a pity.

Although I scored a lot of goals in the league, I'd been unable to transfer this form to the national team. Maybe it was because in Vitkovice I was used to being on the ice most of the time—I played every power play, every important moment. The national team doesn't work like that. As a young player, you get only two or three shifts per period to show what you can do. Your position improves only if you can take full advantage. Regrettably, I just didn't know how to deal with this.

I wasn't experienced enough to sort these important matters out in my mind. I didn't lack talent, and I was very well prepared by my club; but to make more of an impression at the international level, I needed to mature. At 21, few players have what it takes. The coaches tried to bring me along, but they didn't succeed in unlocking my potential.

What's more, the national team placed great emphasis on well-coordinated lines of players from the same team, or at least pairs of clubmates for whom they found a third. That third was frequently me. I did get to play alongside Lada Svozil, but rarely. My appearances were most often with Ivan Hlinka, with Jaroslav Pouzar as our left wing. Both great players, but we weren't really on the same wavelength. When the two of them got a play started, I was never quite sure where to go.

Although playing alongside my idol was a dream come true and a great honor, Ivan and I tended to get in each other's way. As a skater, he was a slow starter who would accelerate gradually, and he was used to approaching the offensive zone from the right—where I was roaming. My forward route cut off, I hung back, looking on as the play developed in front of me. I hardly ever seemed to get the puck, although I wanted it as much as Ivan did. What was I supposed to do, fight him for it?

At the 1981 world championship in Sweden, my center was Milan Novy, a classic sharpshooter alongside whom I had to adjust to yet another system. Things didn't work out the way I wanted them to this time either. It was a small comfort to me that, unlike in Moscow, I got regular playing time; also, I got to score a goal in the world championship, against the USA. We paid them back for our defeat at the Olympics by beating them 11-2, with four goals from the outstanding Jiri Lala.

Once again, our games against Canada were something special.

Their team was set up in an interesting way. The world championship would be Don Cherry's final coaching assignment before his departure for TV show business. Their team included 50-goal marksman Dennis Maruk, young forwards Mike Gartner and John Ogrodnick, and mustachioed captain Lanny McDonald. Although very little information about the NHL made it through the Iron Curtain, we knew plenty about Larry Robinson and Guy Lafleur, and we had great respect for them; they had played in the Canada Cup in 1976, and besides, I'd seen them for myself in Montreal.

When we shook hands after the game in Gothenburg, I imagined myself saying, "Hope to play against you again soon, guys." My head was filled with thoughts of the NHL.

Robinson and Lafleur may have been superstars, but we were far more concerned about defenseman Barry Long, a strapping figure from the Winnipeg Jets who put the fear of God into us. When we got close to him in the pregame warm-up, he growled like a mad dog, so we took care to keep our pucks away from the Canadians. Things weren't much different in the game itself. We got the puck away quickly, afraid of being caught in possession and pressed against the boards or face-down on the ice. Coach Ludek Bukac must have been delighted—these short, crisp passes were what he'd been trying to drill into us all season!

Maybe it was thanks to Long that we beat Canada comfortably twice, thus putting ourselves among the medals.

On the last day, we faced the Russians, world champions by some distance. We were sure of the bronze. But with this opponent, there was always something to play for. Having beaten them at the Izvestia tournament in December—our first win against the Russians since I'd been on the national team—we fancied our chances. And this time, Vladislav Tretiak would be rested.

This could be the game in which I prove myself, I thought. With the score at 1-1, I broke away and was about to shoot when Slava Fetisov tripped me. The referee indicated a penalty shot.

I messed it up good and proper. Afterward, they said that the moment was too much for me. But that's nonsense. I tried a fake, but it was toward the end of the third period and the ice was breaking down. I skated into a groove and the puck bounced off to the right, ending up in the corner. I went left, then found myself sailing, along with Vladimir Myshkin, into the goal, where I flapped about like a fish in a net. Pretty embarrassing. Had it happened today, I'd be a YouTube star.

My teammates thought it was hilarious. Back on the bench, Ivan Hlinka leaned over to me and said, "Put it out of your mind, Frigo. How many Czechs can be watching a game against Russia? At most, seven or eight … million." I burst out laughing. Next to me, Vladimir Martinec gave us a look, warning us not to give the coaches the impression we weren't taking the world championship seriously.

The score remained 1-1 until the buzzer sounded to end the game.

For a young team with 12 newcomers, the bronze was a success. The dejection brought on by the failure at Lake Placid dissipated. There was hope for the years to come, wrote the press. Hlinka, Martinec and Ebermann, all survivors of the golden era and now in their 30s, were ready to move on, making way for more new talent.

I would also be on my way, although I was only 21. That game against the Soviet Union was my 55th as a senior international player; it was also my last. After those championships, I was removed from the national team for being "politically unreliable," therefore missing out on that September's Canada Cup, an event I'd been very much looking forward to.

But now I'm jumping ahead in the story.

7

Champions of Czechoslovakia

DAD AND I WERE forever talking about hockey. We had hockey for breakfast, lunch and supper. But our talks were never as serious as in the summer of 1978.

Following my second season at Vitkovice, coach Stemprok departed for Landshut in West Germany, and the vacant position was offered to Dad. He had been officially employed by the club since the spring, when he had taken up a position with the youth teams. But he was hesitant about taking this next step.

He was concerned that by becoming head coach, he could make things uncomfortable for me. As everyone knows, no hockey dressing room contains 20 best friends; you'll always find at least one vain, overambitious player who spreads malicious gossip and complains under his breath about nepotism. But I assured Dad he had nothing to worry about—we had a good group, and the players would accept him without problems. Besides, in the past two seasons I'd made a strong case for myself, not least because I'd represented the national team. No one would be able to grumble that I was given power plays just because my dad was coach.

In the end, Dad agreed to take the job. I was glad. Dad loved his hockey and gave it his all. I would have been very sorry if his dream of coaching in the first league had remained unrealized because of me.

Besides, I had the feeling he was just the right coach for us. He would give us more freedom to play and grant us freer rein beyond the stadium, too.

For my two years at Vitkovice, Stemprok had kept us under the whip; the stress had been unremitting. Dad had a softer touch. Having been a long-serving player himself, he knew how things worked on a team, and he could figure out the right approach for any given moment. It was against his nature to behave like a cop. He had more class than to check that the veterans weren't sneaking a smoke, and he had nothing against a player having a beer with his supper. There were still fixed borders we mustn't encroach, but they weren't so close together.

In Dad's first season, we finished third, giving Vitkovice its first medal in 21 years. It was a great moment for the region. People appreciated our dynamic, offensive style of play. They had the feeling we were onto something big, and that still headier times were on the horizon. As is often the case in such situations, greater pressure began to be applied from above.

That summer, Rudolf Peska, general director of the Vitkovice Ironworks, and as such our biggest boss, called us together at the stadium. Having congratulated us on taking third place, he explained that we were expected to improve on it. Basically, he made it our job to do better. It seemed to me idiotic to plan this way, so I stood up and told him that this wasn't how sport worked. "We'll give our all in pursuit of the title, we can promise you that," I said, letting my mouth run away with me. "But it's impossible to make guarantees. We're not working on a production line or at the coalface with quotas to achieve. Anything might happen." I was young: this could be taken as impudence.

Probably I had a special gift for attracting trouble. And I got plenty of it.

Today when I think of young Frycer, I realize he would drive me mad. I certainly wouldn't want to coach him. He was headstrong, always in the right, with an opinion on everything. He was very confident in his abilities. And he had a partner who was the same in all these regards. Lada Svozil and I believed that Vitkovice couldn't manage without us, and we took full advantage. Sometimes we went too far.

On the day of a game in Brno, we got home from a night out at five in the morning. Zetor was a difficult opponent at the best of times. We slept off our hangovers on the bus (fortunately, the drive to southern

Moravia took quite a long time in those days). That evening, we scored all three in a 3-2 victory, so no one could reproach us. After the game, we returned to the bus and slept all the way back to Ostrava.

Of course, if we'd lost, there would have been hell to pay from the others, and we'd have been fined, too. That's the way it is. In every sport. If you're doing well, your weaknesses are excused. But once you start playing badly, people delight in counting your slip-ups against you.

The coach is also important in all this. If he's a psychologist and a diplomat, it certainly helps.

Once, Milos Holan came to Sunday practice directly from a dance, with glitter still in his hair. He popped some chewing gum into his mouth and stepped onto the ice with confidence. Dad's choices were to give Milos a dressing down, make an example of him, make him eat dirt. Or to turn a blind eye and hope his benevolence would be rewarded on the ice. Usually, he chose the second course, and he rarely regretted it.

I can't say that I made things easy for Dad at Vitkovice. Our relationship had changed. There was a big difference between the 12-year-old peewee and the adult pro. I had my strengths and I had my weaker moments. I know my antics were sometimes difficult for him to take. I never talked back or snapped at him—I respected him too much for that—but there were times when we didn't have much to say to each other.

Dad's main worry was that I'd get into the kind of trouble that couldn't be handled by the club. Once again, he gave me a great deal of advice, but this advice differed from the kind he gave me in Karvina. *If you go to a bar, you don't have to stay until it closes. Don't drink and drive—call a taxi. If you get into a fight with someone, don't cripple him, for God's sake. And make sure there are no cops about.*

In some things, he was stricter with me than with the others. Where punishments were involved, the fact that I was his son made no difference. Some of my transgressions attracted a fine, others the temporary withholding of my win bonus, or its removal altogether. I had to bow my head and accept what was coming to me.

My troublemaking came to a head early in the 1979-80 season. After five games, I'd spent more time in the penalty box than any other player in the league, although Lada wasn't far behind me. I'd racked up a total of 32 minutes, 20 of which were for unsportsmanlike conduct.

This was overdoing things.

I've always hated injustice, and in those days I would get really mad if I felt someone was trying to put one over on me, which was often. It's a good thing for young players to care deeply about what happens on the ice. But we took it to extremes. We lorded it over everyone and took offense at everything. If I disagreed with the referees about a penalty call, it occurred to me—brat that I was—to explain to them the rules of hockey. Naturally, they refused to speak with me, which angered me even more. I'd slam my stick down on the ice, so earning myself 10 minutes in the penalty box.

The older players had a go at us for weakening the team for nothing. Like naughty schoolboys sent to the principal's office, we received repeated summons to meet with officials at divisional HQ. Sometimes I was sent for, sometimes Lada; usually, the two of us appeared together. The scene was always the same: the president behind his desk, flanked by four yes-men. And they would always give us the same lecture, straight from the handbook, on how the socialist athlete should behave.

The public, too, began to take an interest in our disciplinary problems. Josef Mikolas, a great goaltender of the past, wrote an article about us in the local press. Called "Seekers after self-discipline," it was none too complimentary.

At the time, such criticism really got on my nerves. I realize now, of course, that critics of my behavior were absolutely right. Fortunately, after a while Lada and I became less hot-headed, which worked to our own advantage as well as Vitkovice's. I'm not claiming that we became models of good conduct, but we paid more attention to the play and less to what went on around it. We stopped being spoiled brats.

We finished that season in fourth, which we considered a success even though we hadn't fulfilled the task set by our comrade the general director. I scored 31 league goals and finished sixth in the *Zlata hokej-ka* (Golden Hockey Stick) poll for best player in Czechoslovakia. Not bad for a seeker after self-discipline.

———

In summer 1980, Dad was unexpectedly relieved of his post at Vitkovice. It had nothing to do with results—although we'd earned four points fewer than in the previous season, fourth place was no disgrace, and it would hardly set heads rolling.

The association had decided that from the next season on head coaches of league clubs would require the highest form of license or at least be studying toward it. Dad refused to play along. At 52, he had no interest in returning to the study of coaching, he explained. He resigned his post and went back to Karvina.

His position was taken by Jan Soukup, who had been Stemprok's assistant, then Dad's. Soukup took on ex-player Karel Metelka as his right-hand man. With all due respect to these gentlemen, I believe anyone could have coached that team, just as anyone could coach Canada today. The team was ready and hungry for success, its composition ideal. After what Stemprok had started and my dad had fine-tuned, it would be enough to bring the harvest home.

The 1980-81 season was like a ride on a roller coaster. Incredible. Twists and turns, hopes and dreams, mess-ups, emotions. And once again, it happened that I played a leading role in all of it.

Take our October game in Kladno, when we beat our hosts—4-2—for the first time in ages. Their excellent team challenged for the title most seasons, usually successfully. Not surprisingly, Lada and I decided that our result was worth celebrating. We spent the night after the game in Prague, where we hit a few bars. This time, our safety valve didn't kick in: off the leash in the capital, we didn't get back to the hotel until the early hours. The coaches were livid with us, and we were fined on the spot.

And that wasn't all. That morning, our bus was due to leave for the airport from in front of the White Swan department store. We decided to pop into the bar next door for a quick beer, to straighten out the level of alcohol in our blood. Unfortunately, we ended up having about five beers. Instead of sneaking to the back of the bus and pretending we weren't there, we sat down right behind the coaches. All the way to the airport, we giggled like idiots, at any crap that occurred to us. That finished the job nicely.

On our return to Ostrava, the management and older players came up with a further punishment. On top of our fines, we would each be suspended for the next match. I could do nothing but accept. What bothered me more was that news of our disgrace had gotten into the papers. The headline read: "Frycer and Svozil banned by division for game with Slovan Bratislava after dietary lapse."

I don't know who leaked the information—perhaps the coaches, or one of the management who was sick to the back teeth of us. Though we could hardly be proud of what we'd done, it wasn't so unusual. Such things happen everywhere, several times a season. Typically, they are dealt with by a fine, or by the coach laying into the culprit the next day. In worse cases, a short suspension, concealed from outsiders by the excuse of a high temperature. What happens within the team stays within the team. If it didn't, the newspapers would be full of it.

On this occasion, I was so upset that I cleared my locker and told the coaches to stick it. Then I went home to Karvina, to my dad.

The whole affair came to a head with an open letter addressed to "Comrade Miroslav Frycer, hockey player with TJ Vitkovice and the CSSR," which appeared over half a page in the daily *Mlada fronta*, penned by well-known sports journalist Vaclav Pacina. His sermon, an analysis of the mess we'd gotten ourselves into and my reaction to it, ended with the idea that I should ditch my higher-education studies and instead go into the army, where, as one of the greatest talents of my generation, I'd not only become a better hockey player, I'd mature mentally, which could only benefit me.

Ridiculous. When I read it today, over 35 years later, I can't help but laugh.

I didn't go to the army, but I did soon return to the team. The situation settled down—I just had to get used to being mocked by fans. "Roll out the barrels, it's Vitkovice!" they would cry. Or they would curse us as drunkards. Athletes must learn to ignore such taunts.

―――

There was a special magic about our Christmas holidays in 1980. As a pleasant diversion from the demands of the domestic season, we flew out to Davos, Switzerland, for the Spengler Cup. We shopped for the family and played in a prestigious tournament in beautiful surroundings. In a curious way, too, we prepared for an assault on the league title.

It started innocently enough, with our traditional game of shinny. Wherever we were playing, on the day of the game, the same group of us kept the custom of ending the morning tune-up with a short five-on-five. Sometimes the stakes were 10 crowns, at others the price of that evening's beers. Several times it happened that the shinny was more important to us than the game against some Swedes or Finns— then, our main battle began at 10 a.m., and it left us sweatier than the game that evening.

In Davos, the shinny reached its high point when Jaroslav Vlk and I disagreed over whether a goal should stand. He said it shouldn't; I said it should. The argument escalated into a screaming match, followed by a veritable explosion that had us laying into each other with our fists and sticks. Our teammates dragged us apart, but the damage had been done.

"I've played on the same line as him for the last time! Never again!" I yelled.

It may have been over a trifle—a meaningless game of shinny—but I was deadly serious. Teammates and coaches alike told me I was out of my mind, that when we talked it over tomorrow I'd see things very differently. But I was unmoved and insistent. "No. No way. Out of the question."

So ended the celebrated line of Frycer-Svozil-Vlk.

The coaches had no choice but to put Lada and me together with Frantisek Cernik. Surprisingly, this change worked to the benefit of the whole team. Ours had been a good line before, but now it had added aggression and firepower. We were much better for it. Vlk went to the second line, which improved, too, with him on it. Thanks to my refusal to back down, now we had two strong lines that would cause opponents all kinds of problems. Crucially, the incident at the Spengler Cup didn't spoil the atmosphere in the dressing room. Vlk and I continued to go for a beer together. We got along fine as long as we weren't playing together.

Another turning point came that February, at the training camp for the national team in Nymburk. It wasn't at all unusual for such gatherings to take place while the season was in progress. The clubs had nothing like the power they have today; it went without saying that everything was subjugated to the needs of the national team. I seem to remember that the coaches called us up for 10 days. It was a slog from the very first moment. Practice three times a day, a real tough workout. We were less than happy about having to do this before the league season was over.

At the beginning of the training camp, Jaromir Sindel came down with tonsillitis and went home, encouraging us to follow suit. I stuck it out for about three days. Then, during a skating drill, I skated straight into some pucks arranged in the corner of the rink, took a tumble, grabbed my groin—and before long I was scooting back to Ostrava. Lada Svozil and Frantisek Cernik did something similar. It wasn't entirely bogus—we were carrying a few knocks from the league—but the early departure did us good, as it allowed us to rest up and let our aches and pains heal.

League leader Ceske Budejovice, whom we sought to challenge for the title, had nine players in Nymburk. All of them lasted till the end, which I think cost the club the title. They simply ran out of steam. When they came to Vitkovice, it was obvious they were drained and their legs were heavy. We thrashed them 7-3 and moved up the standings. After that, we won on the road at Sparta and Pardubice, followed by a home win against Kladno. All these victories were by a single goal. Three games from the season's end, we led the standings by two points.

Things went quickly after that. First, a crucial game in Bratislava against Slovan, fighting tooth and nail to stay ahead. We won the game 8-5, but poor Lada ended up in the hospital following an unfortunate clash with Jozef Bukovinsky, a good, decent guy who away from the ice wouldn't have harmed a fly. Although each had tried to get out of the other's way, Jozef had caught Lada's ankle. A very nasty injury that marked the end of Lada's season. So bad, in fact, that he was lucky to return to hockey at all.

In the next match, we overcame Plzen at home 5-3. Before the final round of games, we remained two points ahead of Ceske Budejovice. To make Budejovice's result meaningless, we needed to win our game against Gottwaldov. In other seasons, one point would have been enough, but in that season no single points were awarded—after the failure in Lake Placid, the association had decided that tied games would go into 10 minutes' overtime, then, if need be, be decided by a shootout—giving the winning side two points and leaving the defeated one with nothing. This was supposed to teach us to play under pressure, so driving us to victory.

Apparently, the association had little faith in us, or maybe they didn't want us to win: although we were the league leader, the championship trophy was taken to Litvinov, where Ceske Budejovice was playing its last game. This annoyed us, but we decided to ignore it and think only of ourselves.

In the game against Gottwaldov, we knew that the success we'd worked for for so long was ours, provided we took that last step. But that very knowledge seemed to hold us back.

The home players were relaxed. With no danger of relegation to the second league, there was nothing for them to play for. We were off our game from the start, struggling to control the puck, late in the battle along the boards; nothing came together for us. Then Gottwaldov went up 1-0, making the weight on our shoulders that much greater.

Although we had no news of the score in Litvinov, we doubted Ceske Budejovice would slip up. Because our goal differential and head-to-head results were worse, we had to turn our game around. There were about 3,000 fans from Ostrava in the stands, and they drove us forward. In an atmosphere like this, to fail was unthinkable.

The clouds didn't part for us until the 45th minute, when Milos Riha tied the game. Thirteen seconds later, I added a second—my 33rd and most important goal of the season. After that, we didn't relax our grip. The game ended 4-2 for us, Milos having clinched the result with an empty-net goal.

It was March 15, 1981, and Vitkovice was celebrating its much-longed-for title! Its first in 29 years, and so far its last.

The euphoria knew no bounds. Before the celebrations bore us back to the dressing room, our wonderful fans poured out of the stands onto the ice. It's for moments like these that we play hockey. Unqualified happiness, joy, relief, a great sense of sporting achievement. Even years later, I get goosebumps just thinking about it.

Frantisek Cernik knew from his time with Dukla Jihlava and the national team how such successes should be celebrated. Within minutes of the buzzer, he brought out champagne and cigars he'd bought earlier but hidden from us so as not to offend the hockey gods.

Everything flowed freely. It was fantastic.

We had dinner at the Moskva hotel, where the fatigue and stress finally caught up with us. We were so mentally drained that we lacked the strength to carry on celebrating. For weeks we'd been planning the spree we would embark on once the title was ours, and suddenly all we could do was sit there looking at each other. Besides, Frantisek, Jaromir and I would soon be heading off to join the national team for the pre–world championship training camp, while the rest of the boys would go directly from Gottwaldov to play in some nonsensical tournament. There was no chance of our going on a bender.

I drank two beers and ordered a third that I didn't finish. Then my parents drove me home. That historic title belonged to Dad, too. How happy I was that he was at that last game!

We finally got our hands on the championship trophy about two weeks later, at a gala event at the Atom hotel in Ostrava to mark the end of the season. We received a bonus, a champion's medal and a certificate, plus about four other types of medals. There were lots of bigwigs there, so we soon made ourselves scarce, finishing our title celebrations in a bar. I got home in the early hours. As I was undressing, I found two Model VZKG Employee medals pinned onto me. I've no idea where these came from and why I ended up with them. So far, none of the boys have been in touch to say they are missing from their trophy cabinet.

For me, this celebration was tinged with a strange melancholy, as I knew I wouldn't be defending the title. I had a different plan for how my career would progress. I wished, hoped and believed that in the fall I would be scoring goals in the NHL.

Whatever it might cost me.

8

Escape

IT MAY BE THAT ALL important things start unexpectedly, with a large helping of luck involved.

Take the Sweden Cup in April 1980. As it was an Olympic year and there was no world championship, the international season was to end with a tournament in Gothenburg. Taking part would be us, the Soviets, the Swedes, the Finns and a Canadian team. We ended up in third place, but I wasn't concerned about the result. A low-key encounter on a Gothenburg street had a much more powerful effect on me.

Before one of the matches, Lada Svozil and I were out walking when he was approached by a stranger on the street. They exchanged a few quick words before parting.

"Who was that?" I wanted to know.

"Some guy from Canada. He's looking for players ready to flee to the NHL, and he wants me to be one of them. It's not the first time he's spoken to me."

"I'll go with you!" I burst out.

"For real?"

"Absolutely, if they'll take me."

I'd longed to play in the NHL for ages. At least since late 1977, when I made the team for the world junior championship in Canada, I'd been convinced that I wanted to play hockey overseas. And I was also convinced that I would do it. If I set my mind on something, I go for it head on and without thought of compromise. Which is just what I did with this great dream of mine.

It was clear to me from the outset that it wouldn't be easy for me to get to the NHL. General secretary Husak was in Prague Castle, Brezhnev was in the Kremlin, and the Soviet army was in Czechoslovakia and had recently entered Afghanistan. We all believed that communism was here to stay. In 1980, there was no question of traveling legally to the NHL. It was possible to slip through into western Europe, but only if you were over 30 and had played at least 150 international matches, or you were a world champion.

I fell short of qualification by 123 internationals and nine years of age.

I wasn't intending to wait that long. I didn't want to depart as a 30-year-old relic of the golden generation of the '70s—exhausted and battered, with dodgy knees. Besides, you can't plan like that in sport. One bad injury and not only are you out of the international picture for good, you're happy just to be playing for your club team again; all hope of playing abroad has gone.

There was nothing else for it—I would have to defect.

The guy who had spoken to Lada in the street was called Ludovit Katona. A Slovak living in Toronto, he had an arrangement with teams in the NHL to sort out contracts for them with players from Czechoslovakia. He hung around the national and club teams with the intention of tapping players who, so he believed, didn't buy into the regime's cock-and-bull stories about life in the fairest society in the world (i.e., the advanced socialist state).

Lada and I were two such players. We were both well aware of what we were living in and why. If we'd had any choice in the matter, we wouldn't even have joined the Socialist Union of Youth. For a long time, we resisted the executives at Vitkovice, telling them we didn't have time for meetings because we had to practice and play. But Frycer and Svozil, leading athletes in the worker's paradise city of Ostrava, would need to be unionized, and that was that. One day we arrived in the dressing room to find, lying on the table, a brand-new union member's card for each of us. These cards bore not only our photos but our signatures too, which came as quite a shock to us. There was nothing we could do about this.

Lada took me along to his next meeting with Katona, at a bar on an out-of-the-way city street. There was no question of his picking us up at the reception and having coffee with us in the hotel restaurant: we needed to be careful.

We were closely watched on every trip we took abroad. Our party would include gentlemen none of us knew but whose role was clear to all of us. Sometimes they were introduced to us thus: "This is Dr. Novak." But if we went to them to ask for a pill, they would wave us away in horror. These doctors had been trained at a very different kind of school.

The snoops were forever following us around, to find out who we were associating with. The only associates they were interested in were émigrés and people who looked like managers from teams in the West. Nor did they care if we partied too long or smuggled home a few pairs of jeans. Their reports concerned matters of great importance, matters that could destroy careers in sport—and lives.

At the meeting with Katona, he revealed that he was representing the Quebec Nordiques, a team new to the NHL. And he wanted to know if I, too, was interested in leaving my homeland. "Of course," I assured him. "At the very first opportunity." I wanted him to know I was deadly serious.

Before we parted, we agreed that he would get in touch with us when the time came. And he gave us a few hundred dollars, as a token of the Nordiques' appreciation of our interest in joining them.

I was so obsessed with the NHL that my instinct for self-preservation deserted me. It never occurred to me that Katona could be a fraud, even less an *agent provocateur* for the State Security police; I would make these connections only later. I longed to get out and he was my ticket to Canada, so I simply had to trust him. In time, there would be no doubt about the kind of crook I was dealing with. He was no idealist out to make the sporting dreams of players from the East come true, that's for sure. For him, it was all about business, and we were just warm bodies for whom Canadian teams paid him a king's ransom.

That meeting in Gothenburg was my first step toward my grand hockey dream. I hadn't the slightest idea of the difficulties that awaited me before my first appearance on NHL ice.

———

It's not as if emigration is like buying a new TV. Regardless of the motivating factors behind it, it's a complex decision with many consequences—because it affects the lives of others. At the moment of first contact with the Nordiques, I was married and my wife, Vera, was pregnant. And there were my parents besides.

As soon as I got back from Sweden, I sat my father down and told him about the offer from Quebec. He encouraged me to take the chance, which might not come a second time. My mother agreed with him. "Go, you're young," they told us. "We'll get by without you somehow."

But I didn't want them to have to get by. I knew that if we left, the regime would take it out on them. There were plenty of similar cases among people I knew. It would mean the end of my father's career as a coach. The best he would be able to hope for was a job as a PE teacher at a school for trainee miners.

For this reason, right at the outset I made it a condition that my parents would go with us.

We weren't the only players with an offer from abroad—before long, most members of the national team had gotten one, and the NHL wasn't the only interested party. But most of the lads decided to stay at home. I fully understand why. Unlike the lives of others in the years after the Soviet occupation, ours weren't too bad. Not only did we enjoy playing hockey, it paid well. Our salaries were above average, we traveled to the West several times a year, and our apartments were equipped with electronics from the Tuzex store for luxury exported goods. At 20, I was driving a Fiat 131, also known as the Mirafiori.

The only other citizens of Ostrava to drive one were my teammate Frantisek Cernik and singer Marie Rottrova.

For me, though, one basic thing was missing—freedom. I wanted to be able to speak my mind in public and go on vacation wherever I chose. It's part of my nature to want to live life my own way: when someone tries to limit my freedom, I can get pretty angry. For some, *freedom* is just a word. Not for me it isn't.

The thought of what I would do after the Vitkovice club presented me with my retirement gifts was a depressing one, too. I couldn't imagine my future at all. How would I make a living? What would a certificate in economics get me? How would I adjust to a desk-bound office job after years of being as free as a bird? The uncertainty surrounding my future was another factor in my desire to leave.

Our bold plans were dealt a first blow in late August 1980, at a training camp with the national team in Hluboka nad Vltavou. One of the guys came running into breakfast one day with his eyes wide. "Have you heard about the Stastny brothers?" he said. "They've gone! Peter and Anton are in Quebec!"

Lada and I just stared at each other. That's the end of that, then, I thought. If the Nordiques have signed the Stastny brothers, they won't be wanting us.

Of course, we'd had no idea that Peter and Anton were bound for Quebec—such things weren't spoken of over a beer, even among friends. There was no way of finding out which of our teammates had something on the side going on in secret.

The Stastny brothers had been in touch with Katona for longer than we had. Their escape had been planned for the Europa Cup in Innsbruck, Austria, to which, surprisingly, the management of Slovan Bratislava had allowed Peter's pregnant wife to travel. The three of them reached Canada—via Vienna—after a pretty adventurous journey. A third hockey-playing brother, Marian, returned home.

A few days later, a message arrived from Quebec telling us that our plans were unaffected—the team was still interested in us. We arranged to meet again in December to go over the details of our agreement, at the Spengler Cup in Davos.

At the meeting in Switzerland, we were joined by Gilles Leger, the Nordiques' director of player development, who was behind the whole scheme. He had coached Vaclav Nedomansky and Richard Farda in the World Hockey Association, which had attempted to compete with the NHL. Leger was one of the first to realize that players from Europe could provide North American leagues with welcome new blood, a view that he held to in Quebec. After his first season in the NHL, it was clear to him that if his new club was to succeed among the elite, he needed experienced players. There was no time for nurturing immature talent, which was why he had started the so-called *Projet Européen*, which focused on players in Czechoslovakia who were willing to emigrate. The project's first stage had been the defection of the Stastny brothers; bringing over Lada and me was to be the second. I discovered later that he had been following me for three years, since the world junior championship in Canada, when he had been general manager of the Birmingham Bulls in the WHA.

We met in a smoky Davos bistro, again at the instigation of Katona, who had latched onto us at the stadium and mumbled the name of the bar and the time of the appointment before disappearing. Having confirmed to Leger that we were willing to go to Canada, we agreed to sign contracts the next day.

Our arrival at Leger's hotel room was like a scene from an American movie. Leger was sitting in an armchair under a cloud of cigar smoke, with Katona alongside to translate.

"Here are your contracts," he said. "I suggest you take turns, with one waiting in the bathroom while the other signs."

We refused to do it this way. *If we're to defect together, we'll sign up together. We've nothing to hide from each other.*

Katona translated the content of the contract for us and we signed it. I was to earn $150,000 for each of four seasons. I didn't give much thought to this sum, having no idea whether it was large or small by

Canadian standards. I didn't even care—I would have signed anything. Now that my dream of playing in the NHL was another step closer, money was the last thing on my mind.

As we were preparing to leave, Leger impressed upon us that the contract would come into effect only after we arrived in Quebec.

There was just one more thing to do—come up with a way of getting there.

I see it all as if it were yesterday. It's March 1981, and Lada and I are lying on hotel beds in Bratislava, thinking of our wonderful futures. Ahead of us are three more league games and the world championship. After that, welcome to Quebec, boys!

Then came the misfortune of Lada's injury, leaving me in little doubt that I was on my own.

Sadly, this was not the only complication. I'd agreed with the Nordiques that I would defect in September, during the Canada Cup. But in late spring, things started to get a bit hairy. With Peter and Anton going great guns in the NHL, a rumor that Quebec had signed more players from Czechoslovakia was making the rounds.

It wasn't hard for the brass at the Czechoslovak Ice Hockey Association to figure out, by process of elimination, who these might be. It couldn't be any of the older players: Ivan Hlinka and Jiri Bubla were the first to get permission to leave for the NHL since 1970 (another result of the defection of the Stastny brothers, incidentally), while Vladimir Martinec and Bohuslav Ebermann had arranged transfers to West Germany and Switzerland, respectively. No one thought it probable that newcomers to the national team would defect. That left the eternal rebels Svozil and Frycer. As Svozil had a broken leg, it was logical to assume that I was the most likely candidate.

The assumption hit the mark, and unfortunately for me it meant I was dropped from the national team. I could forget about the Canada Cup. I couldn't even take my planned vacation to Yugoslavia, where the regime was more liberal than at home, making it easier to travel to the West: I was the only member of my family to be refused an exit permit. An obvious precaution. "Go to the Tatra Mountains," the comrade at the passport office snapped at me. "It's nice in Czechoslovakia, too, you know."

My two best chances of getting out had fallen through.

Once the season ended, I was in more frequent touch with the Nordiques. Messages were sent to Canada through Ota Kubik, my father's best friend, who had stayed in West Germany after the Soviet occupation. We met up with Ota every year in Yugoslavia, and now we were arranging to leave our homeland with his help.

Because we feared the secret police had put a tap on our phone, we made calls from the post office. At first, so that I wouldn't raise suspicion by frequent visits there, my father placed the calls, although later I had to get more involved. We went to different post offices, on different days of the week and at different times of day, trying not to draw attention to ourselves. We preferred to speak in codes we'd agreed on earlier. What if the post office phone booths were monitored, too? Conversations between Dad and his friend covered familiar ground, such as their children, hockey and the weather, into which they inserted messages only the two of them understood. *It's lovely here with everything in bloom* meant that all was going according to plan. If the talk turned to unexpected frost, this was a sign that there were complications.

In this way, we got a message to Quebec that my escape would be made not on the pretext of the Canada Cup or a vacation by the Adriatic but during a stay in Switzerland, where Vitkovice would play a few preseason exhibition games. The rest of the family would get out through Yugoslavia.

The new plan looked hopeful—until the start of the summer and the defection to West Germany of my teammate Milan Mokros, together with Josef Volek from Karvina, who had played for Vitkovice until the previous season.

The club was thrown into chaos. All kinds of stories were spread about who would be fleeing where and when. As the most suspicious of the lot, I was summoned for questioning to the conference room, where Rudolf Peska, general director of the iron and steel works, was waiting for me in the company of flunkies from the executive council of the sports division.

Although it was only nine in the morning, I could smell the plum brandy on them. On the table in front of Peska was a team picture titled "TJ Vitkovice—1981 ice-hockey champions of Czechoslovakia." Pointing at this, he said to me, "Tell us, comrade, who on this poster wants to get out." I was taken aback.

"How should I know?" I replied. "Do you think such a person would tell me?"

"But we know that you know. Point them out to us."

When he asked me a third time, I turned the poster toward him, pointed at a couple of coaches and said, "Those two."

"You're making fun of us, comrade, surely?"

"What do you take me for, a 16-year-old? Do you really think I'd tell you, even if I did know?"

A momentary silence. Then Peska spoke up. "You're sweating, Frycer."

"I've felt better, to be honest. I've been running a temperature for the past few days."

"In '45, when the tank I was in entered Ostrava, I was running a fever of 40, and I had to fight!" Peska announced, in defiance of logic. A veteran of Svoboda's army, he had walked from Eastern Front to Prague, and now it seemed he compared everything he encountered in life with his wartime experience.

The unproductive interview went on a while longer. When at last I was released, I was told they would let me know later whether I was on the trip to Bern.

I couldn't sit at home, waiting and helpless. In case I was pulled from the Switzerland trip, we came up with a fourth escape route. By far the riskiest and most desperate.

It occurred to me that if I couldn't enter Yugoslavia legally, I might get there from Hungary along the Danube, which formed a natural border between the two countries. I would simply jump into the river and swim across.

That summer we took our vacation in Hungary, so I could explore the riverbank. I spent hours making my way along the Danube, looking for places where the river was at its narrowest. The frontier wasn't as tightly guarded as the Iron Curtain—a good sign. If all else failed, I would swim across the Danube. As I was at peak fitness, I believed myself capable of doing so. Besides, I'd spent practically every vacation since early childhood by the Adriatic, so I'd swum many miles in the sea. After that, what difficulties could a calm river cause me? I didn't like to think that guys with Kalashnikovs might turn up on the bank at any time, though.

Still, I didn't really believe that this fourth course of action was the one I would take.

In Vitkovice, my case was still open. As the date of departure for Switzerland drew nearer, I realized I would have to gamble. I had one last trump in my hand. The military.

For two years now, coaches from army clubs Dukla Jihlava and Dukla Trencin had been hovering around me, but I'd put off my military service by enrolling at university. I'd enrolled at three universities, in fact. It goes without saying that I didn't go to class. I'd turn up at registration for the mandatory stamp on my ID, and then I'd visit the dean for a list of classes. Whenever the school threatened to throw me out for my failure to attend class, the club arranged for me to transfer to another course of study.

The thought of military service was enough to give me nightmares. Although the lads had explained to me that I'd have nothing to worry about in Jihlava or Trencin—after the induction program, all I'd do was play and practice—I was bothered by the thought that any old trouble could put me in a tank. In fact, I was terrified by it. I had enough of being reined in and bossed around in civilian life. Two years in green? No, I just couldn't imagine it.

But now the military seemed to me a good way of pushing Vitkovice into a corner. These civilian officials would have nothing to answer the army with. One's duty as a patriot trumped everything.

"Let me tell you something," I announced at one of our many interviews. "When you get back from Switzerland, you won't find me in the dressing room. I'll be in the army."

It worked. The Party big shots may have had as much of me as they could stomach, but there was still the championship to defend. Lada Svozil was injured, and who knew if he'd ever return. If I went off to the army, they would be down by 49 goals, which they would hardly recover by putting in a couple of juniors. They would need to change their behavior toward me.

Besides, my uncle Rudolf Otava, a good guy and great athlete, declared that he would vouch for me. He was the managing director of the huge Ostrava-Karvina mining company, and his word really meant something in Ostrava. In spring, when we met in Prague before the departure for the world championship in Sweden, the 16th Congress of the Communist Party of Czechoslovakia was in progress. We were staying in the same hotel as senior members of the Party. That evening, my uncle invited me to his room, where he introduced me to some big cheeses as his nephew the international hockey player. Maybe this encounter helped me, too.

In the end, I was allowed to join my teammates in Switzerland.

The council of the sports division took their time over the verdict, no doubt concerned that if they didn't, I would prepare my escape. They brought the announcement to my home the day before the team's departure. I invited them in. I wanted them to see that we hadn't sold the furniture, as people preparing to emigrate sometimes do. The TV and the hi-fi system from the Tuzex store stood where they always had, and the Fiat was parked in front of the building. I couldn't afford the slightest shadow of suspicion.

"See you tomorrow, then," they said as they took their leave.

As soon as they were out of the door, I dashed to the car. I had a great deal to do before evening. My first stop was the post office, where I dialed a West German number I knew by heart. "Tomorrow I'll send a package. Another will follow two days later," I said into the receiver. The person on the other end of the line knew this to mean that I was on my way to Switzerland and the rest of the family were heading for Yugoslavia.

Then came the hardest part of the whole escape. Saying goodbye to my grandma and grandpa. I couldn't tell them the truth, but I think they realized that my dropping by for coffee and a smoke was no casual visit.

I appear to be a self-confident person, but on that occasion my self-confidence was greatly exaggerated. This was one of those situations that pull at the heartstrings, and it really shook me up. As we sat together outside, I had a lump in my throat and couldn't drive the thought from my mind that we would never see each other again. When you got out in those days, the curtain closed behind you immediately. Some families were divided for decades. It made me very sad.

On leaving Hrusov, I drove straight to Lada's place. Another tough moment. He was my best friend, and he knew exactly what was going on. Again, I tried to persuade him to do what I was doing. "And what would I do there?" he said, pointing to his crutches. "Do you think invalids are welcome in the NHL?"

In the five years we'd known each other, we'd been through some incredible stuff together, successes and fuck-ups alike. People said we were like twins. On trips abroad, we'd go out shopping separately and come back with the same things—shoes, jeans, red jackets. Actually, though, we're very different. Lada is a placid, jovial type from the Hana region; I'm a cowboy from Karvina who shoots from the hip.

Looking back today, I'm not sure Lada would have gotten out even if he hadn't broken his leg. I had the feeling that his NHL dream wasn't as powerful as mine, and that he wasn't prepared to lay everything on the line.

The risks were great indeed. It was clear to me from the start that if my escape backfired, I wouldn't be able to put it right by paying a fine and sitting out a few games. Rather than returning to the Vitkovice team, I'd be going to court and then to jail. No one would give a damn about me. But I'm an only child and selfish enough not to let anything stand in my way. I'm also stubborn and able to take risks without consideration for others. Often, I'll start to think things through only after they go wrong.

In later years, Lada and I would meet up on vacation in Yugoslavia. He'd make a full recovery and get back to his best, making the 1984 Canada Cup team. I encouraged him to get out; his contract with Quebec was still in force. But he no longer wanted to do it. Pity. I think he'd have done well in the NHL.

———

The following morning, my wife went with me to the bus station. Our 10-month-old daughter came along in her pram. To allay any suspicions, in front of everyone she handed me a list of what she wanted me to buy in Switzerland. The driver started the engine and we waved to each other as the bus drove away. The most thrilling few days of my life had begun, and there was no way back.

Shortly afterward, a friend, one of the few who knew what we were planning, drove my wife and daughter to the airport, where they boarded a plane for Zagreb. Meanwhile, my parents were sitting at home with their luggage, waiting for news.

In the bus, I just couldn't relax. I was bathed in sweat and my nerves were at the snapping point.

To my great relief, we crossed the border into Austria without difficulty. Soon afterward, we made a toilet stop at a roadside service facility. I was the last to return to the bus. The lads made a joke by clapping me back on board. "What a surprise! Frigo's come back!" I had to play along. "Calm down, lads. It's too soon to make a run for it."

By the time we reached Bern it was evening, and I ran straight to a phone. My first call was to Yugoslavia, to hear that all had gone well and my wife and daughter had arrived at the home of acquaintances.

Then I dialed my parents' number. "The first package has arrived safe and sound," I reported.

"That's good. And how are you feeling? Better?"

"Yes, my fever's gone. My temperature's just over 37, so it's not so bad."

The mention of a package meant that my wife and daughter were in Zagreb. The words *just over* were code for *in Switzerland*. My parents got in their car and sped through Hungary to Yugoslavia.

The next day, a message reached me from Zagreb that the second package had arrived. Again, I felt great relief. The only part left to play was mine.

I spent the evening before D-Day in a hotel room with Milos Riha, Jaromir Sindel and Antonin Planovsky, playing cards, as we usually did. I wasn't much of a card player, and I tended to lose more than I won. But now I hit a lucky streak. I tossed crazy money onto the table, and still I kept on winning.

"What's going on, Frigo?" Jaromir wanted to know.

"I don't know. Money seems to like me today."

"Come off it! There's something wrong. Out with it!"

It was getting late, and we'd had a few drinks. Should I tell them? I decided that what I had to say wouldn't leave the room.

"As we've known each other for ages, guys, I'll tell you. I'm getting out. Tomorrow. I'm going to Canada."

No one spoke. Antonin looked stunned. Jaromir started to cry.

Milos was the first to pull himself together. All day he'd been wondering why I kept running to the phone, so maybe it came as less of a shock to him.

"Have you got all you need?" he asked.

"You know very well that I don't have a thing."

"Not even a passport?"

"Not even a passport."

Things had changed since the Stastny brothers defected. When we travelled to the West now, the management kept hold of our official passports. And I hadn't brought a private one.

Then Milos did something I'll never forget. He reached into his pocket, pulled out his passport, ripped out the photo and handed the passport to me. "Maybe it'll help you," he said.

Fortunately, I never did have any need of it. But Milos has my undying admiration. Because of what he did for me, he had the secret police on his back for a whole year.

We finished our drinks and went to bed. After that, I didn't touch another thing in the hotel, not the water in my room, not the breakfast. It may seem to you like paranoia, but at that time we were hearing stories about rowers who had ended up in Prague in a drugged-up state after an evening drink in West Germany, having let slip that they were planning to defect. Maybe these were nothing more than stories. But as I had no way of knowing the truth, I preferred to suspect the worst. I was almost at the end of a journey I'd been on for a year and a half, and my dream was within reach—I wasn't going to underestimate a single thing, no matter how small it was.

The next afternoon, a bus picked us up at the hotel to take us to our first game. I boarded with a small bag containing underwear, a pair of jeans, a T-shirt and a toothbrush. I left the rest of my things in my room.

On my way down in the elevator, I met Jaromir. He was still upset and tearful. We'd known each other since we were kids. First we played against each other, then together—for Vitkovice, for the juniors, for the national team. All that was about to end; we'd never share a dressing room again.

"Please, don't cry, or you'll set me off, and that'll make everyone suspicious," I told him. But my voice, too, was unsteady.

Fortunately, none of the team officials or the snoops took the bus with us, preferring to go shopping instead. I suppose it didn't cross their minds that anyone could make trouble right before a game. I went all the way down the aisle to the back of the bus, passing Zbynek Neuwirth, a great guy who had taken me under his wing when I'd moved up at the age of 16 from Karvina to the Vitkovice first team. "Zbynek, I'm getting out," I muttered. He nodded, his eyes shining.

Old buses had a door at the back. Carefully, I eased the door open, just a crack, and I held it that way for the whole drive. I'd decided that if anything should go wrong at the last moment, I would leap out and run away.

We moved through the streets of Bern at walking pace. As the game would begin at five, we'd caught the afternoon rush hour. It felt like time was standing still. I was drenched with sweat and my brain was going a mile a minute.

We had agreed that Petr, the son of my father's friends, a kid I knew from our regular vacations in Yugoslavia, would be waiting for me at the stadium. As we entered the final stretch at last, I spotted his red Passat parked some distance away. Glory be! Now I needed to keep my head and calm the adrenaline that was bubbling in my veins. While the others were exiting by the front door and going for their kit bags, I would leave by the back and approach Petr without drawing attention to myself.

My resolution carried me about two paces before I broke into a sprint. I reached the car, jumped in and yelled, "Drive!"

Petr stepped on the gas, the tires squealed, and we were away.

I was out. At last.

We'd gone only a few hundred yards when Petr slammed on the brakes. "For fuck's sake! My brother!"

"Your what?"

"We left him at the stadium." He explained that when I made my dash for freedom, his brother had been mingling with the autograph hunters around the front door. With a sign stating that Petr was waiting on the other side of the bus.

"Wait here by this tree and don't move a muscle," he commanded me. "I'll be right back."

The few minutes of waiting that followed were among the longest of my life.

Then Petr took me to his aunt's apartment, where I called Quebec with the news that the team could fly in for me. Then I drank two small beers and fell asleep in a state of mental exhaustion.

The rest of the family reached Bern later than planned. Katona was supposed to get them out of Yugoslavia, but he was playing a strange game that almost foiled my escape. Although the Nordiques had provided him with plenty of money for the bribing of important people, so ensuring that everyone got over the border without difficulty, he'd blown one thing after another. And he planned to outfox the local communists so that more dollars would end up in his pocket.

The first attempt to cross the border into Italy failed. My family looked on as Katona played up to the border guards, so getting himself arrested. Then they turned the car around and drove back inland. It was a close shave.

That idiot made a real mess of things for them. And when the police threw him in jail for the night, his role was over. I'll never forgive him for putting my family in such danger. And I'm not the only one with bad things to say about him: it's the same with the Stastnys—he led them on a merry dance, too. Remarkably, Katona would later sue the Nordiques, claiming they owed him $100,000 for his part in our escape; he also demanded a fee in excess of the original agreement for the Stastnys. But I only read about that in the papers.

My father was forced to take matters into his own hands. He sought out the help of friends in Zagreb. It was arranged that at a given time on a particular day the border guards would turn a blind eye to the documents of four people from Czechoslovakia and let them through.

There's no need for me to describe the joy and relief I felt when we all came together at last, safe and sound.

We'd done it! With the help of many others, from Czechoslovakia, Germany, Yugoslavia and Canada. My dream was so powerful that it spread to people around me, and those people did all they could to make it happen.

We'd pulled off an incredible feat. And how I relished the fact that we'd gotten two families out, not just me alone! While still in Bern, I sent the team executives at Vitkovice a postcard with the following message: "All's well with me. The door to the West is open. Thanks for everything."

We'd taken the comrades to the cleaners. And boy did it feel good!

It still does.

9

The Fourth Stastny Brother

THE MANAGEMENT of the Vitkovice club found out about my flight half an hour before the start of the first game in Bern. Later, I learned from the boys that the officials and the "eyes" entered the dressing room, shopping bags in hand and all smiles. Then they noticed the discarded bag with my number on it.

"Where's Frigo?" one of them snapped.

The boys just shrugged. "Dunno."

The stakes were raised. They picked out the youngest and told him that if he didn't tell, he'd be in all kinds of trouble. "I saw him in front of the stadium, getting into a red car," he said.

Panic ensued. The officials went back to the hotel, where they went through everyone's things. Some of the players had private passports, and these were found. The phone lines to Czechoslovakia were called into action.

The first call was to my mother-in-law. On learning from her that her daughter and granddaughter had flown off on vacation to Yugoslavia, the officials began to realize what had happened.

The next call was placed to Karvina. They wanted to speak with Coach Frycer. "The team left for a game in Gottwaldov," someone in the club's secretary's office explained. "With the assistant in charge. Coach Frycer didn't report for work."

It was plain to them now that all of us were gone. And there was nothing they could do about it.

At least they could take a measure of revenge on me by adding to my 18-month sentence (for my illegal departure from the republic) two years for stealing property from the socialist state. It's hardly surprising that the boys took their pick of my things and sold them on, with the result that the bag with the number 16 was returned to Vitkovice empty. The clowns insisted I'd stolen the stuff—maybe they thought I'd fled to Canada in full uniform.

It was absurd: I get a three-and-a-half-year custodial sentence while some guy gets to show off his black-bladed Graf skates at the rink in Ostrava. Only national-team players had skates like these, so it was surely obvious to everyone whose they had been and how their owner came by them.

Whenever I received information like this, with a time lag, from various sources, it always made me smile. As for the punishment they thought up for me, even if it had been 10 years, it would have been all the same to me.

I was living elsewhere. I'd moved on.

My parents spent only a few days in Bern before departing for West Germany, where Dad intended to resume his coaching career. In this, he received a helping hand from Dr. Georg-Heinrich Kouba, a German from Opava and an old friend, who, having defected after the Soviet occupation, had set himself up as a private surgeon in Freiburg and become president of the local hockey club.

I was glad that my parents were being taken care of. It's no easy matter to emigrate at aged 53 and start again from nothing, and I admired them for it greatly. In an interesting twist, Dad signed up for a coaches' training course in Cologne, having a year earlier believed himself too old to do the same in Czechoslovakia. He did it in German, too—and was duly granted the license. In 1982, he was given the chance to coach Dusseldorf in the Bundesliga; further coaching stints followed, in Frankfurt, Kassel, Stuttgart, Freiburg, Neuss and Heilbronn.

I was delighted that things worked out for him. Back in Czechoslovakia, the communists removed all mention of him from encyclopedias and books about hockey. It was as though he had never coached Vitkovice and Karvina, or been one of the first Czech coaches in Yugoslavia; in fact, it was as though he had never existed. The Germans were more appreciative of him.

———

As soon as the Quebec Nordiques brass got the news that I was free, Marius Fortier, one of the team's six founders, flew over to arrange my move to Canada.

It wasn't as simple as we'd imagined it. I was in Switzerland with no papers, a wife and a 10-month-old child. Immigration minister Lloyd Axworthy refused to make an exception for me, as he had done for the Stastny brothers a year earlier. There was no chance of our flying to Canada immediately.

I was forced to wait until the Swiss and Canadian authorities worked out a solution. The process seemed endless. We were urged from all sides to be patient.

Although I knew they couldn't send me back to Czechoslovakia, I remained anxious. The situation was out of my hands. I was dependent on others to do everything for me. That I knew nothing about what was going on behind the scenes and who was pulling the strings only added to my stress.

For weeks I sat on my backside, powerless. And I gained weight.

Our lodgings remained a secret, and for safety's sake we moved every few days—from hotel to apartment, from apartment to hotel, then on to another apartment. I couldn't even go out for a run. No one knew how far the tentacles of the Czechoslovak secret police reached, and it would have been foolish to take risks.

The only time the boredom was relieved was when people from the Nordiques came to visit. What a welcome change it was for me to be taken to the embassy to sign a few documents!

This was my mood at the end of September, when I celebrated my 22nd birthday. The only gift I wished for was permission to leave for Canada as soon as possible.

On October 2, after a month spent in Bern, the Canadian embassy issued us with provisional documents. But even at the airport in Zurich, the guard around us remained in place: three policemen escorted us all the way to the plane.

Only after the aircraft lifted off the ground and the captain confirmed that our destination was Montreal did I begin to relax. The weeks of uncertainty and nervous tension were over. Even so, we weren't in the mood to pop open the champagne. We sat on our own in silence, not wishing to draw attention to ourselves. Besides, I'd been warned by the people from Quebec that the great fuss made of me on landing would be difficult for me to deal with.

We reached Montreal in the afternoon. As we made our descent and I looked down on the outlines of the city, it dawned on me that my new life was truly starting—I was here at last, and my first steps on the ice were fast approaching. I was worried. Would I be able to cope? Not just with hockey in the NHL, but with life in a country I knew little about? I wasn't sure. What I did know was that flying to Canada for a week-long tournament and living there were two different things.

And there was no going back. It was time to look forward. To look forward only.

The Nordiques had called a big press conference in the Château Mirabel hotel. Just as they had a year earlier, to mark the arrival of Peter and Anton Stastny; just as they had a few weeks earlier, when Marian had succeeding in reaching Canada. They knew how to make the most of these occasions. Above all, they were sending a message to the Montreal Canadiens: "We've taken on another reinforcement. The days of our playing your younger, weaker brother are well and truly over." The rivalry between the two francophone clubs was enormous, as I was soon to discover for myself. Compared with the Battle of Quebec, Prague's Sparta-Slavia rivalry is pretty insipid.

The press conference was attended by the whole management team, including team president Marcel Aubut, who was bursting with pride at having brought over a fourth Czechoslovak international in the space of 14 months.

Goalie Dan Bouchard, whose contract with the Nordiques had just been extended, sat down next to me. His signature was a big deal for the team, too.

Things got started. A first, second, third, fourth question. TV cameras purred; still cameras clicked. I felt like I was in a trance. In Czechoslovakia, I'd never seen such a fuss made about hockey. With an interpreter's help, I managed to convey that I was looking forward to arriving in Quebec and playing in the NHL at last. Then Aubut handed me the number 15 jersey. As I pulled it on, I noticed that my name was spelled with the diacritic hook: FRYČER. This courteous attention to detail pleased me. Perhaps Peter had mentioned it. A reporter asked me to strike a pose; without giving it much thought, I showed the "V for victory" sign. The next day, this image appeared in all the local dailies.

Before the conference ended, I shook hands with coach Michel Bergeron for the cameras. By the time I reached the car, I had given out so many autographs that my right hand hurt. At last it was over—my first day in the circus known as the National Hockey League. A couple of hours on Canadian soil and I was beginning to understand the kind of show I was stepping into. And they say that hockey is the same everywhere! This was something much bigger than I was used to.

The limousine delivered us to Quebec late that night. We were accommodated at the Château Frontenac hotel, one of Quebec City's most impressive buildings. So this was the city that was to be my new home! I looked from the window at the street below for a long time. I didn't get much sleep that night—I'd experienced a great deal in the past few hours, and my mind was full and racing.

———

Early next morning I ran down for breakfast. I wanted a quick bite to eat before the guy arrived to take me to practice.

As I walked into the restaurant, the people at the tables turned toward me. Then they stood up and started to clap. Still a little drowsy from the six-hour time difference, it took me a while to realize what was happening. The applause was for me! Looking down at the table, I saw a copy of *Le Journal de Québec*, with a photo of me on the front page. That explained it. I made a little bow to express my thanks.

This was another culture shock. Although I'd played in the Czechoslovak league for five years and at some major international tournaments, no one in Ostrava took me as a celebrity. I was known by the 10,000 people who went to Kotas Stadium, but I was of no interest to anyone else. And here I was, being given a round of applause before I'd so much as touched a puck!

It began to dawn on me that the pressure I'd be under here would be very different from the kind I knew; in fact, I struggled to imagine it. As well as being accountable to myself and my teammates, I would need to prove myself to the people from the Nordiques who had brought me to Canada, plus all the new fans. My immature behavior would have to be a thing of the past. It was time for me to grow up.

After breakfast, the taxi delivered me to the old Colisée arena. I was praying that at least one of the Stastny brothers would be there—all I could say in English was "hi," "bye," and "how much?" and I was feeling pretty overwhelmed. It would really help me to have someone I knew by my side.

But there was no sign of them. I would learn soon enough that Peter and Anton were forever battling against time. If a team meeting was called for half-past nine, they tended to turn up at 29 minutes past, just as Coach Bergeron was preparing to lock the dressing room door. They're still like this today.

I walked into the dressing room and said hello. I felt anxious right from the start. Michel Goulet and Dale Hunter were doing stretches on the floor, the kind of exercises you might see from a gymnast. Both with bodies honed to perfection, abdominals like six-packs. And

I stood next to them, my face swollen with the 20 pounds of extra weight gained during my month of idleness in Bern.

My place was in the corner. The guy sitting next to me introduced himself as André Dupont. I stared at him, too—but for a different reason. I doubted I'd ever seen a belly as large as his on a hockey player.

Although his name was new to me, I soon learned that he had played for the Philadelphia Flyers in the years when they had been known as the Broad Street Bullies and twice bludgeoned their way to the Stanley Cup. His massive championship rings would soon be a source of my silent admiration. By now, Dupont was 32, playing out his career in Quebec, and obviously winding down—hence the belly. But as soon as he got out on the ice, the giant in him awoke and he went for every puck, entering every battle as if his life depended on it. He was a true captain. He was also a big joker, a great guy to have around. He helped me a lot in the beginning.

I was as impressed by his stick as I was by his rings. It was as long as a pole. When I stood mine up straight next to me, it didn't even reach my chin; his reached over his head. "Why do you need such a long stick?" I teased him later in the season. "In games, you don't pass, you don't shoot …"

"Let me show you," answered Moose, as he was known. He invited me to try to get past him on the ice. That wasn't too difficult—I was faster and good with the puck. But then, just as I was thinking the deal was done, he hooked me, sending the stick crashing from my hands. "That's why my stick's so long," he grinned. "You may be a fast, skilled player, but you won't get away from me."

Marian turned up in the dressing room about five minutes later, with Peter and Anton hot on his heels. They gave me an emotional welcome, with hugs all round. Moments later, the teasing started. "That's enough!" they cried. And "Took your time getting here, didn't you?"

They, too, were glad that I was there.

After practice, we sat down together for a while. We had a great deal to tell each other. To start with, they had a warning for me: "There are things in Canada, Frigo, you will have had no idea about at home, so be prepared."

They couldn't have been more right.

For almost half a year, I kept having the same nightmare.

An airplane stands on the tarmac, a set of steps leading up to an open door. I run toward it at full pelt. I'm pursued by Czechoslovak police in green uniforms, their heavy boots clumping across the concrete, and they are closing in on me. I'm almost at the plane when I come to a sudden stop. I can't move—my legs have turned to stone. The police officers reach for me, I feel their touch … and then I wake up. Scared senseless and covered in sweat.

Fortunately, I would then look out of the window at a garden with tall trees nodding in the breeze and know myself to be in the safety of Quebec. And I would feel tremendous relief. But I never managed to get back to sleep. I would go downstairs, smoke a cigarette, and wander about the house till morning. For the rest of the day I'd be like a bear with a sore head, unable to shake off this classic émigré's dream.

Because of this nightmare and all the sleepless nights it caused me, I have immense admiration for those who fled to the West without a contract in their pockets.

Things must have been so much harder for them. All they could look forward to for sure was a stay in a refugee camp. They didn't know which city, in some cases even which country, they would end up in, nor if they would find work in their field of expertise (maybe they would start out washing dishes) or if their children would adapt to their new life. Only after I'd heard what some of them had to say did I realize how complicated some situations were.

Things must have been tough, too, for Petr Svoboda, Petr Klima, Frank Musil and Michal Pivonka, who signed with NHL clubs where there was no other Czech or Slovak. Unfamiliar with the language, they took their first uncertain steps in a new land alone. And they couldn't call and ask their parents to fly over for a couple of months to help out.

How fortunate I was to have the Stastny brothers!

In the early days, Peter, Anton and Marian were a tremendous help to me; I'll be grateful to them till my dying day. Sometimes I call myself the fourth Stastny brother. It's hyperbole of course, but it feels about right. They took me into their family and treated me as one of them. The precious friendship we formed holds strong to this day.

I don't know what I'd have done without them in those first few months. Although I could look after myself on the ice, I struggled away from the rink. I was ignorant of Canadian customs, and I had a hard time communicating.

Team administrators were kind and helpful. They helped me find somewhere to live, and for the first season they gave me a car. But no one in the office was entrusted with my care. That wasn't the way things were done in the NHL. The rule was clear: we give you a very good salary, and your private affairs are your own concern.

In Quebec you can't get by with English only; it isn't fully bilingual like Montreal. You may strike lucky with English in certain downtown stores, but it's more than likely that clerks will hear you out before answering proudly in French. In moments like this, I was lost. But everyone told me to concentrate on English—if I tried to learn two languages, they said, I'd get confused.

Luckily for me, Peter could speak French by now, and he went with me wherever and whenever I needed help. Without him, I wouldn't even have been able to open a bank account. Plus, I needed papers, doctors, insurance, credit cards …

Perhaps the biggest change from my life in Czechoslovakia was in how much I got paid. From one moment to the next, I was able to buy practically anything. It's no wonder that in certain cases sudden riches made newcomers lose their good judgment and sense of reality. They bought a Cadillac with their signing bonus, then a luxury apartment. Within a month, they would be sent down to the farm team in the

AHL and find themselves living from hand to mouth. Or they would be plagued by freeloaders, masquerading as friends, who would bleed them dry. Some of the stories are pretty sad.

To my good fortune, the Stastny brothers became my financial advisors. At the very beginning, Peter convinced me to invest my signing bonus in a pension fund. This was excellent advice: my money was kept safe. Today it pays me a pension, and it will continue to do so for as long as I live (provided Canada doesn't go bankrupt).

I didn't dare make bigger investments. Marian, for instance, opened the Dix-Huit bar (after the 18 on his jersey) four months after his arrival in Quebec. Such things weren't for me. I lacked both the business sense and the experience, and I was afraid of sinking my money into something I didn't understand. Besides, in those days I had a real taste for alcohol; if I'd opened my own night club, before the month was up I'd have found myself in a mess.

It took me a while to learn the value of money. As to the check I received from the team every second week, I had part of it paid into my account and the rest paid into my hand. Several months passed before I got the hang of the prices in the stores and understood that when I shopped at a supermarket, I didn't need wads of hundred-dollar bills in my pockets.

I think back to the end of my first season, when Peter and I went to the tax office about something or other. I asked him to wait for me while I went to the bank to draw out some cash; my family and I were flying to West Germany to see my parents the next day.

"How much do you want to take out?" Peter asked.

"Dunno. About $30,000, I suppose."

"Why so much, for God's sake! Are you planning on buying a house there?"

I was clueless. I had no idea about the exchange rate, how many Deutschmarks I'd get to the Canadian dollar, or how many of them I'd need for a month-long trip to Europe. I was just as clueless about lots of other things, too.

Fortunately, one of the Stastnys was always on hand to point me in the right direction and offer advice.

Thanks, boys.

10

Four Hat Tricks and a Trade

I WAITED ALMOST TWO WEEKS for my first NHL game—a game I'd dreamed of for so long. Coach Bergeron didn't want to throw me into the deep end. The others had a training camp behind them, while I was fighting to get back to full fitness after my weeks of idleness in Switzerland.

Besides, I needed to find my feet in a world of hockey that was new to me.

Basically, I was pretty clueless about it. There's an incredible difference between how things were then and how they are now. These days, Czech boys who go to play overseas know all there is to know about the NHL. They have seen lots of games on TV and read heaps of articles and interviews. They can ask older players about their experiences, and their agents give them all kinds of advice and instruction. In my time, we knew the names of the clubs and the biggest stars, and we knew that the rink was narrower and sparks flew on the ice. That was all. For us, the NHL was a step into the twilight zone.

My first practice session taught me a lot. Peter warned me beforehand that I'd need to get used to a very different tempo. He wasn't wrong. In Quebec, we trained at full tilt, the whole time. Sessions were short but intense. Even before games. At Vitkovice, I'd been accustomed to taking it pretty easy on the eve of a game; things couldn't have been more different in the NHL. Sprints were a regular feature of pregame preparations. Had a coach in Czechoslovakia demanded such efforts, he would have provoked disbelief and the accusation that he was wearing his players out. In Canada, such matters weren't even up for discussion.

No one took the liberty of sounding off, even out of the coach's sight and hearing. Everyone knew the farm team had four candidates for every position, just waiting for the call. A blind eye might be turned to a first offense, but for a second there would be a warning. A third would be rewarded with a bus ticket. They say it's only a hundred miles to the farm, but it's a thousand to get back.

This was one of the reasons we gave our all in practice, as though we were playing to a stadium full of fans. Everyone wanted to prove his worth to the team. And sometimes they overdid it. "In a one-on-one, you'll get a glove in your face or a slash," Peter Stastny warned me. "And don't be surprised if you get the odd smack or two."

I found this hard to believe at first. But in the middle of practice two guys would throw off their gloves and lay into each other with their fists before the others pulled them apart. "Fuck you! Fuck you! Fuck you!" would be hurled through the air. And five minutes later they'd be laughing about it like a couple of kids.

In the early days, too, I had to get used to being watched closely by my teammates during every drill of every practice. They knew that Peter was a superstar: he had scored 109 points in his very first season, and he'd won the Calder Memorial Trophy for NHL Rookie of the Year. But who was this new European whose name they had never heard before?

Let's be honest: they didn't exactly welcome Europeans with open arms.

And this was an especially sensitive topic in Quebec, where the team was composed mostly of French Canadians.

Two days after my arrival, Maurice Richard, one of the greatest figures in hockey history, wrote a column in *Le Journal de Montréal* in which he claimed that by signing Europeans, the NHL was shooting itself in the foot. "It won't be long before there are more Europeans at Quebec than Canadians," he wrote. "Most recently, last Friday, the Stastny brothers were joined in Nordiques colors by Miroslav Frycer.

There is something tragicomic about how NHL bosses are welcoming a wave of Europeans when they can see that this welcome is destroying the careers of Canadian players."

Richard had old-school views. Besides, in his day—the '40s and '50s—it was a rare thing for even an American to play in the NHL. And now here we were with four Czechoslovakians on the same team! I wonder what he'd say about all the Germans, Danes and Swiss of today …

He was right about one thing, though. We really were taking work from Canadians. My coming to the Nordiques meant a homegrown player had to leave for the AHL, where he would earn far less. Each thousand dollars he lost would make a big difference to him—NHL salaries in the early '80s were not nearly as high as they would be 10 years later. Or are now. To keep their families, a lot of players had to work through the summer; they would find jobs as bouncers, at the docks, or on the family farm.

It didn't help matters that we were given inflated contracts—my salary was 50 percent higher than the NHL average. On the other hand, the team was using money to compensate us for having left our homeland and everything in it—apartment, car, savings and so on—by defecting to Canada. And as we were pretty experienced, they hadn't brought us over for the third line—another fact that would not have endeared us to some.

Although none of my teammates said to my face that I was an alien who was occupying the place of a Canadian, the way they looked at me in the early days spoke volumes. Peter had warned me not to let them get too close or open myself up to them. It would come back to haunt me if I did, he said. There was a lot of talk about our being a team; everyone wore a happy face, but this was a pretense that wasn't difficult to see through. It was every man for himself, the slogans they drilled into us notwithstanding. Each was playing for his own points, his own career, his own money. The atmosphere in the dressing room wasn't like it was at home. We weren't such a close unit. We'd put on a show in our two hours together at practice, then we'd go off and do our own thing.

Although teammates kept their views on Europeans to themselves or voiced them where they wouldn't give offense, opponents had no such reservations. They went in on us hard, sticks flailing. Which we didn't take lying down. Indeed, it was necessary for us to pay them back, so showing them we had as much right to play in the NHL as they did. It took me a year to gain respect on the ice. I was accepted only after they saw I had no problem throwing off my gloves and, if need be, poking my stick between someone's legs.

Even then, the badmouthing continued. For opponents, I remained a *European shit* or a *fucking communist*.

Some of the comments were born out of ignorance and lack of education rather than intent to hit a sensitive spot. More than a few Canadians had no idea where Wisconsin was, let alone an awareness of what life was like behind the Iron Curtain. Those who had never flown to Europe for a world championship or weren't second-generation immigrants knew precious little. There was no point in explaining to these people that the currency of Czechoslovakia wasn't the dollar, or that when it was nighttime in Canada, it could already be daytime in Europe.

In later years, a teammate asked me straight-faced if we'd had floors and windows at home. The idiot probably thought I'd grown up in a mud hut. What's more, he liked to badmouth Europe. "What are you, then?" I shot back at him. "I don't suppose you're a Native American. Judging by your name, I'd say you were some kind of European shit."

But the best place to answer such talk was on the ice. With a goal or two, ideally.

I made my NHL debut against the Minnesota North Stars. My long-held dream became reality on October 12, 1981, at Quebec's Colisée arena.

For me, the pregame warm-up was a treat in itself. No helmets, hair flowing. As we circled the ice, I felt the eyes of 15,000 people on me. For two weeks now, the people in the stands had been reading in the newspapers about a new player who had defected from Czechoslovakia. At last the time had come for me to show them what I could do.

I wish I could go on to give details of the great game I played and the unforgettable moments I took away from it. Unfortunately, though, I can't remember a thing. My memory is one big blank. What I do know is that we lost 4-2, and I appeared on a line with Marc Tardif and Réal Cloutier. The rest is lost in the mists of time.

I may have already experienced an Olympic Games and world championship, but this was something else. I found myself at the center of my own dream, and it was as if I couldn't quite believe where I was. I tried not to feel the atmosphere, but it was impossible. I was entirely wrapped up in it. I was so overwhelmed that I didn't know if I was in Ostrava, Sweden, Quebec, or Timbuktu. The game just flashed by me. From time to time I touched the puck, passed it to a teammate or took a shot, but I didn't put in much of a performance, that's for sure.

After my first game for Vitkovice, I had no doubts that I was good enough for the Czechoslovak league. But after my first game in the NHL, doubt gnawed away at me. Everything was different: the dimensions of the playing area, the pace of the game, the competition, you name it. At six feet tall and 185 pounds, I was a pretty big guy at home; here, the ice was filled with players bigger than me.

Our next game was in Buffalo, but as I still lacked a work visa for the USA, I had to stay behind in Quebec and spend a few days training with the Remparts junior team. This was the best thing that could have happened to me. Although they had us skating around the ice like crazy, and I worried that such intense practices would render me incapable of playing, it did me no end of good.

When I stepped onto the ice to face the Toronto Maple Leafs, I sensed right away that it would be my day. My legs were working and the fog had cleared. I took a pass, returned it, made a deke, and it was as though a weight fell from my shoulders. I'd broken free. I concentrated on my play and enjoyed the game.

With 17:34 on the clock, Marian Stastny took the puck to the end boards and played it back between two defensemen, and I fired it past Bunny Larocque from close range. Amazing! I was so delighted with the goal that I did a pirouette and kissed the blade of my stick. The crowd went mad. After the game, Toronto's coach Mike Nykoluk would complain that I was a showman, calling me a "hotdog." But I was used to putting my emotions into my play and my celebrations. After all I'd been through, scoring my first goal in the NHL was too big a deal to be celebrated by a slap on the back on the way to the bench.

As my confidence grew, I took ever more liberties. In the 32nd minute I darted through the offensive zone and added a second goal. Now my delight knew no bounds. To crown it all, five minutes later, I scored a third, converting Marc Tardif's flip pass off the right-hand boards. There could be no greater joy than this. Just my second game in the NHL, and I'd scored a hat trick. We won 6-4, I was named the game's first star, and the crowd chanted my name.

I wondered no longer if I had what it took for this league.

In the dressing room, the boys offered their congratulations. Then I was surrounded by journalists. Coach Michel Bergeron arrived. "Good game," he said, clapping me on the shoulder and wishing me lots of luck for the games to come.

"Give him six months and he'll be a better player than Peter," Anton told reporters. He was joking, of course. But it was good of the Stastnys to speak of me in glowing terms, to praise me wherever they could. This, too, was a great help to me. It made it clear to others that I was a force to be reckoned with.

This was particularly important to me in more trying times. Which came immediately after my famous hat trick.

Suddenly, I couldn't score a goal to save my life. I had chances, but the puck would escape me at the last moment. Or I'd fire it inches over an open net. Or straight at the goalie, who had gone down and believed himself beaten. My form fell through the floor. Maybe that lost month in Switzerland was catching up with me.

When this had been going on for a few weeks, Coach Bergeron decided to send me down to the farm team. I was less than pleased about this and took it as a major disappointment, even though he assured me it was only for a few games.

In Fredericton, I mounted a recovery. We had to take a bus to games, which was tedious, but the hockey itself was child's play. I put plenty of points on the board and dared hope I'd soon be on my way back to Quebec.

It never crossed my mind that the Fredericton Express might be the end of the line for me. I would just have to grin and bear my stint in the AHL. In any case, there was nowhere for me to return to. Even West Germany was closed to me—the 18-month IIHF suspension imposed on me after my defection applied to all European competition. Maybe the fact that there was no way back for us worked to our advantage. All we could do was knuckle down, keep fighting and hope.

Later, of course, I met former teammates from the national team who had been allowed to leave for the NHL legally. Among them was forward Igor Liba, whose view of matters was very different from mine. "Here, they'll play any old lummox, but they won't give me a proper chance. I may as well as pack it in and go home." Which was what he did: after one season with the New York Rangers and the Los Angeles Kings, he went back to Kosice. Some of today's youngsters, too, soon become disillusioned. Rather than fighting their way out of the farm team, after a year or two they choose to follow the money to Russia. I tell them that if they want to stay in the NHL and establish themselves, they need to think the way we did. That there's no way back, so I must endure whatever is thrown at me.

I was supported in my patient work toward a return to Quebec by Jacques Demers. A great guy and one of the best coaches I've ever had. He told me again and again to believe in myself, as my place wasn't in the AHL.

"Mirko Frycer is for us what Wayne Gretzky is for the Edmonton Oilers," he announced after a game against the Hershey Bears that had worked out really well for me—I'd scored six points. Quebec took notice, too. The newspapers wrote about it, and Peter called my hotel to congratulate me and say how much he was looking forward to playing with me again.

My stay in Fredericton helped settle me down. I played 11 games, scoring 14 points. After another phone call, this time from general manager Maurice Filion, I was on my way back to Quebec. Where I was ready to play as if my life depended on it.

Although I didn't score a goal in my first game, against the Minnesota North Stars, I did appear on a line with Peter and Marian, as Anton was injured. We played well, we had plenty of chances, and my self-confidence grew a little.

One week later, I had a dream weekend. On Saturday we hosted the Hartford Whalers, winning 7-3, and I scored two breakaway goals. Both on fakes. I was surprised by how easy it was to do this—Canadian goalies weren't ready for a technical finish. They were used to two-on-ones and solo breaks that ended with a shot; it was a long time before they caught on to my trick. All I needed to do was twitch my shoulders, move to the side, deke the other way, and push the puck into the open goal.

The next day we won 6-1 in Boston, and I scored a hat trick—my second in the NHL. That weekend, I recorded five goals and two assists.

I was back. I knew no one would be sending me back to the farm.

———

My crash course in the NHL and its laws continued. It took me several months to figure out the rules of the hockey business, to get accustomed to the pace and what went on behind the scenes, and to learn what kind of opponent I was up against.

There were times when I paid dearly for my ignorance. In one of my first games, a well-built player pinned me in a corner. To show I wasn't scared, I gave as good as I got. And why wouldn't I? Bold, aggressive hockey was in my blood.

But that guy really laid into me. When I returned bloodied to the bench, I saw the Stastnys tapping their foreheads.

"Why did you fight him? Are you crazy?" one of them said, before going on to explain: "That nutcase picks up 200 penalty minutes a season!"

"How was I supposed to know?"

But after that I was careful not to get into fights with players outside my weight classes.

I got used to the way things worked in the dressing room pretty quickly. After a game, I would undress and drop my clothes on the floor; before long, they would be hanging up or tidied away in bags. By the next day, everything would be carefully laid out in its place. We didn't even need to carry the shoulder bags containing our sticks. So that we could concentrate on our work only, the club had people to take care of everything. The showers were pretty amazing, too. The first time I saw them, I was reminded of the state-run luxury goods store in Czechoslovakia—we had several brands of shampoo, aftershave, shaving cream and razors to choose from.

What disappointed me, however, was the lack of care for players' fitness. At Vitkovice, we had a trainer and went regularly to the sauna and the pool; the level of comfort provided by the national team in this regard was higher still. Yet the wealthy NHL was ignorant of such conveniences in 1981. You need a massage? Then call up a masseur and go to see him in your free time. When my legs were aching, I had to massage them myself at home …

Nor was there any medical provision to speak of. For every ache and pain, there was one simple cure: ice and heat. If this didn't help, we were given a pill. There was never any rest or any time set aside for treatment. As long as there were no broken bones and we were mobile, we would play. If I had a groin problem, for instance, there was no one I could take it to. My overstressed groin might be blue, but still the doctor and the coach would wave me away. "That's a European ailment," they would tell me dismissively. A groin strain wasn't a problem, it was an excuse made by mollycoddled Europeans. The fact is, the Canadians never complained. It wasn't that they felt no pain. But they would slap on the ice, strap themselves up, and keep their discomfort to themselves.

Our dressing room differed from others in that it was also a *vestiaire* and a *šatňa,* the French and Slovakian translations. Three signs on the door made clear the composition of the team: we had 14 francophone Canadians, three anglophone Canadians, one American, and four players from Czechoslovakia. By the standards of hockey in those days, a veritable United Nations.

That one of the signs was in Slovak, was confirmation of the team's hierarchy. In the dressing room, the voices of Canadians Moose Dupont, Marc Tardif and Mario Marois carried the most authority, but Peter Stastny wasn't far behind them. He had achieved this position of respect in a single season—not only for his goals and assists, but also for his personality. He'd always been a leader, and he had no fear of taking on that role in Quebec. He learned the language quickly, he was strong in his opinions, and he wouldn't take any nonsense on the ice. When the other guys I named left the team, it was the most natural thing in the world for him to take on the captaincy.

Although Canadian frankness and sincerity had their limitations, I wouldn't say the Nordiques players I knew were a bad bunch. Marc Tardif gave me a lot of help; he spoke slowly to me and guided me as Vladimir Vujtek had once done. Seeing how nervous I was on my first trip to Madison Square Garden, he assured me that this game was nothing special in the NHL; I should just concentrate on my own play. Thanks to him, I got through it fine. He praised me after the game. Then we went on to the next challenge.

Marc and I often played together, usually accompanied by Réal Cloutier, a broad-shouldered heartthrob with a nose for the net. Both had starred for the Nordiques in the old WHA days. Tardif was the leading scorer in the history of that league, while Cloutier once scored 75 goals in a single season. They were great to play with. As were Michel Goulet and Dale Hunter.

But I felt best with the Stastny brothers by my side. We had the same hockey DNA, and our understanding on the ice was such that we could have been playing together for years. Whenever one of them was injured, or Coach Bergeron needed to shuffle the pack, I'd be move up to the first line. The points seemed to score themselves.

But once I'd gotten the hang of the league and grasped some of its rules, I realized that things couldn't go on like this forever. Right wing on the first line could be played by either me or Marian; there wasn't room for both of us. And it wasn't hard to figure out who was the favorite. The whole point in bringing Marian to Canada was for him to play with his brothers. "The Stastny brothers" were a well-known NHL brand. They attracted the crowds—Quebec was selling many more season tickets than ever before—and above all, they were great players at the top of their game. In December 1981, Peter was second only to Wayne Gretzky as the league's most productive player, while Anton and Marian were both in the top 20.

Nor was I helped by the fact that the coach and I didn't understand each other. In more than one sense.

Bergeron's English was poor, and he gave all tactical instructions in French. I had no idea what he was talking about. The boys would explain some of it to me afterward, but the rest I had to try to work out for myself. Whenever we disagreed, he would yell at me in French, I at him in Czech. It was like a bad comedy.

Our relationship was complicated from the start. Bergeron made it clear at the outset that he didn't think much of me—I was there only because the president of the team had brought me over. Even when I was scoring he would make things uncomfortable for me and give me too little time on the ice. This wound me up. I didn't need the same amount of ice time as Peter or to be out for every power play, the kind of treatment I'd been used to at Vitkovice, but I was convinced I deserved a bigger role.

Bergeron also disliked my style of play. He wanted me to forget about dekes and throw everything at the end boards; he had other players who could play with the puck. My line was instructed to play classic dump and chase, which was against my nature. And I refused to accept it.

In February, I scored two hat tricks, against the Colorado Rockies and the Winnipeg Jets, but this wasn't enough for Bergeron. Not even my goals could convince him to allow me to play the style I was used to, the style in which I was most productive.

It hadn't taken me long to gain the respect of my teammates and the fans, but I would never get it from him. A point was reached in our relationship when we were practically allergic to each other. I took offense at his behavior and he took offense at mine. Yelling at each other obviously wasn't going to solve anything.

At Bergeron's urging, general manager Maurice Filion called a meeting at which we would say everything out in the open. Not trusting myself to mount my defense in English on my own, I took Peter along. I said that if all they needed was someone to toss the puck into a corner, they should pull someone out of the crowd. And if they continued using me for just two or three shifts per period, there was no point having me on the team.

"You really want me to translate *that*?" said Peter in amazement.

"Of course. I didn't run off to Canada to be afraid of expressing my opinion."

But the meeting didn't make any difference. Bergeron and I still didn't get on. He was a good coach—he took the Nordiques into the playoffs seven times and the conference final twice. It was just that the two of us would never see eye to eye.

We were both at fault. Looking back on it today, I know I should have been more patient. I didn't understand his mentality. I was ambitious and wanted to play. I couldn't accept that there were things I needed to learn about the NHL, and skills I needed to develop, before I could be given more space. But he wouldn't let me play my game. As a rookie, I'd scored 20 goals in 49 games, but it wasn't enough to win him over.

It was only a matter of time before I left. I was expecting the situation to play itself out over the summer. In March, however, when Bergeron roared at me that I shouldn't change for a game against the Calgary Flames but go to the general manager instead, I had a good idea what was about to go down.

It was a pretty short conversation. Filion explained that the Maple Leafs had offered them Wilf Paiement, a power forward who was a better fit for the team, and that they had decided to trade me for him. He handed me a ticket to Toronto, telling me I'd be flying out at six the next morning so I could play in the evening.

It was cleared up at last. One second I was a Nordique, the next I wasn't.

I thanked him for everything he'd done for me. Then I turned to leave. As I was going out the door, I called back to him in jest, "When you come to Toronto, I'll put a hat trick past you. You'll see."

It was a strange feeling. We'd planned our escape to Canada for a year and a half, at great risk to the whole family, and at last we'd gotten away. And how long had I lasted in Quebec? A mere five months. I'd been expecting to stay much longer. I liked both the city and the club. As we paid the highest taxes of all NHL players, half the team would have welcomed a move, but I didn't care about that. I'd enjoyed playing for the Nordiques and hadn't given the taxes a second thought. It's a shame that things didn't turn out better.

I don't have a bad word to say about the management team. They— Gilles Leger, Marcel Aubut, Marius Fortier, Maurice Filion, and others—helped me escape from Czechoslovakia and gave me my chance in the NHL, for which they have my undying gratitude.

If I'd understood certain things earlier, maybe my relationship with Michel Bergeron and my life on the team would have been different. It's hard to say. As things turned out, they marked me down as a troublemaker, and they traded me out of the team at the first opportunity, before I had a chance to cause them more serious problems.

That evening I called in on the Stastnys, who continued to encourage me and to build my self-confidence. Being traded was no disgrace in the NHL, they explained. I'd been given a fresh chance, and maybe

Toronto would suit me better. A different part of Canada, the people there had a different mentality.

All these years later, I know that those five months with the Quebec Nordiques gave me an amazing education. I took a crash course in professional hockey and wasn't found wanting. Maybe it worked in my favor that I faced so many difficulties at the very beginning: adapting to a new environment, problems with the language, being sent down to the farm team, a coach that didn't believe in me, and finally being traded. I began to take a realistic, illusion-free view of my work. I understood that the NHL is a business, where the player is treated like a piece of meat. If you're merely a good player, not the kind of superstar teams are built around, you can be sold to the other end of the continent at any time. All it takes is one phone call.

Fortunately, my time in Quebec was brief, so leaving wasn't as hard for me as it would have been if I'd lived there for five years and made lots of friends, and my family had set down roots. In the end, I was pleased that I'd rented a house in the city rather than buying one, even though people had kept telling me what a great investment it would be; at least that was one less thing to worry about.

The next morning, I packed only the things I needed and went on my way. On landing in Toronto, I bought a newspaper in which I read that team owner Harold Ballard couldn't understood why Paiement had been traded for Frycer. "We've already had two Czechs, and they didn't do very well," he declared, in reference to Jiri Crha and Slava Duris. "I'm surprised we haven't learned our lesson."

This next gig would be an interesting one, too, I realized. I was unwanted in Quebec, and there were no fanfares of welcome for me here either.

As it turned out, I spent longer with the Maple Leafs than any other club in my career. Six remarkable years, in the course of which there was never a dull moment.

11

Taking My First Steps in Toronto

I APPRECIATED THE OPPORTUNITY to play for the Maple Leafs from the
word go. If I had to leave Quebec, I could think of no better place to go
than Toronto. It was a bit like signing for Barcelona as a soccer player.
That is, if you can imagine Barcelona regularly finding themselves at
the bottom of the standings.

The Maple Leafs is a club known to every hockey fan. It is the biggest, the most popular, and, despite its lack of success in recent decades, one of the richest. It is one of the so-called Original Six (members of the NHL from 1942 through 1967)—along with the Montreal
Canadiens, the Detroit Red Wings, the Chicago Black Hawks (spelled
as Blackhawks since the 1986-87 season), the Boston Bruins, and the
New York Rangers. In those days, teams traveled to games by train,
they played each opponent 14 times in the regular season (which must
have added spice to rivalries), and players like Gordie Howe, Maurice
Richard and Stan Mikita graced the ice. Some refer to this time as
hockey's golden era.

No doubt it's great, too, to play for the Vancouver Canucks or the
Buffalo Sabres, but with those teams a sense of belonging to hockey's
rich and illustrious history is harder to come by.

I was never more aware of this history than when Toronto assigned
me the number 14 jersey. At the time, more than a few amused comments reached my ears. Number 14 had been worn by Dave Keon,
four-time winner of the Stanley Cup and one the Maple Leafs' greatest
legends, even though he had left the Leafs under a cloud. It was an
honor for me to be given such a number. I tried not to think about

whether I was expected to emulate Keon's achievements, though—the weight on my shoulders was big enough already.

Perhaps the greatest privilege connected with my time in Toronto was the opportunity to play at Maple Leaf Gardens. There was no better-known building in Canada. Frank Sinatra, the Beatles and Elvis Presley had performed there, Muhammad Ali had boxed there, and it had been visited by Elizabeth II and Winston Churchill. But above all, its ice had hosted many famous hockey battles, from Stanley Cup finals to tense duels with the Soviets. The locals were proud of the place, not least as it had been built in a mere five months in 1931, at the height of the Depression.

Unlike other arenas, Maple Leaf Gardens didn't stand alone in an open space. It was in among the other buildings on Carlton Street, part of the pulsating downtown. If it hadn't been for the illuminated MAPLE LEAF GARDENS sign that also bore the name of our next opponent, it's unlikely an uninformed tourist would have realized what a gem it was.

It was a true cathedral of hockey. The first time I went in through the side entrance, my jaw dropped. History breathed from every inch of wall. Every floor of the building was decorated with photos of champions and maple leaf emblems. The banners hanging from the roof were a constant reminder of 11 Stanley Cup victories. It never crossed my mind that I would see for myself the end of all this magnificence just 20 years later, when from Yonge Street I peeked inside to be confronted by the sight of one set of stands in a state of demolition and a bulldozer working on another. How sad that was! Today, there's a Loblaw supermarket inside, and whenever I walk its aisles, I say to myself things like, "A-ha, that's where the blue line used to be."

The décor in the arena wasn't our only reminder of the glorious past. Stars of the past like Eddie Shack, Frank Mahovlich and George Armstrong would come to watch us train; born-again Christian Paul Henderson would bring Bibles into the dressing room; Johnny Bower, famous goaltender and all-round great guy, worked for the team as a scout. And the fans who supported us from the stands were extremely proud of their club's history. For these fans, we would give our all. I remember certain national-team players in Czechoslovakia agreeing on the result before a game and taking it easy, and I also remember how we played at half-speed to make a point to an unpopular coach. People in Toronto would never have stood for that.

In comparison with Quebec's, the dressing room was quite modest. Just a vestibule, some showers at the back, a sauna and an ice bath, and a small weight room next door. The players' room contained a fridge, a cola vending machine and a TV. The dressing room was small but cozy. If I wanted to say something to a teammate, I didn't have to shout it over 60 feet, as players do today. And what an indescribable feeling it was to sit down on one of the wooden benches and imagine all those who had sat there before me …

I often wonder how I would have started off in Canada if, instead of having those five months in Quebec, I'd gone straight from Vitkovice to the tradition-steeped Maple Leafs. As it was, I arrived having gotten the hang of the NHL. And I'd played one game at the Gardens already, so I had at least a vague idea of what to expect in Toronto.

My knees weren't shaking before my first appearance. I believed in myself. I knew that with the Leafs at the wrong end of the Norris Division, competition for roster spots wouldn't be as intense as it had been with the Nordiques. Besides, I'd been promised time and space on the ice to show what I could do.

At that time, the team was undergoing extensive rebuilding. New general manager Gerry McNamara had been brave in getting rid of older players, including some leading figures of the '70s era. In November, experienced defenseman Ian Turnbull left for the Los Angeles Kings, and a few weeks before my trade, the Leafs had traded superstar center Darryl Sittler to the Philadelphia Flyers.

My arrival was to be seen in the context of these changes.

Club owner Harold Ballard wasn't the only one raising his eyebrows in surprise. As ever, the press and television were discussing which side of each trade was the winner and which the loser, whether the move was evidence of far-sightedness or a cardinal sin. I don't suppose I had many sympathizers at the beginning.

Wilf Paiement, who had left for my sake, was one of the league's most recognizable figures. A classic Canadian tough guy, he wasn't afraid of blood and had plenty of dirty tricks up his sleeve. The Czech boys who came up against him at the 1977 world championship in Vienna could tell you a few stories. But he was also a good goal scorer. Just one year earlier he had played the season of his life, amassing 40 goals and 97 points. But noting that his performance levels were declining, Toronto decided to trade him. In exchange, they got me—a rookie from Czechoslovakia whose name meant nothing to most fans.

McNamara explained the trade thus: "Frycer is 22 and Wilf is 27—that makes a big difference to us. Our hockey team is getting younger and younger. That's the only way we feel we can improve." But I don't believe he chose me just because of my age. If I hadn't scored a hat trick against the Leafs in October, it's unlikely I'd have been given the chance to pull on their blue and white jersey.

I made my first appearance for the Maple Leafs the day after the trade. Although we lost 7-6 to the Chicago Black Hawks, I was happy with my debut. I had a few chances, I assisted on three goals, and after the game I was approached by the old gentleman himself. "Congratulations, and welcome to the Maple Leafs," Ballard told me with a smile. At that moment, I knew I'd be fine in Toronto.

Just a week after my arrival, I had a chance to prove that the Frycer-Paiement trade wasn't a disaster for my new club. That's right, we had a game against the Quebec Nordiques. In the dressing room, remembering the "promise" I'd made to general manager Maurice Filion on my way out, I joked that today was a day for me to score a hat trick. It was. I scored two goals in the space of 39 seconds in the second period, the third in the 58th minute of the game. It finished 6-3. I couldn't have been happier. Although goalie Dan Bouchard knew my tricks,

I'd beaten him three times. And why shouldn't I admit it? I felt pretty pleased to have gotten one over the Nordiques.

In the final period, the fans at Maple Leaf Gardens were on their feet. Not only because of my goals—it was the Leafs' first win in 10 games. We'd given the journalists, who weren't used to such shows every week, something to write about.

That hat trick against the Nordiques was my fifth. At the time, only Wayne Gretzky had amassed more—and that season he scored 92 goals, a record that will likely stand forever.

It wasn't that I'd struck on a miraculous recipe for scoring three goals in one game. Luck had a lot to do with it. And teammates. Sometimes I'd play really well, all three goals were beauties, and I could say with pride that it was my game. At others, things went less well for me, but I succeeded in latching onto a couple of rebounds and converting a breakaway, giving me a hat trick even though I was less than impressed with my own performance.

Only much later did I come to realize what a feat I'd achieved. Hat tricks shouldn't be taken for granted. I know lots of great players who were 30-plus when they scored their first, or are happy to have managed two in their career. I ended up with nine NHL hat tricks. The table of Czech scorers of hat tricks is a parade of our greatest forwards. Sometimes I happen across it in a newspaper, and how glad it makes me to see only Jaromir Jagr above me!

———

I added only one more goal that season. But what a goal it was! We were playing against the St. Louis Blues, needing a win to keep our playoff hopes alive. The final minute began with the score at 3-3; if it remained tied, we could start packing for our vacations. So the coach pulled the goalie. It was now or never. We piled on the pressure. Twelve seconds before the buzzer, I took Ricky Vaive's pass from the right and fired a shot past goaltender Mike Liut. We won 4-3.

Everyone clapped me on the back. I'd become the hero who saved the day for Toronto.

I'm not sure how happy Ricky was about my goal, however. In that very game, he became the first player in Maple Leafs history to break the 50 goals in a season barrier, an amazing achievement that even the likes of Darryl Sittler and Frank Mahovlich never matched. And I'd stolen some of his thunder. Maybe that's why he never took to me.

A great forward, Ricky was also a right winger. His stick was as heavy as a dumbbell, but nine times out of 10 he put the puck exactly where he wanted it. And he had a shot like a rocket. A classic sniper, he could shoot from anywhere. He could play hard, too, allowing him to score many times from in front of the net, where players often got hurt. In some games, he'd record a hat trick even though only one of his shots went in—the other two would deflect behind the goalie off his pants or skate.

And he was vain. He and I were often at odds.

Although I scored fewer goals than Ricky, I scored enough for people to take notice. I was good at fakes and dekes, plus I knew how to celebrate a goal, which the fans enjoyed. Journalists tended to seek me out. Maybe Ricky had scored three goals, I'd scored one, and half the reporters outside the dressing room would be waiting for him, the other half for me. As he was speaking into the microphone, he would cast a sidelong glance my way. This glance told me all I needed to know about his jealousy of my successes and popularity. Sometimes, he'd have a go at me verbally. At first, I'd ignore this, but later I learned to give as good as I got. Always within the bounds of what I could get away with in the dressing room, of course.

We didn't celebrate family birthdays and go on vacation together, but I respected him, as one of the best forwards in the NHL and as my captain—before he lost the captaincy, that is. On a trip to Minnesota, the whole team spent a night in a bar. But only Ricky had so much to drink that he missed morning practice. The C was taken from him immediately.

The glory of my goal against St. Louis didn't last long. I may have revived our hopes of reaching the playoffs, but the odds were still about one in a thousand. To go through, we needed to win our last five games and the Blues to lose all theirs. Mission impossible. We lost them all and finished fifth in the division, 16 points short of advancing …

For the first time since 1973, the Maple Leafs had failed to reach the playoffs. And our tally of 56 points made this the worst season in their history. Who could have guessed that in the next few years we would keep this sorry record going?

On the other hand, no one was making a tragedy out of this early elimination. Journalists and fans alike understood that many experienced players had left, and a team was being built for the future. At our last meeting of the season, the general manager informed us that next year we would be expected to reach the playoffs, not just fight for a place in them. Then he announced the dates of training camp and we were free to go our separate ways.

Even after the historic failure, no one doubted the suitability of Mike Nykoluk as coach. He was given Dan Maloney, a forward who had just finished his career, as his assistant.

So I had a second season to look forward to under the idiosyncratic Nykoluk.

He was more of an assistant type, having in this role twice helped the Philadelphia Flyers to the Stanley Cup title and the New York Rangers to the final. Maybe he should have remained an assistant, because he certainly wasn't suited to the role of head coach. Head coach of the Toronto Maple Leafs least of all. He was like everyone's favorite uncle. How many times did I see him angry? Twice?

Before a game, the opposition and tactics were the last things on his mind. No sooner had an employee delivered a box of cookies and chocolates to the dressing room than Mike would race to the table, push the rest of us out of the way, and choose the best for himself. Then he would disappear into his cubbyhole with a smug look on his face. Although this cubbyhole was part of the dressing room, we could tell that Mike was in it only by the clouds of smoke that would appear above the door.

He smoked his cigars any time, any place. Which wasn't so unusual in those days, when people smoked in movie theaters and airplanes, even in the waiting room of the doctor's office. Coaches in Czechoslovakia may have been surprised to learn that certain players—including stars like Denis Savard and Guy Lafleur—made no attempt to disguise the fact that they were smokers. I wouldn't smoke on the day of a game until I got home at night, but some of the boys would light up during breaks, in the restroom or in front of the dressing room. No one called them to task about it. (Later, I had a teammate who would return from the restroom with traces of white powder under his nose.) In the early '80s, the NHL took a free-thinking approach to a lot of things. After a game, we'd return to the dressing room to find two crates of cold Molsons waiting for us—win or lose. No one told us how to manage our diets; as professionals, it was up to us to make sure we stayed in good shape. If our habits got out of hand, no problem. There were plenty of others waiting to take our place.

Nykoluk didn't go to town where training was concerned either. Canadians are well known for seeing strength in simplicity, but he took this to an extreme. We practiced power plays more or less on our own, with Swedish veteran Borje Salming directing things. Then we performed a few simple drills and did a bit of shooting practice. That was it. Mike looked happiest when we were enthusiastic and working together, taking this as a sign that we were training properly. His approach was incomparable with what I knew from Vitkovice. It was like being back with the juniors. Sometimes I had the feeling he wanted to get practice over with as quickly as possible so he could get back to his cigars.

Nykoluk's tactical preparation was similarly minimalist. He would pick up a piece of paper, walk around the dressing room and shout: "We fight! We work! We win!" The same words every game. Moments later, cigar smoke would be wafting around the dressing room …

Mike was better at enjoying life than he was at coaching in the NHL.

When Maurice Filion announced that he'd traded me to the Toronto Maple Leafs, not for a moment did I worry that my game wouldn't be good enough. My concerns were about life in a big city. Quebec was a small city, not much bigger than Ostrava. I had gotten used to it quickly. Suddenly, I was faced with a move to a metropolis of three million people, a kind of Canadian New York.

But I fell in love with the place. We found an apartment in the downtown, a few blocks from Maple Leaf Gardens. After four years, we moved to the suburb of Etobicoke. I still consider Toronto my second home.

It was the center of the Czech community in Canada, another reason I was able to make myself at home there.

I got to know some members of this community soon after my trade, when I was invited to a large banquet for my compatriots. It was held in the magnificent historical surroundings of the Royal York Hotel, and the proceeds were used to support refugees from Czechoslovakia. Everyone wore a suit—it was a pretty grand occasion.

Some of the better-known immigrants were introduced, including me. As my name was said, Tomas Bata stood up from his table and gave me a wave of welcome, a gesture that delighted me. His shoe empire had its headquarters on the edge of Toronto; Mr. Bata not only attended events of this kind but went to Maple Leafs games, too. Sometime after the year 2000, we met in Prague by chance, at the entrance of the Marriott hotel. He and his wife were coming out; I was going in. Mr. Bata stopped and said: "*Dobry den*. Don't we know each other from Toronto?" I was astonished. Such an important man who must have met a million people in his life, and he recognizes a hockey player he saw once at a banquet 20 years previously and perhaps in the NHL a few times after that.

People from Czechoslovakia often met at a Czech restaurant in the famous Masaryktown part of the suburban district of Scarborough. I went along to these events only rarely—all the talk of the old homeland, the folk songs, and the overall sense of nostalgia were a bit much for me. I was 22 years old, and I'd left for Canada to live my own life. I didn't feel a need to mingle with all Czechs and Slovaks. Besides, almost every conversation led to the question: "So how much do you earn playing hockey?" If there was one thing I didn't miss in Canada, it was the simple Czech envy.

But I very much enjoyed my visits with Mirek Cervenka and his wife, Veronika, to whom I'd been introduced by my teammate Slava Duris. That winter, they invited me to try bear. Taste it, not hunt it. A friendship began that lasts to this day.

They kept great company. At their place, I dined with writer Josef Skvorecky several times. Filmmaker Vaclav Taborsky and his wife, Dagmar, a respected editor and director, were frequent guests. There was piano-playing, singing, storytelling. The time I spent at the Cervenkas' home was a pleasant escape from the world of hockey.

George Gross, sports editor of the *Toronto Sun* and one of the most influential hockey journalists, was very much part of that world of hockey. Born in Bratislava as Juraj Gross, he changed his Christian name following his escape to Canada in 1949. I can't say that we were friends exactly, but we got on very well. We played tennis, went to a steak house after a game, and sometimes he took me along to Toronto clubs of which he was a member. He was an amiable and entertaining companion, and I always enjoyed our conversations—which weren't only about hockey. But I didn't get any special treatment from him: if I'd had a wretched game, he'd write that I'd played poorly, making no excuses for me. He always judged us with respect, however. He wrote as he behaved in society.

Someone else I saw regularly was tennis player Ivan Lendl. He would play at the indoor tournament at Maple Leaf Gardens in winter and the Canadian Open in summer. He was half a year younger than me, and we'd known each other since we were little kids. Our fathers did their military service together. While Ivan's mother Olga was still playing competitive tennis, they would call in to see us in Zagreb on their way to a tournament in Yugoslavia. Ivan was keen on hockey. As a boy, long before he became one of the world's top athletes, he would go to Kotas Stadium to support Vitkovice. And now here we were years later, both of us emigrants living on the other side of the ocean. We always had something to tell each other and memories to share.

On court, he may have seemed like a cold machine programmed for victory, but in private he was an amusing, easygoing guy. Once after a game, we were chatting in the corridor by the dressing room when the promoter came up and apologized for interrupting us. Mr. Lendl's press conference was about to start, he explained. Ivan turned to him, switched from his smile to the mask of the aloof professional, and said, "The press conference will begin when I'm ready." Then, with a chuckle, he turned back to me and finished his story.

Meeting up with other Czech NHL players had a special magic for me. In my very first season, I would meet Ivan Hlinka and Jiri Bubla, who played for the Vancouver Canucks. Whenever they flew into Toronto, we would go out to dinner together. And enjoy some really great laughs. On one occasion, Jiri remembered making a prediction as we were flying into Lake Placid: this would be his last Olympics, but I was young enough to play in three more, he had said then. "Doesn't look like you'll be playing in any more Olympics after all, Frigo," he laughed now, as we sat together in our adopted home.

Like other players who had turned 30 before they made it to the NHL, Ivan and Jiri didn't have things easy. I had a difficult start, but theirs must have been twice as hard. They had realized their dream of playing hockey in Canada, and they had made some money. But the Pragosport state agency took a big cut, and their performance levels were no longer a match for the stars of the league, as they would have been five years earlier. They were getting on in years and their bodies were starting to feel it. Plus, it was harder for them to adapt to a different style of play. As world champions and the erstwhile elite of European hockey, as they came to the end of their careers it was difficult for them to accept a coach's instruction to chuck the puck at the boards …

In later years, I saw Milan Novy of the Washington Capitals, albeit only for a few moments, as their coach forbade his players to speak with the opposition before a game. I came up against Miroslav Dvorak on a number of occasions. Our battles with the Philadelphia Flyers were always worth seeing, and I would make fun of Miroslav for the Cooperalls he played in for two seasons. And there was Jaroslav Pouzar, of course. He won the Stanley Cup with the Edmonton Oilers three times, but he didn't have things easy either. The role they insisted on him playing was like purgatory for him—as I knew from the many hours we spent talking together.

Vaclav Nedomansky and I were never close. I was introduced to him in Quebec by the Stastny brothers. Marian knew him best: they had played together for Slovan Bratislava. After my arrival in Toronto, we would acknowledge each other, but we didn't speak much. All we said, in fact, was *"Dobry den"* during the warm-up. No wonder, really—to Big Ned, who was 15 years my senior, I must have seemed still wet behind the ears.

My strangest encounter with a compatriot was with Frantisek Cernik, who played one season alongside Milan Chalupa for the Detroit Red Wings. When they hosted us, Frantisek was tasked with keeping close to me. "What was the coach thinking, asking me to mark a mate I played with for years? Holy shit!" he laughed, as we shared a beer or two afterward.

I enjoyed this moment of nostalgia for Vitkovice. We lost 7-6; I scored two goals, Frantisek one. I still have the official game report at home.

12

A Goal for Dad

EVERY YEAR, TEAM owner Harold Ballard gave us the same Christmas present. An airline ticket to anywhere in the world. All we had to do to sort out our vacations was go to the Air Canada office and state our destination.

I thought it a wonderful gesture that I got one too in my first season, even though I'd still been a Nordique at Christmas. Classic Harold generosity. It didn't take long to decide where I wanted us to fly. At the end of the regular season, I returned to Quebec for a few days to bring the affairs related to my move to a close and to see how the Stastny brothers were doing in the playoffs (extremely well—the Nordiques upset the Montreal Canadiens in the first round and eventually advanced to the conference final). Then we headed off to see my parents in West Germany.

Dad had just started a new job in Dusseldorf—where, by coincidence, Vitkovice would be playing in the Europa Cup tournament in August 1982. I couldn't miss the chance to go along and say hi to everyone.

It was like a scene from a farce. At the stadium, I took up a position next to where the buses parked and waited for the boys to arrive. Their reaction was priceless. Some of them didn't even look at me; they headed for the dressing room with heads turned away, pretending I wasn't there. Coaches Jan Soukup and Karel Metelka stopped to ask how I was getting along in the NHL. The conversation lasted about half a minute, but I understood why they wanted to keep it short. My best friends on the team, notably Lada Svozil, Jaromir Sindel and Milos Riha, came running up to me. We were all delighted to see each other.

A year ago, we hadn't known if we would ever do so again, and now we were going for a beer together. I've no idea what the snoops put in their reports, but I do know that my friends didn't get into trouble for spending time with a convicted emigrant.

We flew to West Germany every year. Before we did, we would go somewhere warm, like Hawaii, Florida or Jamaica. Wherever Dad was coaching, I would go out on the ice with his team in the summer. Once, I was joined by Peter and Anton Stastny, who spent a week in Freiburg on their travels in Europe. This was great for the boys on Dad's team, players in the 2nd Bundesliga who suddenly had an opportunity to train with pros from the NHL. They went all-out to impress us, Peter in particular.

But in the summer after my first season in the NHL, it was a while before I stepped things up in my training. Maybe I just needed a rest after 10 very demanding months in which I'd fled to Canada, struggled to make my mark in Quebec, been sent to the farm team and then traded to Toronto, where I'd had to acclimatize to a new team. Maybe, too, I enjoyed being able to do as I chose in the off-season, with no coaches to send me to the athletics track or the weight room.

For two months, I played a little tennis and soccer, but otherwise I relaxed. I paid the price for this at training camp, where I spent the first ten days in agony. I swore I would never let this happen again. Every summer after that, I toiled away conscientiously, although I would take things a little easier in the first month. It wasn't enough for me to train with a German team. To avoid the worst of the July heat, I would get up at five in the morning and go for a run in the woods. And I really disliked running. I had thighs like blocks of wood; every mile was misery.

Among the Maple Leafs, I was one of the few who pushed himself like this. Most of the Canadians treated the period between the end of one season and the beginning of the next as a vacation. They would travel, play golf and have fun. Those not involved in kids' summer camps wouldn't put on their skates until September.

It may have been the official line that training camp was about fighting for places on the team and the chance for 60 ambitious souls to prove they should make the team, but this was nonsense. The roster was known in advance. We knew very well whose spot was assured—by length of contract, reputation and level of performance in the previous season. Maybe a couple of places in the fourth line were up for grabs, but nothing more.

The main point of the camp was for players to get back into shape after the idleness of summer.

Some came back in a sorry state—so overweight they could hardly fasten their pants. To today's players, with their personal fitness coaches and diet consultants, this would be inconceivable. But to give credit where it's due, these out-of-shape players gave their all from the first day of camp, improving their diets, cutting out the beer, and staying in the gym after practice. Within three weeks, they were unrecognizable from the men who had reported to camp. Their well-chiseled bodies were ready for NHL action.

It took the Canadians a long time to realize that the melting of the ice signaled the beginning not of vacation but of preseason preparation. There's more and more money in and around hockey these days. The connection has been made that if players work hard in July and August, it's possible they will be able to play until they are 40, and so earn enough money to set them up for life. Club management, too, has come to understand this. At some point in the mid-1980s, the physical fitness tests we had long been used to in Europe were at last introduced. At the start of training camp, we'd be taken off to a university and made to pedal an exercise bike; they would measure our range of movement, the strength of our arms and legs, our speed and stamina.

Life was carefree no longer. During the season, players would now be fined for carrying too much weight, and lights-out was introduced on our road trips. But we had a heightened sense of our own professionalism.

Before my second season in the NHL, I was joined on my line by Peter Ihnacak, a pal from Czechoslovakia. Known as Iha, he, too, had been forced to defect, of course.

I'd had an idea that something was in the pipeline in spring, when general manager Gerry McNamara asked me about him. I knew Peter from Sparta Prague, as one of the best forwards in the league. We hadn't played together much for the national team, for a simple reason: half of Iha's family lived in America. His grandfather had been among the many Slovaks to leave the country during the Great Depression to seek their fortune overseas. Peter's brother Jan and his two sisters had defected in 1968, after the Soviet occupation. As a result, he was allowed to represent the national team only on the less fortunate side of the Iron Curtain. Whenever the team traveled to the West, he was out.

An exception was made in 1982, when the world championship was held in Finland, a country that didn't accept refugees from communist countries. In Helsinki, however, Iha sneaked onto a ferry and traveled to Sweden, where his brother and some people from Toronto were waiting for him. His path to the NHL was open. According to the new rules, he had to pass through the entry draft; with the pick they received from Philadelphia in the Darryl Sittler trade, the Maple Leafs took him 25th overall.

Peter spent the summer at his brother's in the USA. In September he flew out to join the training camp. I picked him up at the airport. We drove to the hotel, with the bright lights and skyscrapers of downtown Toronto in front of us. As we studied this great panorama, I said, "This is the Mecca of hockey. If we do well here, it's ours for the taking."

We were young and living our hockey dream; quite simply, we were riding a wave of euphoria. Our NHL careers were ahead of us, and we believed they would be long and successful. As it turned out, Iha and I spent six seasons together, under three different coaches and two general managers. Usually we played on the same line; even when the coach shuffled the lineup, we would end up next to each other eventually. Peter would go on to record 267 points for the Maple Leafs to my 268.

Iha wasn't the fastest skater, but he was a well-built guy with a forceful style of play, and he was good at making space for me. We clicked because we had the same grounding in how the game should be played. We weren't greedy with the puck, and we knew the right time to make a pass. In our private lives, we followed different paths. Peter was very sociable and liked lots of people around, while I preferred to spend time with closer friends.

Walt Poddubny, a Canadian bear with Ukrainian genes, became the third member of our line. Walt came to Toronto at the same time I did, from the Edmonton Oilers. He was a hefty guy and a powerful skater, and he was pretty selfish, like most of the Canadians in those days. If we were two-on-one on the opposition and he had the puck, I might as well have made a U-turn and headed for the bench, as I knew for certain that he'd shoot on goal. The best I could hope for was a deflection. But we soon brought Walt around to our way of doing things. If he made a pass to us, we explained, we'd return the puck to him. Before long, it was clear to him that our style was in his interests too.

In the 1982-83 season, the three of us formed a solid second line, scoring 81 goals (the first line was made up of Ricky Vaive, John Anderson and Bill Derlago). Iha recorded 66 points, which would remain a club record for a rookie for the next 34 years; it was eventually eclipsed by Auston Matthews.

My statistics improved to 25 goals and 55 points. I was beginning to feel more comfortable in the NHL. I was coming to terms with a different hockey culture and style of play, and I was getting used to life in the big city. Plus, a year and a half after leaving Czechoslovakia, I had become confident in my English. I have a certain gift for languages, so I relied on picking it up in the dressing room and from TV. The speaking went well from the start, but as for the writing, even today the most I can manage is an SMS text message. Unfortunately, I was too lazy to learn grammar, spelling and the like. I had to admire Marian

Stastny, who would work his way through a newspaper with diction-
ary in hand.

The high point of my second season came in March 1983, with a visit
from my father. How I looked forward to finally showing him what I
could do! And he was more than curious about the NHL. He'd devoted
his life to hockey, but he'd never had the chance to see this league for
himself. And he would get to see his son in a Maple Leafs jersey in a
game against the high-flying Oilers, who were beginning to dominate
the league.

He saw me in action for about 10 seconds before I made a fool of
myself. During the first shift, I collided with defenseman Don Jackson,
who bawled me out about it. I gave him the finger. The officials might
have let me off on a cross-check to the neck, but not this gesture. My
game was over. I joined my father in stands for a while, but we left
before the end.

I was far more successful in my next game at Maple Leaf Gardens.
We beat the St. Louis Blues 5-2, and I scored the game-winner. "That
one was for Dad," I told journalists afterward. It was my 20th goal of
the season.

Dad was proud of me for having made my NHL dream come true,
and he was glad I was doing well. But he didn't acquire a taste for
Canadian hockey. Some of things I hadn't understood in my first
months in Quebec, he never did understand. He appreciated the fact
that the play was fast and dynamic, but he had no use at all for the
dump and chase. Dad was an advocate of technical hockey. In his view,
when a team came in possession of the puck, it should keep it under control and create pressure and chances by building combination
plays. It should never just toss the puck away. "By shooting the puck at
the end boards, you waste energy, because you have to win it all over
again," he would say.

This wasn't the only thing about the NHL that went against the grain
with him. I liked the fact that we played a lot of games and that our
practices were fewer, shorter, and more intensive. With 80 games in

the regular season and a great deal of travel, there was no other way. As a coach of many years' experience, Dad saw things differently. I remember him asking me one morning what time I was going in for practice. When I told him we had two days off, he practically refused to believe it.

Then there was the time we were on our way home from a game and Dad said, "You did great today, Mirek."

I was glad of the praise, but I couldn't agree. "No, I didn't, Dad. I had a couple of good spells with the puck, but I wasn't happy with my game. I can do much better, and they expect better from me."

Dad never stopped rooting for me. He made note of all my goals and kept all the newspaper clippings. We continued to talk about hockey for hours on end. But he knew I could no longer use his advice. This wasn't his world.

———

We finished the 1982-83 regular season third in the division, the best position the Maple Leafs managed in my years with them. By our standards, a total of 67 points was a decent achievement. We won five of the last seven games, putting us into the playoffs with room to spare.

These would be the first playoffs of my career. Another new experience for me. In my day in Czechoslovakia, the league title wasn't decided by a series of knock-out games. The champion was the team that earned the most points over 44 league games, meaning the winner was sometimes known several weeks before the season's end. At that time, the situation was the same at the world championship. Everyone was playing against everyone else; no game was a decider.

The playoffs are an entirely different competition. The start of a new season. All results till then count for nothing. Hockey's great clichés. But that's exactly how things are. I felt the serious atmosphere of the playoffs at our last practice before our series against the Minnesota North Stars. The approach was different. Suddenly, everyone was that little bit more focused and determined. No one joked in the dressing room. We all minded our own business.

On the day of the game, there was a palpable change of mood at Maple Leaf Gardens. Receptionists, ushers and office staff were more serious and unusually anxious. When we emerged from the dressing room and onto the ice, the arena was buzzing. It hadn't been exactly quiet in the regular season, but now the noise of encouragement was intense right from the first face-off.

Things were different on the ice, too. No sooner had the referee started the game than something struck the top of my foot. The next blow was a butt-ending just below the ribs. So this was the playoffs!

I could deal with this kind of play. Every cross-check and foul served to galvanize me. Toughness didn't scare me; I knew that if someone laid into me, I would give twice as good as I got. In fact, I found the playoffs fascinating from the very first minute. Though we were friends away from the ice, Bobby Smith and I went after each other on it. And when Willi Plett struck me a blow, I took my stick in both hands and returned it.

I much preferred a tough fight to the kind of sleepy contest where nothing went right for us and the travel-weary opposition was too exhausted to do anything about it. The playoffs were a class apart. We needed to make every shift count, otherwise it was vacation time. We went into every duel at full tilt. The aches and pains of the regular season meant nothing now. Provided you weren't holding your head under your arm, you were fit to play. We had the whole summer to recover.

The first round was a best-of-five. Our series against the North Stars was pretty equal. They finally sent us home in the fourth game, having beaten us 5-4 three times, two of these games having gone into overtime. We'd almost made it to the next round.

I was happy with my series. I'd scored seven points, making me our most productive player along with Ricky Vaive. This gave me energy and confidence for the next season. Although 55 points was a good return, I reckoned I had more in me. At 24, I had established myself on the team and was no longer an NHL rookie.

The wish never became reality.

My hopes for the season were dashed in the first training session back at Maple Leaf Gardens. Out on the new ice, I skated into a groove—and my knee took the brunt of it. This put me out of action for a month. I never really got going after that.

I played only 47 games that year. My rhythm was that of the injured reserve list—return, injury, return. There was forever something wrong: my knee, a tooth abscess, my neck, my shoulder … At one point, the doctors suspected I was suffering from mononucleosis, so they stuffed me full of pills and I slept all day. For a week I struggled to eat, and I lost a lot of weight. I recovered my health, but it was difficult for me to recover my form. It was like driving with the handbrake on.

A season that had promised so much came to end for me at the beginning of March, when I injured a knee against the New York Islanders.

It drove me crazy. But what drove me crazier still was the talk about the fragile European who didn't have what it took to hold his own in the rough and tumble of the NHL. What nonsense! We Europeans weren't exactly ballet dancers. It was just that there were so few of us that every forced absence was more visible. No one made a fuss when a homegrown player suffered this kind of injury. While we were criticized, the Canadians were keen to emphasize their own resilience and readiness for hockey's ordeals. Yet Peter Stastny and Jari Kurri, for instance, played through their whole careers without serious injury. And few Canadians could take what Borje Salming did on the ice.

Unfortunately, I didn't have Peter's and Jari's good fortune. My medical records were forever being added to. For much of my time in the NHL, I felt like I was negotiating a minefield, worried about what my next step would bring.

I brought some of the problems on myself. During the season, I tended not to spend much time in the gym, keeping the weight-training for the summer in the hope that the strength work I did then would last me the next nine months. Had I devoted more time to it and made my body more resilient, I might have avoided some of my troubles.

Very few of my injuries could be considered typical hockey complaints that are part and parcel of the sport, like broken fingers and battered knees. I seemed to collect nothing but crazy afflictions—a broken bone in my foot, a tooth abscess, a chip off the pelvic bone, a fractured tailbone …

I battled these as best I could. It tried my patience pretty hard. But I never gave up hope that the season would arrive when I would show everyone what I was capable of.

13

NHL All-Star Game

WHEN THERE WERE 21 TEAMS in the National Hockey League, getting through to the playoffs wasn't much of a milestone. When the regular season ended, 16 teams went on and five started their vacation. In the old Norris Division, the weakest in the league, it was enough to finish second from bottom—that is, to ensure that one of the Chicago Black Hawks, Minnesota North Stars, Detroit Red Wings or St. Louis Blues finished below you. For two of the past three years, we hadn't even managed that, so it was logical that there should be a change of coach. Mike Nykoluk reached the end of his spell with the Maple Leafs and of his coaching career altogether. His place went to Dan Maloney.

Maloney was only 34, his only experience in coaching his two years as Mike's assistant. Maybe you're saying to yourself that a Maple Leafs head coach should have a better CV and more experience, but that's how things worked in the NHL. There was no talk of licenses and coaching classes. No one was interested in exams in physiology, psychology and tactics. Confidence was placed in the guy who appealed to the general manager. There were even cases of someone being appointed head coach as soon as his playing career ended. Still playing in May, four months later he'd be leading the training camp and building a new roster.

You could hardly call Maloney a top coach. But I've no complaints about him. It was under him that I had my best two seasons in the NHL. He was quick-tempered and a bit crazy, but I liked him as a person. Even when he set me straight by bawling me out, I respected him. Because he was a straight talker.

Under Maloney, practices had zip. Not that his methods were day to Nykoluk's night—Dan, too, favored Canadian simplicity—but I certainly found them more fun. Everything was faster and more dynamic, the drills a little more demanding; time on the ice made more sense.

Of the things Maloney insisted on, toughness was the most important. He never denied his past as an elite enforcer with a famous right-hand punch. In practice, sometimes we'd go after each other with such fury that the doctors would need to stitch up head wounds in the dressing room. Dan taught us a few dirty tricks for how to get under an opponent's skin, and how to deliver a really painful blow. He'd give me lessons on the best way to play the puck. "When you pass, lift your stick. Your opponent won't spare you, so why should you spare him? If you don't, the next thing you feel will be an elbow in the face."

We did our best, we showed no fear, but even so, sometimes we were given a proper hiding.

Our third game of the 1984-85 season was against the Winnipeg Jets, and they really went after Peter Ihnacak and me. For no good reason. They had nothing to pay us back for from previous games, and there was no particular rivalry between the two clubs. They probably went after us because we were Europeans. Or because their coach was Barry Long, an old acquaintance from the 1981 world championship.

As the insults flew across the ice, it was plain that my midget-like appearance got on their nerves: I kept getting taunted with the name "baby face."

We were taking slashes, spears and cross-checks to the head from the first minute. They broke three sticks on Iha and me. Dave Babych, Laurie Boschman and Thomas Steen took turns as our executioners. Steen was the meanest of the three. He was a great player, but so malicious he was perfectly capable of jabbing his stick between your eyes. I wouldn't have gone out for a beer with him, that's for sure.

By the time the game ended, I was as beat up as the fender of an old car. I sat in the dressing room with one bag of ice on my knee and another on my elbow, plus four new stitches above an eyebrow.

Maloney was tough, but this was too much even for him. He used the press conference to lay into the Jets' players and coaches.

In the context of how our season was going, however, this was nothing. After that game in Winnipeg, we found ourselves in a crisis we couldn't break out of. Between October 14 and January 9, we won just four games. Four games in three months!

Maloney gave it everything he had, but nothing helped—not criticizing us in the press, not punishing us by making us skate without a puck and without water.

We players, too, tried whatever we could. The whole team went out and got drunk together. It didn't help. We tried not drinking and not smoking. That made no difference either. We even went to a strip club together. No good. Later, general manager Gerry McNamara called us in for regular meetings, which was worst of all. The meeting before the meeting. The meeting after the meeting. The meeting between the meetings. Forever the same clichés and hollow words.

Once after practice, I was about to go off to play tennis when someone announced an unexpected meeting. They kept us in the dressing room, where we waited for Maloney and McNamara. It made me mad. More meaningless speeches, more wasted time …

I believe I can take a lot. I don't let things stew inside me, and it always takes a long time before I explode. But the explosion is worth waiting for. That was certainly the case this time. I got so mad, I gave the table a kick and spilled the drinks. The next thing I kicked was a blocker. Gaston Gingras was slumped with boredom on the carpet on the other side of the dressing room, and it almost took his head off.

I'd lost it. Silence fell: the guys had never seen me like this.

"What bright idea will we come up with this time?!" I yelled. "Let's get back to our game. That's the only way we'll crack this thing. Sitting around talking doesn't mean shit."

McNamara had arrived in time to see the end of my performance. "He's right, you know," he said. "It's on you guys." And that was the end of our crucial meeting.

In all my years in the NHL, that was the only time my words made such a telling contribution. Usually, the atmosphere in the dressing room was calm, even when our play was miserable. Surprisingly, it was the slicks from the fourth line who spoke out most. As soon as the coach walked in, they would stand up and shout: "Let's go! Let's turn this around!" But they resumed their silence the moment he was gone. It was the same after every defeat. As we got onto the bus, they would put on their game face, passing the coaches looking suitably crestfallen. Then they would sit at the back and have a grand old time.

When Ricky Vaive was still captain, he tried to lead the way. But all of Toronto knew the team's true leader was Borje Salming. Ricky could scream till he was blue in the face, but by the time we filed out onto the ice, his words were long forgotten.

Such was Borje's authority; his word was law. As he'd been with the Maple Leafs since 1973, when most of the rest of us were still peewees, this was perfectly understandable. When he raised his voice, everyone else shut up. This well-toned, sinewy figure would get to his feet, say a few words, and everyone would nod. No one dared contradict him. God forbid that he should get mad.

The coaches, too, had great respect for his opinion. If there was something Borje didn't like about practice, he'd call it out and we'd go about it a different way. It was a pity he didn't want to be captain. Offered the C several times, he always refused it. He didn't want the aggravation or to lose time on the duties required of a Maple Leafs captain.

He was happier in the role of mentor. At practice, he'd spend a lot of time with the youngsters, and afterward he'd take them for lunch and a chat at the Golden Griddle opposite the rink. Whenever a wide-eyed kid arrived from the farm team, it was taken for granted that Borje would take him under his wing. He was a proper leader.

Borje was such a big NHL star that he was nicknamed the King. But he remained modest and true to himself.

He and I went through a lot together. For a time, we were roommates on our travels. And toward the end of my time with the Leafs, he and

I were the longest-serving players there. Although my respect for him knew no bounds, sometimes we would have a go at each other. At practice especially. Once, we were practicing power plays alongside each other and I was his defense partner, but I was making a mess of it. After the puck had gotten by my stick several times as I stood on the blue line, Borje got mad and yelled at me. I yelled back at him. My position on the team was now strong enough to permit this. We exchanged "fuck offs," threw down our sticks, and marched back to the dressing room.

There we sat, silent and pissed off. Then we started to laugh like loons. "Made short work of that drill, eh?"

A side of Borje not many got to see.

Maloney's first season was the worst in Maple Leafs history. We won only 12 games, putting up a wretched 48 points, the lowest in the entire NHL. When it was over, the front page of the *Toronto Sun* declared "THE WORST TEAM EVER," with the faces of all the players under the headline.

But the cards hadn't fallen so badly for me. Even when we were incapable of winning a game, I was still scoring goals. By the end of January, I had 20 of them; Ricky Vaive and I were vying for first place in points scored for the club.

We were in Chicago for a game when news reached me that knocked me sideways.

I arrived late for the team lunch—I'd been chatting with Peter Ihnacak. I walked into the restaurant and everyone shouted, "Congratulations, Frigo!" I had no idea what was going on. The boys explained that I'd been selected to play in the 1985 All-Star Game. I would be the Maple Leafs' only representative.

It was difficult for me to take this in. I'd grown up dreaming of playing in the NHL, and when at last I got there, I did my best to establish myself and do well. But it had never crossed my mind that I'd be given such an honor. I'd be playing in an exhibition game alongside hockey's greatest stars, including Wayne Gretzky, Marcel Dionne, Bryan Trottier, Mike Bossy and Anders Hedberg. This was more than a dream come true; it was something I'd never dared dream.

When we got back to Toronto, practically everyone with the club came up to congratulate me, from Harold Ballard at the very top down to the person doing the most menial cleaning job. Further proof that selection for the All-Star Game is a great honor. I was called to the office, where I accepted delivery of my official invitation from NHL boss John Ziegler. I was given information about who would pay for my plane ticket and hotel, plus instructions on what to take with me and when the first meeting with coach Glen Sather would be. Then I was all set for Calgary.

The All-Star Game is more than just a sporting holiday—it's a magnificent social occasion. On the eve of the game, we were invited to a welcome banquet where everyone wore a suit and we players were ceremonially introduced one after another. It was a pretty big deal. Everyone who was anyone in the NHL was there. All the splendor made me nervous, and the boys poked fun at me for it. My name was called and I walked to my place at the table. As I passed Michel Goulet, my former Quebec Nordiques teammate, he told me with a chuckle, "Breathe, Mirko, or you'll pass out on us."

Our program for the next day included a Western-style party, where we would wear cowboy boots, a checked shirt, a vest, jeans and a cowboy hat. A very pleasant get-together. Anyone who knew us just from TV and press photos, where we slashed and hacked at each other with our sticks, would have been in for a big surprise. All the animosities and outstanding debts were left at the door. Canadians are brilliant at this. On the ice, they think nothing of brawling with a brother or a best friend, then picking up good relations the moment they leave the rink. For them, hockey is a job that lasts 60 minutes. They put on a show, then leave their roles behind. For instance, Dougie Wilson of the Chicago Black Hawks and I went after each other whenever our teams met, trading all kinds of insults, but in Calgary we had a friendly chat and shared a taxi to the arena.

In those days, the Maple Leafs played in the Campbell Conference (it's called the Western Conference today). So I would be representing a team built around players from the champion Edmonton Oilers. There were eight Oilers altogether, including both goaltenders. Glen Sather was the Oilers' coach. One big name after another. As I sat in the dressing room with Wayne Gretzky and Paul Coffey on one side and Marcel Dionne and Jari Kurri on the other, I felt like I was dreaming. I'd never played on a better team than this. Today, eight of those players are in the Hall of Fame, with some of the others likely to join them there.

As we were warming up, Sather announced that he was putting me on a line with Thomas Gradin of the Vancouver Canucks and Steve Payne of the Minnesota North Stars. Our tactical instructions took about six seconds to deliver. "Make the most of it and have a good time," Sather told us. Then he turned to his Edmonton charges and said, "And you lot make sure you don't get injured."

At the pregame ceremony, it was my honor to be the first of our team to go out onto the ice—to the applause of the sellout crowd at the Saddledome. I didn't tend to get nervous before a game, but this was an exception. My knees were practically knocking together when the stadium announcer proclaimed: "Wearing number 14 and representing the Toronto Maple Leafs, their second scoring leader ... Miroslav Frycer!"

Then I was supposed to skate to the blue line, doff my Stetson and wave to the crowd with it. I concentrated on every step, determined not to stumble or fall. It worked. As I stood in the center of the rink and waited for my teammates, I said to myself over and over, "What the fuck is a kid from Karvina doing here, among the NHL's biggest stars ..." I could barely take in where I was and what was happening to me.

It was a terrific feeling.

In later years, players stopped taking the All-Star Game seriously, and it became a bit of a farce. Games would end in ridiculous scores like 17-12, there was little defense, and goaltenders were made fools of. It didn't interest me as a spectator, and I can't say I take to the current three-on-three tournament either. We went into the game with much greater passion. With respect, too, of course: we didn't go after each other, and we were careful about injuries. But we were there to win. The NHL rivalry between the Edmonton Oilers and the New York Islanders was a fierce one, and the game was a matter of great prestige for guys from those clubs.

What pleased me most about it was being given the chance to play European-style hockey for the first time in years. All 36 guys on the ice knew how to handle a puck and were prepared to show it. In a league game they would have taken a crack at the net, but now they would make a nice pass.

My big moment came in the 17th minute. Mike Krushelnyski made a brilliant play from the left wing and I was in alone with just Tom Barrasso to beat. During the season, I'd scored several times by going five-hole. It's one of the hardest shots to get right—you must strike when there's a gap between the pads, keeping the puck very low. I'd known right away that I would try this with Barrasso. No fake, I'd just wait for the gap to appear between his legs.

As the puck flashed into the net, I felt the same joy and shock as for my first goal in the NHL. I scarcely knew what was happening to me. I'd scored in an All-Star Game! Should I celebrate in an exhibition?

My goal evened the score at 2-2, but after that the team from the Prince of Wales Conference came back at us. For the rest of the game, they were always at least one goal in front. Sather sent on a last shift made up entirely of guys from Edmonton, and with the score at 5-4, he pulled the goalie. Further proof that we were taking this game seriously. It had nothing to do with money—each player on the losing side would get $750, the winners $1,000 each. Peanuts, effectively. But if hockey means something to you, you wish to avoid defeat at all costs, even in an exhibition.

The empty-net gamble didn't pay off—Mike Gartner added another to close the scoring at 6-4.

Mario Lemieux was named the game's MVP. He was only 19, and this had been his first season in the NHL. Commentators often criticized him for his poor defense, saying they expected more from a talent like his. In this game, he scored two goals and set up another. His potential was there for all to see. Over the next few years, he brought it to fruition. Other relatively inexperienced youngsters shone in the Calgary game, too, including Chris Chelios, Scott Stevens and Ron Francis; all would have big futures.

The memory of my part in that All-Star Game will stay with me always. It was the greatest individual accolade I received in my career. It means all the more to me because I wasn't chosen as a joke inclusion or to make up some kind of European quota, as was the case a few years ago with the selections for North America versus the World. It was an acknowledgement of my ability as a hockey player. I didn't achieve all I wished to in the NHL, but that game in Calgary went some way toward making up for certain disappointments and bad seasons. I'm proud to have been there.

I doubt that any fans in Czechoslovakia were aware of my achievement. It was forbidden to write in anything but derogatory terms about athletes who had defected. Successes were met with silence; difficulties were exaggerated. Only after Czechoslovakia separated into two countries, in 1993, did my appearance in the All-Star Game attract any attention. As the first Czech to play in it, suddenly I was taking calls from journalists who wanted to write about my memories of the game. That I was a trailblazer hadn't even crossed my mind. After all, my friends the Stastny brothers appeared in the game a few years before I did; that they were the first Slovaks and I the first Czech meant nothing to us at the time.

I won't pretend that I'm not pleased to be first on the list of Czech players, but I don't regard it as a big deal. It's not nearly as important as my memories of those three wonderful days in Calgary. To remind me of them, I still have the Stetson, the stick and the puck I scored my goal with, plus the number 14 jersey in which I represented the Campbell Conference.

———

On my return from the All-Star Game, I was psyched up and keen to prove that my part in the exhibition was no fluke. I was soon racking up the points. Before I knew it, I had 25 goals and 30 assists, the same numbers as in my best season so far. This is great, I told myself. Thirteen games left in the regular season and I'd reached my career high already. This was turning into a pretty decent year.

We were about to play the Calgary Flames when Peter Ihnacak suggested we do some loosening up. I'd never had much time for such things, so I told him I didn't want to.

But he was insistent. "Come on, Frigo! We'll do some stretching and loosening, and we'll chew the fat."

I was tempted. But when Iha started with jumps in the gym, I told him to forget it. "Just try it!" he urged me. "It's really good for the legs—you'll see."

I did try it. And I paid for it. As I landed one of the jumps, I felt something go in my foot. Then a dreadful pain. I knew right away that I'd messed something up. The foot was so swollen I could hardly get it into my skate. I went out for the warm-up and did a few turns; then I had to go back to the dressing room. It was impossible.

Another stupid injury, and this time a completely preventable one. The doctors diagnosed a broken bone at the side of my little toe, and my season was over. A month after the All-Star Game, I was watching my hockey from the stands. It was infuriating.

But I did have one more pleasant experience in early 1985. And at the time, this was more important to me than scoring goals against the Blues or the North Stars. I became a Canadian. Although I had the right to citizenship three years after my immigration, the process by which it was granted to me dragged on a little. Officials took into account the fact that I'd spent every summer in West Germany and many days traveling in the USA with my team, meaning I failed to meet the three-year requirement.

But in the end, a solution was found. Maybe Harold Ballard appealed on my behalf in the right places, or maybe what helped was the coverage the newspapers gave to my case. Anyway, I was invited to take the examinations that had to be passed before citizenship could be granted.

I had no difficulty learning the words of the national anthem—I'd been hearing them before every game for three and a half years. I was more worried about the test on Canadian history and geography. I took my study materials everywhere we went, so that I could bone up on the constitution, names of the provinces and their capitals, and provincial symbols. I passed this test, too. At the initiation ceremony, I took an oath before a judge and so became a Canadian citizen and a subject of Her Majesty Queen Elizabeth II.

Nothing much changed in my day-to-day life. In Canada, it's more important to have a social insurance number than citizenship. Nothing happened but that I handed in the brown asylum-seeker's passport allowing me to travel abroad in return for a standard blue one. For me, being granted Canadian citizenship was above all an important symbolic moment. I had become a citizen of a country in which I was welcome, one that wished me a life of freedom. One where I had no fear of being reported to the authorities for what was said over a beer, and where I didn't have to stand in a long line at the butcher's when I fancied a steak. This meant a great deal to me.

Once I had my Canadian passport, I decided to buy myself out of my Czechoslovakian citizenship. Although I had nothing against the country of my birth, I wanted nothing to do with the communist regime. I didn't wish to remain a citizen of the Czechoslovak Socialist Republic, which had sentenced me to three and a half years for leaving to play in the NHL and had refused to let me back in to attend my grandfather's funeral.

I had to take my application to the consulate in Montreal, which put me in quite a sweat. By right, the consulate was part of the CSSR. We'd all heard stories … In case it took me a long time to return, I let the management of the Maple Leafs know exactly where I was going. But it all went off without a hitch. The consul was a nice guy and a hockey fan; the main thing he wanted to know was if I could get him a couple of tickets for an evening game against the Canadiens. He helped me put together a short CV. Then I paid something like $2,500—for myself and the schools I'd graduated from, and for my wife and two daughters, although the younger had been born in Toronto. A few weeks later, I was notified by mail that I was a Canadian citizen and nothing more. And that was that.

Who could have guessed that within a few years everything would change? The regime would fall, and I'd be able to go home whenever I wanted to. My citizenship created some absurd situations, though. To cross over into Czechoslovakia at Rozvadov, I needed a visa, whereas my second wife, a German, only needed to wave her passport at the customs officials. There were times I had to go all the way to Munich for entry papers. Later, I arranged a permanent residency card for myself, also an exhausting bureaucratic process. As a Canadian, I had to fill out all kinds of forms and collect all manner of stamps; I even had to sign a declaration that if need be, I would take care of my grandmother (or she of me, as the case may be). We joked that coming home was almost as complicated as it had been to emigrate.

I stopped being a foreigner in my own land in 2003. Following my father's death, I wanted to spend more time with my mother. Also, I'd set myself up as a players' agent, and I needed Czech citizenship to establish a company. I was granted it within 24 hours. It was delivered with confirmation of my state pardon.

14

Play Hard, Party Hard

THERE IS MUCH to admire about the NHL of the 1980s—the amazing scoring achievements of Wayne Gretzky, Peter Stastny, Mike Bossy and other stars; the dominance of the New York Islanders and Edmonton Oilers dynasties; the statistics of defensemen who broke the 80-point barrier with ease season after season. It may never happen again that a team wins four championships in a row. It is very unlikely that the records for offensive play will be rewritten any time soon.

I take my hat off to the high achievers. Not least in the light of my own injury problems, I find it incredible that Dougie Jarvis could play 964 NHL games in a row. That's right, he didn't miss a single game in 12 seasons! And he played for three different clubs. His streak finally ended in 1987, when the Hartford Whalers sent him down to their farm team. Steve Larmer managed 884 consecutive games.

Enviable records both. Especially as they were set at a time when all games had their bloody battles and officials waved play on that today would see disciplinary action taken against the perpetrators. Slashing, cross-checking, checking from behind and hooking were part and parcel of the game. If I got blindsided and went down, the fault was mine for not seeing the opponent who ambushed me. "Keep your head up!" we were told.

I didn't live through the Broad Street Bullies era, but even in our day, games against the Philadelphia Flyers weren't ones opponents looked forward to. In my early years in the NHL, Bobby Clarke and Paul Holmgren were still around, and even after they left, the team was filled with big, strapping guys who inspired fear. Whenever a visit to the Spectrum was due, players would come down with "Philadelphia flu"—out of the blue, they would feel ill and be riddled with aches and pains. They weren't at all keen to play.

But I have one fine memory of an away game against the Flyers.

I performed a couple of dekes in the offensive zone and moments later, before I knew what was happening, my part in the game was over. Glen Cochrane, one of the players I'd deked, caught up with me in the corner, took me by the elbow, and spun me in the air like a propeller. I came down on my head. Knockout.

I lay on the ice motionless, with no idea what was going on.

The doctors took me straight to the dressing room.

"Do you know where you are, Mirko?" they asked.

"Philly," I mumbled.

"Do you know which period the game is in?"

"No."

"And the score?"

"Don't know."

After that, all I remember is the wailing of the ambulance siren. The hospital doctors gave me an injection and kept me in overnight for observation. I rejoined my teammates at the hotel the next morning. I still wasn't feeling great—my head was spinning, and my stomach was in no state for breakfast. It was like the morning after a drinking spree. I didn't need an expert to tell me I was suffering from a concussion. But my main concern was to be ready for the next game. These days, this condition would put me straight on the injured reserve list, meaning no hockey for me for a while. But I wanted to get back out there. At any cost. I was on a roll, and I didn't want to miss a single game.

By the way, Cochrane escaped with a minor penalty.

I played that game in Philadelphia in a Swedish Jofa VM 235, the helmet to which I remained true throughout my career. It was worn mostly by Europeans, although it was Wayne Gretzky who made it famous. The VM 235 looked like a plastic shell, which explains why in Canada a notice on its inside stated it wasn't approved for hockey games and was worn by players at their own risk. It suited me very well. I tried the more robust, cushioned CCM, but I found it too heavy and restrictive. I couldn't get used to it.

I never had a serious head injury in my Jofa. But Michel Goulet wore the same helmet and wasn't so lucky: a head injury ended his career. Even Cochrane's assault wasn't enough to put me in real trouble. I don't like to think how I'd have ended up but for that shell on my head.

I couldn't help but admire guys like Dougie Wilson and Al Secord, who wore no helmet at all. Like everyone who had played without a helmet before 1979, when mandatory protection was introduced, they were excused from wearing one. At the same time, the sight of them made me shake my head. They were like stuntmen. Although from today's perspective the hockey of that time may look like a slow-motion movie, in front of the net and by the boards, where these guys had no fear to tread, the blows fell thick and fast, and of course the puck moved at tremendous speed.

Quite recently, I checked out my duel with Cochrane on YouTube. Not a pretty sight. But it was a trifle compared to what happened to Borje Salming in a game against the Detroit Red Wings.

It was sheer bad luck. A pass was made toward our goal and Borje knelt to stop it, just as Chris Kotsopoulos dealt a blow to their forward Gerard Gallant, sending him tumbling to the ice. Gallant's skate sliced into Borje's face, inflicting a wound that ran from his forehead to his mouth, just missing his right eye. As Borje's blood spurted, the blood of the rest of us froze in our veins. It was dreadful. For a moment, it looked as though Borje had been decapitated. The trainers leaped out onto the ice and set about stanching the bleeding. Before long, the ice was awash with blood-covered towels.

At the hospital, Borje received about 250 stitches for the wound. When he re-appeared at practice a few days later, with his stitches and the swelling, he looked like a zombie. But he missed just three games.

Borje was one hell of a tough guy. In the '70s, the opposition, the Flyers in particular, really went after him, dishing out blows for all the

Europeans who had arrived in the league after him. It was said that Borje's fellow Swede Inge Hammarstrom could go into a corner with six eggs in his pockets and return to the bench with the eggs still whole. Borje was the opposite—he had no fear of the rough and tumble. He'd take no shit from anyone. Bearing in mind his style of play, it's pretty unbelievable that he played 1,148 games in the NHL, plus 81 in the playoffs. For the 30 minutes he was on the ice each game, he would throw himself into shots like a second goaltender. He'd emerge riddled with bruises, and he had stitches all over his body.

So many battles were fought! The worst kind was the bench-clearing brawl, when everyone leaped off the bench and onto the ice, resulting in a free-for-all involving 40 guys. In this way, a game could go on for four hours; a single skirmish was hardly ever enough. Then it would take a while to clear the ice and distribute the penalties. People would arrive at the arena at seven and get home at midnight.

For those of us who took no pleasure in this kind of action, there was one clear way to go. Grab the first available man—ideally one equal to you in size and fighting skills—and try to keep him at bay. Once, I rashly got into a fight with Ray Bourque, who gave me a thrashing, while I barely tickled him.

The biggest brawl I experienced was in January 1986. We were playing against the Red Wings, our main rival. The tense rivalry between these two storied clubs had probably begun in earnest when a young Gordie Howe was dealt a blow to the head from the stick of Ted Kennedy that sent him headfirst into the boards, resulting in him fighting for his life in the hospital. The rivalry with Montreal was less intense—they played in a different division, and we never met in the playoffs. Today, Maple Leafs v. Canadiens games are again a prestigious Canadian showdown, but in our day, Montreal was an opponent like any other. Nothing special. We would face the Red Wings eight times in the regular season and sometimes in the playoffs, too.

Five minutes from the end of this memorable game, we were leading 6-4. It had been a typically intense match from the opening face-off, with the crowd getting to see three fights in the first two periods. The fourth and biggest fight started off as a family squabble. When Wendel Clark collided with his cousin Barry Melrose behind the goal, the rush of adrenaline was palpable.

First to lay into each other were Gary Nylund and Greg Smith. At that point, coach Brad Park gave the command for the players on the Detroit bench to join the fray. Miro Ihnacak was playing in the NHL for just the third time, so imagine his surprise when backup goalie Ed Mio gave him a smack! Meanwhile, enforcer Bob Probert butted defenseman Bob McGill, an offense for which he would receive a four-game ban.

One of the first to jump onto the ice was Lane Lambert, who headed straight for me. I didn't have a chance as his blows rained down on me. But after a while he seemed to tire of hitting me, because he let down his guard. That's when my well-aimed blow broke his nose. There was a great deal of blood.

When it was all over, the Leafs bench was obviously fretting over my appearance. With my white jersey covered in blood, I looked in a bad way. I calmed my teammates down immediately. "It's his blood! Today it's different! Today, I'm the winner!"

That was probably the only fight in the NHL that I actually won. This really wasn't my discipline.

Jim Korn, our tough guy, would sometimes take me in hand after practice, doing his best to teach me a few tricks that would get me through the fights. "It's best to grab his jersey at the right shoulder and twist," he explained. "That will restrict his swing so he can't aim his blows. And if he gets really close to you, grab his pants down low and yank at them. Then he'll struggle to stay on his skates."

I gave this advice a try when the next tense moment came my way—a run-in with Vancouver Canucks captain Stan Smyl. He may have been only five foot eight, but he knew how to fight and was always up for it. "Come on, then!" I shouted at him as I threw down my gloves. Just as Jim had told me, I grabbed his jersey at the right shoulder, twisted, and

… whack, bang, boom! Smyl caught me with a series of blows and the fight was over. He happened to be a left-hander.

Our mass brawl with the Red Wings was the last in Maple Leafs history. League administrators were less than impressed that hockey received its highest media coverage after this kind of slaughter. TV pictures of 40 men brawling on a rink covered with gloves, sticks and helmets did little for the sport's image. The next season, discipline in the NHL would be stricter. Hockey's wildest, most violent days were over. Since then, fighting has been a privilege afforded only to those on the ice. The first to jump off the bench to join in gets a fine and a 10-game ban, with no salary while he serves it. Anyone who vaults the boards after him gets a five-game ban. Nowadays, every player or coach thinks hard before losing his cool.

———

We were wild away from the ice, too. Our era's motto was "Play hard, party hard." For many years, outsiders had no idea about the life played out behind the magnificent curtain of the sacred NHL. In recent years, however, all kinds of things have come out—not least thanks to hockey players who have chosen to be frank in their memoirs.

In the 1980s, the NHL was one big drinking party. I'm not exaggerating. To get by in that league, you had to do business in bars and at parties as well as on the ice. Toronto was no island of vice—it was the same everywhere.

It was a lifestyle dictated by the dressing room and passed down by famed predecessors. It was impossible to go your own way. Anyone who tried to wouldn't have been accepted by the team. In fact, he'd have been finished.

We foreigners were under particular pressure to conform. Any failure to fit in would have been felt on the ice. The others would have made bad passes to us and bawled us out for every mistake. "Why the hell didn't you shoot?" or "Don't you know how to pass the puck?"

No guy who failed to adapt lasted long on the team. He'd play two games, then he'd be off to the AHL. The coach was no fool—if he saw that a player was rejected in the dressing room, he'd pull him.

We took every opportunity to work on team morale. One evening sticks in my mind. I'd come home tired from playing tennis, switched on the TV, and stretched out on the couch. Then the phone rang.

"It's Borje. What are you doing, Frigo?"

"You know, dozing in front of the TV, thinking of going to bed."

"It's no time for bed. Team meeting at my place."

"But Borje, I'm worn out …"

There was no way of refusing. Twenty minutes later, a taxi arrived with Borje in it. Quickly, I got changed. I didn't get home again till seven the next morning.

I don't want to make out that this kind of life went against the grain with me. Quite the opposite.

I did have my limits, though. They concerned the third element of that classic triad: alcohol, women and drugs. Being a smoker, I tried weed, but I held back whenever white powder appeared at the table; I would have a double whiskey instead. I wasn't that big a gambler. My self-preservation instinct has kept me in good stead. I've never allowed hard drugs or motorbikes into my life.

The most hazardous and popular parts of the season were the road trips. We really looked forward to getting out of Toronto for a few days and having a blast, to unwinding and shaking off some of the stress and tension that surrounded us.

We took charter flights up and down the east coast; when flying westward, we used commercial airlines. Long journeys are part and parcel of playing in the NHL, and we were used to them. But there were still hours of boredom to kill. As we waited for our next flight or bus, as we moved from one hotel to the next, we spiced things up as best we could.

Sometimes we were like children. Anyone watching us from a distance would have said all our jokes were straight out of elementary school. But I enjoyed all this.

Putting ketchup on someone's shoes was a classic practical joke. At a team lunch, someone would shout, "Shoe check!" and everyone would look under the table to make sure their own shoes hadn't been targeted. Any victim wearing suede shoes could throw them straight in the trash. And it was better not to fall asleep on the plane—if you did, you might wake up with the end of your tie snipped off and mustard around your lips.

At airports, we were grateful for any stupid thing that took our minds off waiting for our flight. The guys would requisition baggage carts and have "bobsleigh" races on them. In suits, of course, as it behooved professionals from the National Hockey League. Or we would place bets. On everything. A dollar on whose baggage would emerge first from the carousel. The exact time of arrival of the bus. When our gate would open.

Once, when we'd run out of other ideas, we bought a long string and attached one end of it to a five-dollar bill, which we dropped on the floor. Then when tourists reached down to pick it up, we'd jerk the string and watch in amusement as they tried to grab the bill. The looks on their faces were priceless! Great fun for overgrown kids.

On landing in Los Angeles, we knew that in addition to a game against the Kings, we had one big party to look forward to. This was our favorite destination. We would stay at a hotel near the airport, in rooms next to a pool surrounded by palm trees. A delightful change from Canada's endless winter. It was great—except for the mornings. We'd awake to the sight of discarded newspapers, pizza boxes and beer cans; champagne bottles floating in the pool; hockey sticks topped with helmets standing in the sand. Then we'd know we'd had a blast.

When I started out in the NHL, there was no such thing as a curfew. No one took any interest in what we did on our trips. Before we left, we'd be given an itinerary of our flight times and when our bus would leave for and return from the stadium, when practice and the game would take place, and when the team dinner would be. As long as we turned up on time, everything was okay. Later, the coaches did introduce a curfew, but it was only a formality. At 11:00, they would check the rooms and tick off the names, and that was the last of it. If we then chose to go downtown in search of entertainment, or have female company in our room, no notice was taken.

The coaches knew what was what, of course. If we turned up at practice glassy-eyed, guzzling pint after pint of water, they knew something had gone on during the night. But once our skates were on, we were expected to behave as professionals. If we didn't give our everything in practice, there would be trouble.

On the ice, we had to be ready, morning and evening. The rest of the day was our own affair. Provided we did nothing to shame ourselves and the team in public, everything was kept behind closed doors. When a neighboring hotel called to say that one of our players was sleeping on the couch in their reception area, our response would be a laugh and a shrug. What were our coaches expected to do about such things? They could hand down fines, but what good would it do? In any case, when we'd met them at four that morning in front of the bar, they had lit our cigarettes for us ...

Club owner Harold Ballard sympathized with our way of life more than anyone. "You youngsters will never know the half of what we got up to!" he would laugh.

Our away games were akin to a group of sailors returning to port. After the game, it was a quick shower, dinner, then off to our favorite bar. We never failed to have a great time. A few hours earlier, we'd been shoving our sticks in opponents' faces; now we were drinking toasts to each other. Our work was left behind at the rink; now it was time to have fun. Our sitting down together was proof of our mutual respect. We were the same, and we lived the same lives. The difference was, on a few evenings of the week we wore different jerseys.

When I think about the way of the world today, I realize how lucky we were in the golden '80s. As there were no smartphones, none of us ever got snapped in a bar, and none of us ever had our photos sent around the world. People respected our privacy. Canada's tabloid press isn't as vicious as it can be in Europe, and there was no pack of paparazzi at our backs. Besides, NHL games hadn't yet reached Florida, Nashville and San Jose, to say nothing of Las Vegas. If they had, we'd have been looking for some of our guys for two days at a time.

We always knew when to stop. As soon as the playoffs started, everyone reined himself in. There were no more parties. If we went out together after a game, we'd stop at one beer and turn in early. Now we had a clear goal; we could party in the off-season. Everyone felt the same. During the playoffs, I can't remember a single incident of someone turning up for practice high or hungover. If ever there was a need, an older player would take a rookie aside and whisper in his ear, "It's good that you're drinking for the team, but you're overdoing it a little." This mostly did the trick.

There have always been parties, and there always will be. There are drinkers and drug-takers in today's NHL, too. But it's less common today, and the partying is less intensive than it used to be. The great influx of cash into hockey has changed a lot of things, not least the lifestyle of its players. The behavior of anyone in his right mind who signs a contract worth $40 million, so setting himself and his children up for life, is bound to differ from the conduct of hockey players 30 years ago: there is too much at stake to risk his reputation or career.

We played at a wild time, which left its mark on our lives. We had no one to set us straight. We made our way by trial and error. In whatever we did. And not everyone put on the brakes in time. Behind the scenes of the much-admired and idealized NHL, stories were played out that didn't always end happily.

But that is a subject for a different book.

15

Three Goals for Gretzky, Four for Frycer

As soon as I fulfilled my dream of playing in the NHL, I knew it wasn't enough for me to be in Canada, under contract and playing regularly. I had greater ambitions. Above all, I wanted to prove to myself that I was capable of competing with the world's best. I wanted to make an indelible mark.

I was convinced that if I could stay fit, I would achieve this goal. I just needed a season free of stupid injuries and senseless illnesses.

After breaking my foot in March 1985, I was out for a long time, and I gained a little weight. On returning to training after the summer break, I was desperate to get started. This time, I'd done more to prepare myself than just join Dad's training sessions in Germany. The Stastny brothers and I had done some work—very hard work—together in Quebec, all four of us making sure we pushed ourselves to the max in every exercise, with no need for a fitness coach.

Marian and I were able to practice some moves for the new season. After four years with the Quebec Nordiques, their general manager had bought out his contract and allowed him to leave—on condition that he wouldn't move to the Montreal Canadiens. In August, Marian had opted to join the Toronto Maple Leafs.

It was great for me to have a guy like Marian on the team. Sometimes we played on the same line, with me on the left wing and Peter Ihnacak or Tom Fergus at center. Plus, we were roommates on road trips. Unfortunately, Marian didn't find what he was looking for with us. He had a decent season, scoring 20 goals and accumulating 53 points, but once it ended, he left for Switzerland. At 33, he struggled to accept that he no longer had a leading role on the team, and I'm not sure he ever really got over the involuntary end of his time with the Nordiques. And he must have been bothered by our results. In Quebec, he'd been part of one of the NHL's best lines, appearing eight times a season in the spectacular rivalry against the Canadiens and in the playoffs every spring. We were forever at the wrong end of the standings.

The 1985-86 season, too, got off to a less than promising start. We won only two of the first 16 games. We were where we'd been a year earlier. In the end, though, we lifted ourselves out of the basement.

For me, the most important thing was to stay fit. After my minefield of injuries, I was blessed with better fortune, and I missed only seven games. With each game I played, I gained greater confidence. I stopped being afraid of what might happen.

When we played against the Chicago Black Hawks, I delivered a nice body check on Jack O'Callahan, and this time he was the one hurting, not me. The press wrote that my hit was one Wendel Clark would have been proud of. And in a game against the Washington Capitals, I managed to best Scott Stevens. But don't get me wrong—we were both going for the puck, and he wasn't expecting me to rush him.

These were tiny steps—small personal victories—but they added to my self-confidence.

The great performance I'd been waiting for finally arrived on January 8, 1986. At home against the Edmonton Oilers, I played the game of my life—improbable as it may sound, because they were the Stanley Cup champions, and we were one of the worst teams in the NHL.

My great day had a strange beginning. At the end of the morning skate, I stayed out on the ice with goaltender Don Edwards, my task to get him warmed up. The drill was a simple one: two players in the face-off circle taking turns shooting on net. Shot from the right, shot from the left, shot from the right, shot from the left …

On one of my turns, I tried a wrist shot, catching the puck just right but unfortunately hitting Don on the head. Worse still, the shot made a dent in his cage, dealing him a blow between the eyes. His bloody wound required 21 stitches. As there was no way Don could play in the game, the general manager was forced to send to the farm team for a backup.

In the dressing room, the guys joked that my great shooting form boded well for the evening.

As we normally did after the morning skate, we had lunch as a team at the Hot Stove Lounge, where the meal was almost always steak. No one complained—we needed to build up our strength for the evening. There was a year-long experiment with pasta, maybe inspired by Martina Navratilova's famous diet, but the chefs soon went back to meat. I had no objection. Still, I would contend that food is a matter for individuals, and that serving the same meal to everyone doesn't make much sense—everyone's bodies are different. When I played for the Czechoslovakian national team, right before a game Vladimír Martinec would eat two bread rolls with a large helping of a thick mayonnaise-based salad, washing them down with a small glass of beer. After such a meal, I wouldn't have been able to put one foot in front of the other. In Canada, I found out that cheeseburgers were the thing for me—my ideal pregame meal was two of them, plus soup and a salad.

In the afternoon, I would take a nap, smoke a cigarette, and snack on a sandwich before setting out for the rink. I didn't drink coffee before a game. In the dressing room, I'd grab a cola and a chocolate bar, for energy.

My sticks would have been ready since the morning. Like every player, I had to get the length and weight just right. We really do notice if our stick is a couple of sugar lumps heavier or lighter. Mine needed to feel right in my hand, and I was prepared to trim it little by little till I got it that way. Today, I realize that the importance I placed on this was all in the mind. By making these cosmetic adjustments, I was convincing myself that my instrument was perfect.

Choosing the right stick is a matter of trial and error. I'd take a factory-fresh bundle of sticks and discard one or two straightaway because the weight just wasn't right. Sometimes I'd use a stick for one shift before I figured out it wasn't for me. If it was too soft, it would bend like a bow when I took a shot; if it was too hard and heavy in the blade, my touch when making a pass would be too heavy. When playing in the NHL, I tried a few different brands. First Canadien, then Cooper, then Titan, which suited me best. In that game against the Edmonton Oilers, I was toting a Titan.

Having performed a quick check of my sticks, I would change into my uniform.

I had the least trouble with my vest. I always wore the same one—an old, lightweight Cooper acquired in Quebec that lasted me all my years in the NHL. The equipment managers sometimes suggested that we try new things. It was their belief that we would feel better with bulkier pads, but all that padding made me feel as clumsy as an astronaut; I used scissors to modify them this way and that, but in the end, I went back to my shabby old Cooper gear. I liked my gloves to be long and loose, not with fingers so tight that I lost feeling in them. I didn't like close-fitting elbow and shoulder pads either.

I've always put on my skates in the same way. First the left, a tap of the heel on the ground, then the right. This is the only ritual I've stuck to properly. I used to go out onto the ice third or fourth, depending on the current hierarchy in the team. That was how I liked it. When the first Maple Leafs player emerged, the fans would take notice, get to their feet and start to clap. When I reached the ice a few seconds later, the arena would be buzzing. This always gave me a kick. I would feel my adrenaline level rising.

Our games against the Detroit Red Wings and the Chicago Black Hawks had the most electrifying atmosphere. But the guys in the dressing room also made a big deal of the games played at 7:30 p.m. on Saturdays, which were broadcast to all provinces on *Hockey Night in Canada*. This program was particularly important for players who hadn't grown up in Ontario, like Wendel Clark, Jim Benning and Russ Courtnall, as it was a rare opportunity for friends, family and coaches from their childhood to see them on TV. We used to rib them about it. "New bootlaces today, eh? Must be a coast-to-coast broadcast."

We played that game against the Oilers on a Wednesday, but even so it attracted 16,282 spectators, selling out well in advance. Who wouldn't have wanted to see Wayne Gretzky, the world's best player? What's more, he had grown up in nearby Brantford and played two seasons for the Toronto Nationals junior team.

Neither team went into the game with a full roster. We were without Borje Salming, Peter Ihnacak and Ricky Vaive; they were missing Mark Messier and Esa Tikkanen. But this made little difference to the relative strengths of the teams. The Oilers—current champions and stacked with future members of the Hockey Hall of Fame—were the clear favorite.

But after the first period, we were leading 5-1! I'd put us up 3-0 on a rebound, and Russ Courtnall had potted two. After our fifth goal on 11 shots, Andy Moog was replaced in goal by Grant Fuhr. By this point, the crowd had realized this was no ordinary game.

But the Oilers refused to surrender, scoring five goals themselves in the second period. Wayne Gretzky and Jari Kurri led our goaltender Tim Bernhardt in such a merry dance, I felt sorry for him; all he could do was retrieve the puck from his net.

The score stood at 6-6. This was more like basketball than hockey. One attack followed another, and the pucks went in left and right. Some of these goals were amazing. On a breakaway, Wayne Gretzky tried a fake that didn't come off, and the puck slid to the end boards, where Paul Coffey pounced on it and flip-passed it back toward the net. As Tim Bernhardt tried to grab the puck with his catcher, he collided with the returning Tom Fergus, who knocked the puck over the goal line …

We went into the final period up 7-6. But we didn't keep this lead for long. First, Wayne Gretzky struck as only he could, outmaneuvering the defense before sending a blind pass in front of the open goal, where it was converted by Jari Kurri. 7-7. Eighty seconds later, Glenn Anderson scored Edmonton's eighth from the left circle.

This put us behind for the first time in the game. But it wasn't over yet. Far from it. It was time for me to have my say. In the 43rd minute, I took a pass at full stride and converted it in the same manner as Glenn Anderson a few moments earlier. I'd checked out Grant Fuhr's position, controlled the puck, then smashed it inside the right-hand post. Tie game.

Less than three minutes later, I retrieved the puck from Edmonton's net with a broad smile on my face. A memento of my seventh hat trick and 100th goal in the NHL. During a power play, Grant Fuhr had blocked Marian Stastny's shot with his pad and the puck had fallen to me. Defenseman Kevin Lowe's efforts on the goal line were in vain as I scored on the five-hole. Our ninth of the game.

Again, Gretzky instigated an equalizer. In front of the net, he bamboozled both defenders and played the puck to the right-hand post, where the unmarked Anderson stuck out his blade. 9-9. Sometimes hockey is a really simple game.

The drama was reaching its climax. In the 55th minute, Marian tried to send me away on a break, but the pass backfired, and Gretzky and co. mounted another attack. Marian made up for his mistake by intercepting an opponent's pass at the blue line and keeping possession of the puck till I picked up speed. Then he found me at the red line with a brilliant cross-ice pass, leaving me with only Fuhr to beat. Oilers defensemen Kevin Lowe and Lee Fogolin tried and failed to hook me. Quick as a flash, I glanced at the goalie, decided to shoot, not fake, and slotted the puck between his pads.

10-9!

I was in seventh heaven. Another of my hockey dreams come true! Once, we'd beaten the Chicago Black Hawks 10-8, and I'd scored twice past Tony Esposito, but this was something else entirely. Four goals! I'd last managed four goals in one game in the Czechoslovak league against Dukla Trencin, and now I'd done it against maybe the best team in the world. It was so difficult for me to take in, I couldn't stop shaking my head.

We finished the scoring in the 59th minute. The play again began with Marian Stastny. In our zone, he poke-checked Paul Coffey and sent the puck along the side boards on the right to Dan Hodgson. Suddenly, Dan and I were in two-on-one. As I drew the defenseman away, Hodgson deked poor Grant Fuhr from left to right, then slipped the puck into the open net.

The fans were on their feet. Maple Leaf Gardens was in raptures. As the buzzer that would end this crazy game approached, people counted down the seconds as if it were Game 7 in the playoffs. "Ten, nine, eight, seven …" For Leafs fans, this was like winning the Stanley Cup. In recent years, we hadn't given them much to cheer about; they had more often seen us lose than win. This made the celebrations wilder still. I doubt anyone who was there that night will ever forget our 11-9 victory. Even today, so many years later, people come up to me in Toronto and thank me for my part in that unforgettable evening.

Basically, they saw three games rolled into one, with all ending happily for the Maple Leafs. The goals fell as follows: 5-1 (first period), 2-5 (second), 4-3 (third).

After the final buzzer, we huddled around Tim Bernhardt and tapped his helmet, the traditional way of thanking the goaltender. The poor guy hadn't had things easy. Thanks to my having taken out Don Edwards that morning, he'd had to stay on the ice till the bitter end: the coaches hadn't dared play a kid from the farm team who had joined us just a few hours before the game. The record Timmy set that day is unlikely ever to be taken from him. He let in nine goals yet still came out on the winning side.

"How can you explain a crazy day like this? Could it be because of Halley's Comet?" asked Oilers coach Glen Sather. The celebrated comet had indeed appeared near Earth for the first time in 76 years. It won't appear again until 2061, but I doubt the NHL will have seen another 20-goal game in the meantime.

The icing on the cake came after the game, when journalists named me the first star. I waved to our great fans one more time, thanking them for their support. The second star was Jari Kurri, who had collected one goal and five assists. The third star was Russ Courtnall. Wayne Gretzky's three goals and three assists weren't enough for him to make the cut. In the whole of his fantastic career, this may be the first and last time this happened to him.

I got back to the dressing room to find journalists waiting for me there. When the interviews were over, a photographer asked me to pose with four pucks bearing a Maple Leafs logo. I grabbed the pucks and smiled at the camera. The next day, this picture appeared on the front page of the *Toronto Sun*.

So ended the greatest game I ever played in the NHL.

———

I remember one more remarkable match in which I scored the winning goal. It happened in October 1984, and it was Dan Maloney's very first game on the Toronto bench. We beat Minnesota 1-0 in overtime. In the 1980s, such a result was very rare in the NHL. It was the Maple Leafs' first shutout in three years!

Most games were end-to-end stuff; no one had much time for elaborate defense. The game following our gunfight with Edmonton was a 9-7 defeat to the Buffalo Sabres, a month earlier we had beaten the New Jersey Devils 10-7, in February the Oilers would get their revenge over us with a 9-5 win, and we sustained another defeat when we lost 8-7 to the Minnesota North Stars in overtime.

We were urged to strive to score more goals than our opponents, not concede fewer. Practice was mainly about attack and the power play, with little attention given to shorthanded play. As for defense, according to the wisdom of the time, there was nothing to discuss: the center came back, the wingers kept an eye on the blue line, otherwise we had absolute freedom.

It wasn't much fun for the goaltender. Sometimes he would be all on his own as the opposition brought down an avalanche on him. A goalie who kept his goals-against average under 3.5 per game and his save percentage over .900 could consider himself to have had a great season. Indeed, with narrow pads, a minimum of equipment, and no special training for goaltenders, such a feat verged on the miraculous.

How blatant the differences between goaltending then and now! Today's ideal goaltender is Carey Price—at six foot three, he's such an imposing figure that his goal is almost impossible to breach. In our day, goalies were smaller and valued for their agility and dexterity. Grant Fuhr, Andy Moog, Reggie Lemelin, Bob Froese, John Vanbiesbrouck, Billy Smith, Kelly Hrudey ... None of them more than five feet, 11 inches tall.

The NHL expansion, too, was good for the goal-fest. Between 1967 and 1979, the league grew from six teams to 21, which naturally had a diluting effect on the quality of play. Players who had previously been glad of a place on a farm team now had an important role to play in the league. Better players were nowhere to be found. After the Miracle on Ice gold at the Lake Placid Olympics, American hockey made careful progress; reinforcements from Europe were limited by the political situation in Czechoslovakia and the Soviet Union.

The NHL was dominated by the offensive-minded Edmonton Oilers, a team of quick young skaters who regularly scored over 400 goals a season—a remarkable five per game. Even players whose names are today mostly forgotten scored 40. Netting 100 points was no guarantee of putting you among the season's leading scorers.

I enjoyed these great times to the max. Stubborn defense was definitely not in my blood.

But as a team we struggled to compete. We took unnecessary risks, and our play was inconsistent. In early January 1986, besides the Edmonton Oilers, we beat the Montreal Canadiens (that season's Stanley Cup champions), but then we lost to the Detroit Red Wings and the Los Angeles Kings, the two worst teams in the NHL.

We psyched ourselves up for games against strong opposition, then reveled in our victories over them for the rest of the month. In the dressing room, we were forever going on about how amazing it was to put 11 goals past Wayne Gretzky and co. Meanwhile, we dropped point after important point against weaker teams.

Of course, we always went out wanting to win. But we didn't have things properly figured out. This was apparent in the approach of certain players who, having recorded an early goal and an assist, seemed to take it easy for the rest of the game.

Maybe we took more pleasure from our hockey and our lives in general than was good for us. And maybe it was the wrong kind of pleasure.

Still, in the 1985-86 season we did make it to the playoffs. By 17 points, a comfortable margin. The miserable performance of the Detroit Red Wings was largely to thank for this; they managed a measly 40 points, a low point in their history. So we finished fourth in the Norris Division and went through—with 57 points and no fanfare. Buffalo Sabres fans must have been particularly galled by this; the 80 points their team had accumulated in the super-competitive Adams Division weren't enough for a playoff berth.

We played our last game of the regular season in Detroit, and it's another that will remain long in my memory. Although we lost 4-2, of more interest to me than the result was my personal battle with Tom Fergus for the Leafs' scoring leader. I had 74 points, he one point fewer. Our place in the playoffs was already guaranteed, and St. Louis was out of sight in third place, so we were free to express ourselves.

But for me, the game didn't go as expected. I spent most of my time on the bench. The coach sent me out three times per period, whereas Fergie was on for every power play. What the hell was going on? Finally, it dawned on me. Someone with the club didn't like the idea of a European winning the team's scoring title for the first time in Maple Leafs history. This was politics.

Maloney treated me like a kid on the fourth line for the whole of that game. But it didn't do him any good. In one of the few moments I got on, I scored a goal. Fergie failed to find the net—as he had in the previous nine games. First place was mine. In the 73 games I'd played in the regular season, I'd managed 75 points (32 goals and 43 assists).

Till then, only one European on an Original Six team had led his team in scoring—Vaclav Nedomansky of the Detroit Red Wings. This time out, I and Mats Naslund of the Montreal Canadiens had achieved this feat.

What pleased me most about this was my sense that I'd broken my NHL curse at last. Now I would really show what I could do! I joked with journalists that hockey was starting to be "fun," not "fuck," for me.

And I wanted to carry this great feeling into the playoffs.

———

We were due to face Chicago in the first round, and we were very much the underdog. The Black Hawks had made the playoffs every year since 1969, they had a great team, and in the regular season they had accumulated 29 points more than we had.

But I believed we could beat them. They were my favorite opponent. I don't know why, but I always played well against them. Particularly at the Chicago Stadium, a lovely old arena where steps led to the ice and goals were announced by the sounding of a ship's horn. Plus, the fans were crazy in the right kind of way. They would sing the anthem in chorus and yell and boo at the opposition, creating an atmosphere that really got me going.

We and the Black Hawks always took it to each other. I had lots of battles with Dougie Wilson in front of the net, and their checking line of Steve Ludzik and Tim Higgins certainly gave as good as it got. I minded none of this—it all drove my motivation.

When things weren't going my way—I hadn't scored a goal in 10 games, say—I'd grab a calendar and check when our next game against the Black Hawks was. Why despair when I knew a game against them would set me straight? On the other hand, nothing ever went right for me against the Vancouver Canucks. I don't know why, but they just didn't suit me. I may as well have stayed in Toronto. I suppose I went out there convinced that the best I could hope for was a check mark in the games played column.

Of the nine hat tricks I scored in the NHL, three were against the Black Hawks. And two of those were in the 1985-86 season. Their goaltender, Bob Sauvé, must have hated the sight of me. In our eight meetings in the regular season, we beat Chicago six times. We didn't do so well against anyone else.

We had nothing to lose.

Maybe they underestimated us, or maybe we really were their Achilles' heel. Anyway, we won the first two games in Chicago 5-3 and 6-4. An upset was in the making. We went from being everyone's laughing stock to one game from eliminating Chicago from the playoffs (the first round was a best-of-five). We'd gotten under their skin. At the end of Game 2, we saw Steve Larmer and Denis Savard having a real go at each other on the Black Hawks bench. Savard must have been particularly mad—he'd had a brilliant game and scored four goals, yet he'd ended up on the losing side. Their spat was a further sign of hope for us. Their nerves were fraying because they didn't know how to handle us.

For Game 3, at Maple Leaf Gardens, the atmosphere was electric. It gave me goosebumps. The crowd, scenting victory in a playoff series for the first time in seven years, drove us on. Since 1979, the Maple Leafs had either failed to reach the playoffs altogether or gone out in the first round.

We didn't give the Black Hawks much chance this time either. I scored in the 32nd minute to put us 4-0 up. They tried playing rough but still couldn't solve us. The high point of the game came in the third period, when Walt Poddubny and I broke through with just their goalie to beat before making it 6-2. There was no way back for them after that. Then Russ Courtnall added a seventh.

Toronto was seized by hockey fever. In my four years in the NHL, I'd never known anything like it. The fans truly believed we could do it this year, and the press, at other times so critical, shared this belief. What's more, in the Norris Division final we'd be up against the St. Louis Blues, an opponent we surely had a chance against; in the regular season, we canceled each other out 3-2-3.

During the series with the Black Hawks, the atmosphere in the dressing room changed, too. In previous seasons, our thoughts had turned weeks in advance to where we'd be going on vacation; no one mentioned such things now. Having been in the basement and told that we were "the worst team ever" for years, we were united in the desire to do something great and put an end to jokes like: "What do the Maple Leafs and the Blue Jays have in common? Neither can play hockey."

We made a promising start against the St. Louis Blues. We were up 2-1 in the series and Game 4 was at the Gardens. If we won, surely a 3-1 lead wouldn't be overturned. But we messed up, losing 7-4. The series was tied. In our next game against St. Louis, we led 3-0 before going down in overtime.

Our second-round performance was blighted by problems with my line. This was a perennial Maple Leafs problem—one line would play really well, then the next two would bomb. Maloney laid into us in the press, but I didn't mind that—he was right, we were playing really badly. He even healthy-scratched Walt Poddubny for one game. In practice, Peter Ihnacak and I slogged away and urged each other on for all we were worth, but we just couldn't get things to click. The coach had words with us, although there was no need—we knew what was at stake and what was expected of us. I got really mad and frustrated with myself. So much of the team's performance was riding on me, and I was coming up short.

We had to wait for Game 6 for our next win. Staring elimination in the face—what's more, at home—we managed to beat St. Louis 5-3. Walt scored the winning goal off my pass. Something had gone right at last.

For Game 7, we flew back to the USA. Winner takes all. There's nothing better in hockey. It was either on to the conference final or off to a four-month vacation.

Rarely are such duels exhibitions of splendor, and nor was this. Both teams created plenty of chances, but the goalies stood firm. Both teams struggled, too—we more than the Blues, who went into the final period leading 2-1.

Not long ago, I met Bernie Federko, one of their forwards, and we looked back on this battle. He had a vivid recollection of me from near the end of the game. There I was in the penalty box, so devastated by events that when a cameraman came in for a close-up of me, I put my helmet over his camera rather than telling him where he could stick it. I was upset for good reason: I'd spent a lot of time on the ice, and I'd had two decent chances that I'd failed to put away.

We couldn't find an equalizer. Our time in the sun was over.

I remember the dejection in the dressing room after the game. The silence was occasionally broken by the hiss of another can of beer being opened. Everyone wallowed in his own despair and disappointment. No one felt like saying anything. You get thrashed 7-2 and you take it on the chin, go for dinner, hop on a plane to start your vacation. You put it behind you. But a 2-1 defeat in Game 7—that hurts. Our playoff performance had exceeded all expectations, and we'd been within striking distance of the conference final, where we would have faced the Calgary Flames. I was sick with rage.

Maybe we sensed even then that our generation would never make it so far again.

16

Leafs Nation

SPRING 1986 MARKED the end of my contract with the Maple Leafs, signed during the Spengler Cup while I was still with Quebec Nordiques. The meeting to arrange a new one lasted barely 10 minutes. I told general manager Gerry McNamara that I'd like $50,000 more. I could afford to demand a raise because I'd just had my best season ever.

"Okay, I've no problem with that," said McNamara.

"For four years?"

"For four years."

But the bargaining wasn't over. "And if I'm among the club's top three scorers, I'd like a bonus," I tossed in.

"Sorry, Mirko, but that I can't give you," McNamara replied.

Never mind. To end on, I played my joker. "I'd like the club to pay for airline tickets to Europe and back for my whole family once a year."

The GM ended the meeting with these words: "Hey, on your money you can afford to buy them yourself."

So that was that. We shook hands, a secretary typed up the conditions for the new contract and I remained a member of the Maple Leafs organization.

I was glad. I liked it in Toronto, and there was no reason for me to leave. McNamara would be satisfied, too: not only had he retained one of his key forwards, negotiations hadn't dragged on for weeks and months, as in other cases. He could cross my name off his list and devote himself to other work.

I never had an agent to take care of my contracts and money matters. Alan Eagleson and Don Meehan, who represented half the Maple

Leafs dressing room, offered their services to me, but I thought I could manage well enough without them. So what if they could get me an extra $20,000? Such things really weren't important to me. I was happy with what I got, and when I discovered what the others were making, I knew myself to be well paid. I had no cause for complaint. I wasn't such a star that I had piles of promotional offers to work through. Occasionally I'd get a few thousand for playing in different gloves, or some company would buy me a barbecue for our backyard. But that was all the business my career in hockey brought me.

The next day, we went to club owner Harold Ballard to get my contract approved.

"I'm glad you're staying," he said with a smile. Then he wished me lots of luck.

He was a special guy; in fact, he was one of the most remarkable personalities I've ever met. At that time, he was 83 years old and suffering from diabetes, but he ruled the team he'd owned since 1971 with as firm a hand as ever. When he lit a cigar, he looked just like a caricature of a capitalist in the Czechoslovakian popular press. But for me, his most important characteristic was his big heart. He was forever donating to charity, and he never hesitated to come to the assistance of his staff, no matter how lowly their position.

He and I got on extremely well. He was fonder still of Borje Salming, but Borje was Borje—great guy, brilliant player, loyal soldier. What Harold liked about me, apart from my hockey, was my cheerful disposition: I never worried too much about things, and I knew how to enjoy myself. But more than anything, he appreciated the courage I'd shown in defecting. "What I admire about you, Mirko," he would say, "is that you had the balls to get out of Czechoslovakia.

On display in Harold's office was a photo of him with Ronald Reagan. He hated communists, Russian ones most of all; we had this in common. I remember his anger in 1983 when a Soviet fighter plane shot down a South Korean civilian aircraft, killing all 246 passengers. It was as though he took it personally. Because the Moscow Circus had reserved the arena, we were due to practice for a few days in North York on the edge of the city. But Harold canceled the performance, forcing the Russians to gather up their tigers, elephants and monkeys and leave.

At that time, he swore that no Russian would ever again set foot in Maple Leaf Gardens in his lifetime. And he kept his word. In 1984 and 1987, he refused to make our stadium available for Canada Cup games, and we were one of only a few NHL clubs not to play exhibition matches against CSKA Moscow, Krylya Sovetov and other Russian teams, from which the profits were shared equally. "I won't give them a dollar," he declared.

Only shortly before his death did he relax the ban, when the league threatened to fine the Maple Leafs if they failed to play against Dynamo Moscow. The game took place on December 31, 1989, a few weeks after the fall of the Berlin Wall. Six months later, another Ballard taboo was dispensed with—the Maple Leafs drafted Soviet players for the first time. But by then, Ballard was following the proceedings from Heaven.

There was one drawback to the old man's affection for Borje and me: he reserved the right to block our trades, should the situation ever arise. "Salming and Frycer aren't for sale," he told the general manager. I would come to regret his stance, as the Pittsburgh Penguins twice got in touch to say they wanted to put me next to young Mario Lemieux on their right wing. The answer was always the same. *No way.* Pity—it could have been an interesting experience that moved my career in a completely different direction. Who knows, maybe I'd even have won the Stanley Cup. But the boss had the final say, so that was that.

Ballard actually lived in Maple Leaf Gardens—he'd had a large apartment built under the roof. He had an office at the far end of the stadium, although he didn't spend much time in it. But he liked to come to the dressing room in the morning. One of the first to arrive, he'd feast on milk and a donut while he chatted with us and the coaches. Sometimes he'd get one of the trainers to give him a pedicure. Because of his advanced age, he couldn't bend, so he'd sit on the table where we put our drinks and the doctors stitched us up, take off his shoes and socks, and there the trainer would cut his nails. Then he would watch us practice for a while before going about his business.

It must have given the coaches and general managers quite a headache to have their superior following them around. Indeed, he interfered with their work more than was good for us. He got involved in every detail, even deciding who would be an assistant coach or manager of the farm team. The team was his plaything. He moved everyone around like puppets, which was one reason the Maple Leafs never won anything under his leadership.

Another problem was that Ballard didn't know how to choose the right people. For six of my years in Toronto, the general manager was McNamara, who liked Czechoslovaks because he was confident he'd find one to raise the team's profile, as Peter Stastny had raised the profile of the Quebec Nordiques. He placed a lot of faith in Vladimir Ruzicka, whom he drafted in 1982 in the hope that he would get him to the West, which in the end he failed to do. McNamara brought me to the Maple Leafs, and I'm grateful to him for it. But unfortunately, he never set the team up so that it ran really smoothly. If we needed someone to crack the whip over us, the coach who led us would be too laid-back. When the lineup was full of young lads who would have benefited from a more patient, teacherly approach, our coach would be the crazy type who breathed down players' necks and relished a brawl. When things were going famously up front and we were scoring 300 goals a season, we would be weak on the back end.

It was as though we couldn't get ourselves in gear. The team bought players and waited for what would happen. In most cases, things ended badly. Our excellent youngsters included Wendel Clark, Vincent Damphousse, Al Iafrate, Gary Leeman, Steve Thomas, Ed Olczyk and Russ Courtnall, none of whom fulfilled their potential in Toronto but often went on to have great careers with other NHL clubs. Things may have been different if we'd been coached by someone like Scotty

Bowman. It's said he turned down an offer to coach the Leafs, knowing he'd never be given full rein.

Harold was disappointed with our results, of course—particularly as journalists delighted in pointing out that the club's seasons had been average or below average ever since he took over. When we were playing poorly, he swore that he'd replace the whole team. But this resolution would soon be dissolved by the sight of full stands. People kept coming and business was good. And above all, Ballard was a great businessman. Hadn't he once persuaded the Beatles to play two concerts at Maple Leaf Gardens in one day, as he'd sold double the number of tickets? And he ordered vendors at the stadium to add more salt to the popcorn to make the crowd thirstier, therefore increasing beverage sales.

He may not have been able to compete with other owners in terms of number of Stanley Cups won, but there was one thing he beat them at hands down. Surely none of them had seen as many NHL matches as he had. If we were playing on the east coast, the old man would fly out to attend our away games as well. He felt good in our midst. In the company of players half a century younger, he could forget about his age and worsening health.

He would sit at the front of the bus, as I would. Once, on the way from the airport in New York to Manhattan, as we approached a tunnel he declared: "If there's one thing I can't stand, it's tunnels. They make me feel like I'm dead and they're burying me in the earth." And he really was shuddering.

He told amazing stories from the Original Six era, when hockey was even more "rock 'n' roll" than it was in our day. About how he and King Clancy would drive naked women around on the Zamboni in the middle of the night, for instance. Clancy was a pretty interesting guy, too. Officially, he was the club's vice president, but in effect he was Harold's salaried buddy. Clancy was one of hockey's greatest legends. We youngsters could scarcely believe that his career in the NHL began in 1921. He won the Stanley Cup three times as a player and three times as an assistant general manager. He was also a referee for a while, as well as a coach in Toronto.

Those two got up to all kinds of nonsense together … On Clancy's 80th birthday, Ballard amused himself by giving his friend a 10-year contract with an option for an extra season. They were two grandpas from the Hockey Hall of Fame who just refused to get old. Behind the net, to the right, they had their own windowed box (the famous bunker), where they watched the game, nattered about hockey, and recalled the days when the Maple Leafs terrorized the NHL.

Harold loved publicity more than anything, and it's no exaggeration to say he was a household name in Canada. Sometimes he gave the impression that he was determined to make the front pages of the newspapers at least once a week. When he didn't happen to be at war with the NHL executives, he liked to interfere in politics, argue with journalists, and lambaste his children for being freeloaders. His relationship with his Slovak girlfriend, Yolanda, was tumultuous and played out in public.

Ballard was no lover of peace and quiet. He needed excitement in his life. Whenever he got bored, someone paid the price. Before the start of one season, he came up with the great idea of impressing his palms and his dog T. J. Puck's paws in some freshly laid concrete in the middle of the rink. After that, the ice wouldn't freeze properly, and it developed cracks and holes. Ballard worked himself into a frenzy about it. He bawled out the maintenance men for being a bunch of good-for-nothings, fired a few of them, and hired new ones who knew nothing about the work. Problems with the ice remained. As a result, practice was moved to North York.

The annual team photo at Maple Leaf Gardens was another source of amusement. Conducted by Ballard, of course, it would take all afternoon to achieve, making it more demanding than practice. Harold kept finding things wrong: we weren't smiling as we should, the photographer was taking us from the wrong angle, and so on. Moreover, our mascot T. J. Puck would be whimpering and fidgeting because

Harold had sat him on the ice and his balls had frozen, and we would have to wait for him to calm down …

Harold Ballard was a very interesting man, and I consider myself honored to have known him. Many people found him difficult to take, and some don't have a good word to say about him. Some fans have never gotten over his treatment of club icons Dave Keon, Lanny McDonald and Darryl Sittler. Maybe much of the criticism is justified. But the Harold Ballard I knew was very different from the self-satisfied egotist written about in the newspapers, and I'll always stand by him.

And I'll never forget how he helped me in early 1986, when I got myself into a real mess.

―――――――

Stupidity must be paid for. And multiple stupidities must be paid for in multiples. In my case, this meant a week behind bars.

It all began one night when they were checking the downtown traffic. I got pulled over and given the Breathalyzer. In Canada, the legal limit is 80 milligrams of alcohol in 100 milliliters of blood, and I was shown to have exceeded it. It was pointless for me to deny it, as I'd had a few drinks. But when the cops turned their flashlights on my driver's license and saw my name, they let me go. Hockey players could get away with all kinds of stuff in Toronto, and in this case my offense went unreported.

The second time it happened, I was given an official warning.

The third time, they caught me after tennis. We had two days off; I'd been playing with friends and we'd shared a few beers. My home was a couple of miles away, along a straight road. But on the way I turned off to call on—well, let's call her an acquaintance. On leaving her place and reaching the main road, I turned left rather than right onto the streetcar deck. Lights went on immediately: there was a police car right around the corner.

This was bad, I knew. A uniformed woman got out of the car, her expression stern. She used her walkie-talkie to call for reinforcements. Two more cops arrived. As soon as they realized who I was, they attempted to persuade her to turn a blind eye and let me go. "I'm almost home," I added. "A right turn at the lights and I'm there." Unfortunately, she was unmoved. I breathed into the tube and failed the test.

I found out later that she was on duty for the first time and suspected she was being tested to see how carefully she would adhere to the law in the face of attempts to influence her. My car was confiscated, and I was taken to the station, where I was photographed head-on and in profile, had my fingerprints taken, and was made to walk along a line. Then I signed a report of the incident. The case would continue in court.

I'd gotten myself into a real mess. This much was clear to me the next morning, when I heard, in a taxi on the way to practice, that Maple Leafs forward Mirko Frycer had been caught driving while under the influence of alcohol. The dressing room was full of talk of my offense, and the lads delighted in pulling my leg about it. Then the general manager came in.

He didn't waste time talking about what I'd done—after all, it had happened during two days off, not on my way home from a game. But he warned me that the papers would be on my case. And he was right about that.

Harold Ballard reacted very well indeed. He told me not to worry about a thing—he would put his best lawyers on the case and ensure that I got off with the lightest sentence possible. Having spent a year in jail himself, for fraud and tax evasion, he knew quite a bit about trials. "When I was in the can, I had a lovely TV, and they fed me the best steaks," he said, to reassure me. "And I ran the Maple Leafs on the phone. Don't worry, I'll look after you."

This was a generous gesture even for those laid-back times. Although I hadn't killed anyone, or even driven like a madman, other teams may have taken the opportunity to get rid of me. Problem players aren't popular with many bosses. When Dougie Gilmour of the St. Louis Blues was accused of sexual assault, the club traded him to the Calgary

Flames straightaway, without waiting for the law to take its course. (Gilmour was never indicted.)

The court hearing was postponed until June, after the end of the season. As this was a repeat offense, the prosecutor proposed a custodial sentence of between three and six months. When I heard this, I almost passed out. Ballard's attorney could offer me all the reassurances in the world, but the thought of six months behind bars was horrendous. Fortunately, I got off with two weeks and no driver's license for a year. In his summing-up, the judge said I was one of his favorite athletes and he didn't want to make an example of me. Thank God for that.

After the verdict was announced, I was clapped in handcuffs, which is a pretty unpleasant experience, I can tell you. Then they locked me in a cell, where I was to wait for other convicts. My first visitor was the governor of the prison, by remarkable coincidence the brother of our general manager McNamara, and he advised me on how I should behave behind bars. "Don't make any friends, keep your thoughts to yourself, don't allow yourself to be provoked, and never let down your guard," he told me.

That evening, we were taken to the Toronto West Detention Centre. There was a crowd of reporters in front of the court building, and cameras and camcorders wherever you looked. So I pulled my jacket over my head and got to the van as quickly as I could.

The prospect of jail scared me, of course it did. I imagined it like Alcatraz in the American movies—a dark cell with massive sliding bars, filled with lunatics. Fortunately for me, only people serving shorter sentences or waiting for their case to get to court were placed in the jail at Etobicoke, so security was kept to a minimum and the level of comfort was tolerable. In fact, it was more like the Olympic Village in Lake Placid than Alcatraz.

I was put in a cell with a 20-year-old who had smuggled in drugs from Jamaica. He was terrified, poor lad. He'd been given eight years. On my first night, I wasn't doing much better—I tossed and turned and didn't get a wink of sleep. In daytime, I had a special program. The news had gotten out that a Maple Leafs player was serving his sentence here, so the governor forbade me to walk in the yard among the other prisoners. He wanted to make sure I wouldn't get jumped by some numbskull keen to make a name for himself.

I spent the whole day sitting in my cell, reading every line of the newspapers or watching soccer on TV—the World Cup in Mexico was in progress. I was bored to tears.

My only duty was to gather the block's laundry each evening. In normal circumstances, this trip around three floors would take 30 minutes, but it took me an hour and a half: I had to provide autographs on any scraps of paper that could be found. I was obviously a great attraction for the others.

On my second night there, I experienced a raid, when inspectors arrived in the cells to search for drugs. Two nights later, I received another visit—but this time the warden woke me with an apology. "Sorry, Mr. Frycer, but would you mind signing this for me? I'm going on leave tomorrow, and we won't see each other again. And could I have three more autographs for my colleagues?"

In the end, I spent seven nights in jail. My sentence was reduced by a week. Maybe Ballard's lawyers had gotten to work on it.

When I walked free, I was met at the gate by reporters. I donned sackcloth and ashes and told them how sorry I was to have given young people such a poor example, and I added a few more words of apology. And that was the end of the whole affair. I'd served the sentence I deserved, and after that no one said any more about it. Not even out on the ice. My opponents obviously found the traditional insults about communists and crappy Europeans more effective.

———

My DUI conviction provided me with further confirmation that the lot of a hockey player in Toronto was wonderful in many ways and complicated in many others. If I'd had the same problem in Hartford, it would have been reported the next day and then forgotten.

Where the place of hockey in society is concerned, nowhere else in the world can compare to Toronto. Torontonians are fanatical to the point of craziness, but they're also kind and appreciative. As I was given to understand daily.

After I lost my driver's license, I had to ride the subway to practice for a year. When I got on at Islington, the second stop beyond the depot, the car would be nearly empty. I'd sit at the back and immerse myself in my newspaper. As more and more people got on, the more I heard the words, "It's him, isn't it?" By then, I'd been a Maple Leaf for four years, and my face was in the papers about every second day, so I was pretty well known. Before long, the first passengers would venture to approach me for an autograph, bringing others in their wake, leaving me little peace for reading. Many female students and young women traveled into the center of town, so by the time I changed trains at Bloor, my pockets would be filled with telephone numbers.

I had to get used to constant attention from the public. It was part and parcel of our work. I was happy to sign an autograph or shake someone's hand, but I wasn't one of those players who take pleasure in such acts. Fame is nice, but privacy is nicer still.

When we lived downtown, I felt best in the Irish bar close to our apartment. No one there watched my every move. I'd have a beer and some chilli and people would leave me alone. Or I'd wander along to the Croatian restaurant on Queen Street. Croatians care little for hockey, so no one ever bothered me while I was eating.

During games, the fanaticism of Toronto's support wasn't so much in evidence. The games were sold out, of course, and when goals were scored and fights broke out, people would get excited and stand up. But the sound of a Maple Leafs crowd couldn't compare with the roar in Vitkovice's Kotas Stadium, in Litvinov or Kosice, indeed in any stadium in Czechoslovakia. Hockey culture was different there; matches were attended by another type of person. In Toronto, tickets weren't cheap, and season tickets for the best seats passed from generation to generation, hence the heavy presence of checked jackets and shirts and ties. Many fans appeared to be dressed for the theater, not a sports game.

But we felt the interest of the public as we went about our everyday lives, in the street, store and restaurant. Many people couldn't afford tickets for the hockey or couldn't get to the Gardens, so they would show their support for us in a public place. For some who knew us only from newspapers and TV, we were stars. They considered themselves privileged to exchange a few words with us or shake our hands.

If, as some say, hockey is a religion in Toronto, then we were like demigods. Even if our results were poor, our status was assured by the maple leaf on our jerseys. We were members of the family—members of Leafs Nation, as hockey fans in Toronto say. This was difficult for me to grasp at first. In gray, communist Czechoslovakia, I'd been used to an ideal of mediocrity; it was important not to stand out. Here, people praised us to the skies and glorified the fact that we chased a piece of black rubber around a stretch of ice.

Sometimes I found this fanatical devotion embarrassing. For instance, I'd take a taxi to practice and the driver would study me closely in his rear-view mirror.

"You really are him, aren't you?"

"Well, we are heading for Maple Leaf Gardens ..."

"Amazing," he'd say, as if he were chauffeuring the Queen of England.

When we got to the arena, I'd reach into my pocket for my wallet, but the driver would wave my money away. "No, no, no. No need to pay me. An autograph will be enough."

Once, I had a new floor laid in my basement. When the firm learned who the customer was, they insisted on working for me at a knock-down price, saying they were honored to do so. "And would you sign a few photos for us?" they asked.

Unbelievable.

But I had a long way to go to compare with Borje Salming. The fans absolutely idolized him, and the rest of us took advantage of the fact. After a game, we'd wait for him to go to the parking lot, where the crowds would surge toward him. Then we'd make our way unnoticed to our own cars. Borje didn't seem to mind. He was never in a hurry, and he would sign whatever was put in front of him, even by the most tiresome kid. I can't imagine how hard it must have been for Darryl Sittler or Mats Sundin, whose popularity was a level higher even than Borje's.

The life of a Maple Leafs hockey player brings with it constant media attention. Toronto has four daily newspapers, and then there's radio and TV. Our practices attracted more journalists than went to games in some other cities, and they dissected every goal, every mistake, every defeat. They were highly critical—and in our era, they had plenty to be critical about. On the other hand, they were fair. They never dealt me a low blow; they never made anything up about me or put words in my mouth.

It took me a while to learn how to speak to them. In the early days, I took a few calls from the general manager, who wished to explain to me that what I'd blurted out after yesterday's match was inappropriate. At other times, a more experienced teammate would offer me guidance. I believe Canadian reporters appreciated me for my sense of humor and ability to depart from the script. Except for one situation, which I'll go on to describe, I was able to stake out boundaries beyond which my honesty shouldn't take me.

You can't tell journalists everything. Fans make fun of athletes for forever saying the same thing to the point of cliché, but there really is no other way—if they said what was on their minds, they would cause a tremendous stir.

Even at the toughest moments, it's necessary to put on a Hollywood smile and be positive. Or to look crestfallen, if this is more appropriate. I earned four points and played a great game but we still lost? Then I tell the journalists what they want to hear—that I'm disappointed and would happily exchange my goals and assists for a victory, which means much more. I'm on auto-repeat. What does it matter that in the opposite case—we've won but I've scored no points—they criticize me for playing poorly?

Sometimes it was difficult to remain diplomatic. After an unsuccessful game, I would feel like a pressure cooker with thoughts bubbling up inside me, but there I'd stand surrounded by microphones in the glare of the cameras. *Why isn't it working for you? Why is your line so weak? Why? Why? Why?*

I could hardly say the coach was an idiot who bawled us out in practice yesterday and came up with the wrong tactics today. Nor could I say that for the past two weeks my hip had been acting up so badly that if I hadn't loaded myself with pills and two injections, I couldn't have ventured out onto the ice. I had to keep myself in check and make it clear that we were trying, we were fighting, and we were sure to do better next time out.

If you haven't been through it, it's difficult to believe. In 2006, when Czech defenseman Pavel Kubina signed with the Maple Leafs, I warned him that the pressure he was about to play under was unimaginable. He waved the warning away, saying, "We were under plenty of pressure at Tampa when we played in the Stanley Cup Final." When we met a year later, Pavel admitted that the pressure was even worse than I'd described.

Plenty of great players have failed to manage the switch to Toronto. Their performance levels drop and no one knows why. Pressure from the media and the fans really is enormous, from the first day of training camp all the way through to the last game of the season. You feel it most if you come from a club on the peripheries, where you were used to living and playing in relative seclusion.

I remember when Miro Ihnacak, Peter's younger brother, joined us after Christmas 1985.

As he was reputed to be the best left winger in Europe, the club was trusting him to raise the team's play to new heights. His arrival was accompanied by a great deal of hype. All the papers wrote about his escape from Czechoslovakia and declared him a new star whose five-year contract would cost $750,000. What's more, he was given jersey number 27, previously worn by Darryl Sittler. *Dear oh dear, this can't end well,* I thought. And I was right. Under tremendous pressure right from the start, Miro never got over it. The leap from Kosice to Toronto was simply too much for him. When he was playing with Peter and me, we gave him as many passes as we could, thinking that after he scored a few goals, he'd settle in. It didn't help. Before long, journalists delighted in calling him Miro the Zero. He played only 55 games for the Maple Leafs, scoring eight goals; then he was demoted to the farm team. Yet he had the ability. He had been the most productive player in the Czechoslovak league and also a 95-point scorer in the AHL.

This constant pressure may explain why the Maple Leafs haven't been in the Stanley Cup Final for half a century, let alone won the trophy. The burden of expectation and the hunger for hockey never lessen—in fact, in the age of the internet and social networks, they are more intense still. Pity. This city deserves a title. And if it gets one, delighted fans will probably build statues to the players.

I regret the fact we weren't able to be more successful in the '80s. We started every season in the hope it would be better than the last. But it always followed the same scenario. Each September, the papers were full of optimism—the team had a year's more experience, the club had traded well, and promising youngsters had been drafted. By November, the tone of the commentaries would be gloomier. As we started the new year, it was clear this wouldn't be the breakthrough season. From April, thoughts would turn to hope for the new season.

Yet I never enjoyed my hockey more than in those years. Although we never got anywhere near the Stanley Cup, people liked us. It was an honor to play for the Maple Leafs. I'd make the same choice again. Before the arrival of Mario Lemieux, the Pittsburgh Penguins recorded similar results, but when we played there, there were only 4,000 spectators in the stands. It felt like a practice session. That would never have happened in Toronto.

For years we were accused of being the worst group in the history of the club. Today, though, many fans take a more benevolent view of our era. The players weren't the only ones accountable; the roots of the problem lay much deeper. Everything changes—players, coaches, general managers, styles of play and tactics, even the rules by which the NHL is run. Everything except the Maple Leafs' results, that is. At the time of writing, in the past 13 seasons, the club has made the playoffs only three times. The current generation, too, knows what it's like to finish at the bottom of the league. But maybe better times are on the horizon. The team is young, with many promising players; the coach is a good one, and the club is reasonable in its actions.

I'm keeping my fingers crossed that they'll win that cup one day. I want them to experience the magnificent celebrations known to fans in other cities. It's still my club. I'm still cheering for the boys in blue and white.

Once a Leaf, forever a Leaf.

17

At War with Brophy

THE 1977 AMERICAN movie *Slap Shot* is one of the best sports comedies ever. Loved by fans of all ages, it has become a cult. It tells the story of the Charlestown Chiefs, a team in the semiprofessional Federal League that takes to playing a brutal form of hockey in its desire to succeed and survive. When the club makes some money for the first time and wins the title it longs for, its fans are elated.

The lead role—that of player-coach Reggie Dunlop—was played by the outstanding Paul Newman. In writing his character, the screenwriters were inspired by the story of famed bruiser John Brophy, who became our coach in 1986. As a minor-league player, Brophy accumulated almost 4,000 penalty minutes. He'd spent most of his coaching career with farm and second-tier minor-pro teams, too.

As soon as he was appointed Maple Leafs coach, my days in Toronto were numbered. I didn't know that at the time, of course.

It's not always the case that a coach embraces the style of hockey he was known for as a player. I know several guys who as carefree forwards refused to retreat behind the red line, but as coaches became specialists in dogged defense. Brophy and I had gotten along fine during his season and a half as Dan Maloney's assistant. His demeanor toward me had been kindly and jovial, and he had given me praise. I remember him patting me on the back and telling me, "You'll get those 50 goals this season, Mirko. You can do it. I like the way you're a mean son of a bitch on the ice. You're not like those other Europeans, afraid to mix it up."

What could possibly go wrong?

In the first game of the 1986-87 season, we beat the Montreal Canadiens, newly crowned Stanley Cup champions, 7-4 at home. I collected three assists. A promising start. Before long, however, Brophy started playing the big guy. I quickly realized that the joviality had been an act and the words of flattery his way of buttering me up. Now that he was the top man, his approach was very different.

At the beginning of the season, I was appointed alternate captain. But about five games in, Brophy took this from me and gave it to Tom Fergus, saying it was better to pass the responsibility around. I didn't mind—the presence or absence of a letter on my jersey was no big deal to me. Besides, Fergie was a good guy, and I was glad for him.

Then Brophy came up with the idea that I should be more aggressive in games. After each practice, he made me spend half an hour attacking a punching bag. This did bother me. Why was he trying to turn his top scorer into a run-of-the-mill slugger, for God's sake? It was nonsense. "But Johnny, you know me and what kind of player I am," I protested. "I won't duck a fight if it's necessary, but I can be more useful to the team in other ways."

So started the war between us. Brophy turned *me* into a punching bag and held me back wherever he could.

He didn't like the style of play Peter Ihnacak and I practiced. Peter and I tried to adapt to each other; our way of building attacks wasn't that of the Canadians. And it worked. In Brophy's eyes, however, it was "European shit hockey." He wanted us to launch the puck toward the boards. The moment I took a pass at the blue line, he would yell at me from the bench, "Dump the puck in!"

I tried to stand up for my way of doing things. "Why should I play like that? I've been in the NHL for five years, and I've never dumped the puck in, unless I had to." But my complaints fell on deaf ears.

And I spent a few games as a healthy scratch because of them. Six midseason games, to be precise. Brophy relished putting me through this. Once, I turned up at the dressing room half an hour before a game and got changed, ready for action. I was lacing up my skates when he informed me: "You're not playing today."

Just like that. No reason given.

Several times I went to him and asked what I'd done to cause him to pick on me like this. He wasn't able to explain his behavior. "It's just the way things are gonna be," was his answer.

I was soon given to understand that he was bothered by my new contract. In every second practice, he wondered aloud for the benefit of all why I wasn't working harder when I was making so much money. This made me white with rage. I'd take a thousand kinds of criticism from a coach—I wasn't perfect, after all—but no one could accuse me of taking it easy. Ever. I loved the game from the first to the last day of my career.

The conflicts between Brophy and me mounted up. I wouldn't let anything go, and I gave as good as I got. I was well established on the club, so why should I put up with this? In public, I maintained decorum by fobbing off journalists' questions with platitudes. As soon as I started scoring more goals, I'd be fine, I said, adding that it wasn't the coach's fault. But all the time I was seething inside.

Something else Brophy introduced was a regular weigh-in. I had nothing against this—we were professionals, so the coach had the right to ensure we maintained our ideal weight. The problem was, Brophy had no idea what he was looking for. This was way beyond the world he understood—the Eastern Hockey League, with its brawling goons swinging their sticks at each other. He had no coaching certification, and he had no idea about the balance of muscle and fat in a player's body. He gave us all a number and forbade us to exceed it. End of story.

In November, before a home game against the Philadelphia Flyers, he cornered me and ordered me onto the scales. They showed that I was about a pound and a half over. The reason being, the day before I had eaten an especially large dinner.

"You're not playing today!" he hollered.

"You're kidding, right?"

"No. You're overweight. Go home."

So I did. The guys battled to a point, so feeding Brophy's self-confidence.

The next day, we flew off for a short stay on the East Coast. Our first stop was Long Island. In the morning, he informed me and two others that instead of facing the New York Islanders, we would be subject to a special skating training session. He had us racing around the ice for an hour, sprint after sprint. I gritted my teeth and got on with it. But I refused to go to the game. I wasn't going to sit in the stands like an idiot. I'd watch on TV.

So I stayed at the hotel, which was right across from Nassau Coliseum. I got room service to bring me a hamburger, cracked open a beer, and switched on the box. Moments later, the phone rang. Peter Ihnacak was on the line.

"They're looking for you everywhere, Frigo! Ricky Vaive has a fever. You're in instead of him."

"Sure," I said, not believing a word. I imagined myself running into the dressing room, where everywhere would crack up at my having been taken in so easily.

"I'm not joking. They think you're inside the stadium somewhere. They've had your name called over the PA."

I still didn't believe him. But I started to come around when he said, "God's honest truth." *I'd better get over there, just to be on the safe side,* I thought. As I changed, I could still taste the onions from the hamburger. As I hurried into the dressing room, the equipment managers were already panicking about my failure to show up. I got into my uniform in double-quick time, and I reached the bench just as the second anthem was ending. There hadn't been time for me to warm up.

I still believe that Brophy and Vaive, who knew each other from their days together at the Birmingham Bulls in the WHA, had set me up. Ricky would get a rest, and I'd be taught a lesson.

We lost 6-4. Brophy sent me out only a few times in each period, which was just as well: my legs were so sore from the morning's practice, if I'd been given more ice time, I wouldn't have been very effective.

This game didn't go off without conflict either. A minute before the end, someone crashed into me and pushed me into the boards, where I got a nasty blow to the rib cage. It hurt like hell. As soon as the game was over, I got the painful rib iced. The sight of this started Brophy off. "You fucked the game up for us! We lost because of you! You flaked out on us on the ice, and now you're faking injury!" He added something about the ways of Europeans, as was his custom.

All I could say to this was, "Fuck you, Johnny."

The next morning, we met up for breakfast at the Marriott, after which we would fly to Philadelphia for our next game. Peter Ihnacak and I sat together at one table, calmly eating toast, drinking coffee, and reading the newspaper. Silence fell. What was going on? I looked up to see Brophy standing over me. No, he hadn't come to make up. Leaning down, he said, "I know you did it on purpose yesterday. You had hookers in your room before the game, and you were boozed up."

This was nonsense. I felt my blood pressure rise. But I kept myself in check. I mustn't allow myself to be provoked. "Shut up, Johnny," I said quietly.

But he wasn't finished. I faked an injury, I took things easy on the ice, we'd lost because of me, he said. I stood up, grabbed him by the throat, and yelled at him, "One more word and I'll give you such a smack you won't get back up."

I grabbed my keys and went over to where our management team was sitting. "I'm going up to pack and call a taxi," I announced. "Get me a ticket to Toronto. I refuse to play under that asshole."

The execs were taken aback. "Be reasonable, Mirko. It can all be talked out. We've got an important game ahead of us."

But I wouldn't be moved. I flew home, and the others went on to Philadelphia, where they were thrashed 6-1.

Brophy really put me off the game. I'd always looked forward to getting to the arena, having my coffee and donut in the dressing room, chatting with the guys, going for lunch after practice. I enjoyed this life. Now I was going into work with the enthusiasm of a factory worker who couldn't wait to punch his time card on the way out. I didn't stay on at the arena a minute longer than I had to. Hockey became a job, nothing more than that.

I'd had disagreements with coaches before, of course. That's part and parcel of sport. Michel Bergeron and I didn't get on, but I couldn't deny his achievements in the NHL. I didn't think much of Mike Nykoluk as a coach, but I liked him as a person. Dan Maloney had his failings, but he was always fair. With John Brophy, it was a different story. We disagreed on more than just tactics and how to train. He had something against me personally, which I didn't understand then and will never know the reason for. He was the worst coach I ever had. His behavior was bad, plus he didn't get results.

There was the time he made me so mad that I didn't turn up for practice the next day. Nor did I explain my absence. I know this is inexcusable behavior from a player, but at the time I couldn't have cared less. I needed to clear my head, and that was the most important thing.

All day I sat at home wondering what to do next. The easiest thing would be to go to the GM and ask to be traded. There would surely be interest from other clubs. But I didn't want to leave Toronto. If anyone should leave, it was Brophy, I told myself. I also needed to take into account what club owner Harold Ballard had done for me, what the Maple Leafs meant to me, and what would happen with my career. I didn't want to give all this up for the sake of one idiot.

News that I'd missed practice caused a bit of a stir. Journalists came to me for a statement. I didn't open the door. There was nothing I could tell them. In the end, I decided not to push things any further. The next day, I went in early and announced to Brophy that I'd been ill. Let him make of it what he would. Then I turned on my heel, weighed myself, and went out onto the ice. Nothing more was said about my absence.

I wasn't the only one who was sick of Brophy. The whole team turned against him. Except for two or three who swallowed his style.

If we were down 2-0 by the 10th minute, Brophy would always be the first to lose his cool and start panicking. Instead of trying to calm us down and telling us to stick with it because there was plenty of time to turn things around, he would start shouting and cursing. His vocabulary was choice—for him, we were all fuckers, bastards and sons of bitches. You would get more elevated conversation from someone whose education had never gotten beyond elementary school. Brophy's main tool of expression was the word *fuck* in its various guises. Asked by journalists to comment on a defeat in Minnesota, he launched into a string of obscenities. The journalists counted 57 uses of the word in six minutes. I'd played under gentlemen like Ludek Bukac and Pavel Wohl, so this was quite a culture shock for me.

He behaved like a crackpot in the dressing room, too. During intermissions, he would come in hopping mad, take off his jacket, and start tearing it to shreds. Or he'd take off his watch and hurl it to the floor. Wastebaskets flew about the place so often that we barely noticed them. I remember, too, the wounds on his hands, inflicted when he banged them against the Plexiglas behind the bench. And I remember the time in Los Angeles when he was struck on the head by a puck, and the blood was seeping through his white hair, and how he didn't seem even to notice it and carried on yelling; he looked like he was in a trance.

Maybe he meant well, in his perverse way. I can't deny that he genuinely liked hockey and wanted to win. He wanted to energize us and get the most out of us. But he chose the worst of all possible approaches. Young guys in particular were terrified of him. Al Iafrate was a bundle of nerves before every game. I used to keep Gary Leeman calm by telling him to ignore the nutbar and concentrate on his own game.

Even by the standards of the NHL in the 1980s, Brophy was old school. The game was moving in a very different direction; thanks to the Edmonton Oilers in particular, fast, team passing play was coming to dominate. But Brophy continued to rely on what had once brought minor-league teams success—provocation and intimidation of the opposition by use of strong-arm tactics. "Take him down and put him in a wheelchair!" With instructions like this, he would send brawny players onto the ice.

At practice, he liked nothing more than to teach us how to make things unpleasant for the opposition. He showed us how to use our sticks to deliver the most painful kind of slash, and how to poke someone behind the knee so that his legs gave way. "You need to catch him here! Here is where it really hurts!" he would rave.

When we were conceding a lot from the edge of the goal area, he would give us a lesson in how to eliminate opposing forwards. He'd call on Chris Kotsopoulos or some other particularly well-built player and demonstrate his art of defense on them; holding his stick in both hands, he would strike them in the kidneys until they fell to the ground. Again. And again. "You either win that area in there or you don't stay with the hockey club! It's as simple as that," he would say.

During skating practice, he liked to use his stick to slap us across the butt as we skated past. Not hard, and usually when he was in a good mood. But once, he caught me in the very place I had a postsurgical growth. I tumbled to the ice, and an ambulance had to be called. After that, I was out of action for 10 days with a locked knee. This was too much even for Harold Ballard and Gerry McNamara, who subjected him to a lecture on his crazy behavior. Brophy even came to me to apologize. I don't think the apology was his idea, though—he struggled to get the word *sorry* across his lips.

Regrettably, none of my teammates found the courage to stand up to Brophy in the dressing room. I was loudest in my opposition to him; the others merely complained about him over a beer. He'd coached some of the guys at the St. Catharines Saints farm team, so there were a great many stories about him. But the telling of these stories didn't change anything.

That first season didn't turn out too badly. Despite Brophy rather than thanks to him, I'd say. On the ice, we fought for our own reputations and the Maple Leafs logo on our chests. Not for Brophy. In the regular season, we got 70 points, the same as the Minnesota North Stars—but we made it to the playoffs because of our greater number of wins. We went out to the Detroit Red Wings in the second round.

By then, I was no longer involved. My season ended on February 18, 1987. To begin with, I missed 18 games with a knee problem. After that, I was kept out by an injury that at first no one could understand. Typical. I was struggling to push off on my skates. The first assumption was that I had a groin problem. A detailed examination revealed a chipped pelvis. I would learn later from doctors in Germany that the injury had been caused by short-term overstrain—sustained, I surmised, by being made by my coach to race about the ice like a bloated goat. The chip in my pelvis still shows up on X-rays today. I call it my "Brophy memento."

From February on, I went to the arena only when I had to. I was sick of it all. I didn't want to speak with anyone, Brophy least of all. I watched the playoff games on TV. I didn't even go to the end-of-season party, having left to see my father in Germany as soon as we were eliminated. I was mad at my teammates for having put on an act in front of Brophy. I certainly wasn't in the mood to join them in a bar, where I'd have to listen to more of their complaints about the idiot who coached us.

Journalists picked up on my absence, and there was speculation that the general manager would trade me to reestablish calm on the club. But on the eve of the 1987-88 season, Gerry McNamara came up with a different suggestion. He called Brophy and me to the office and insisted that we make peace. We shook hands and promised to give it a try. McNamara had just traded Ricky Vaive and Steve Thomas to Chicago, so it was more important than ever for him that I was playing and relaxed.

It was like shaking hands with the devil. There never was any peace, just a ceasefire lasting a few weeks. Nothing changed, least of all my status on the team.

Yet the season got off to such a promising start. I scored seven goals in the preseason, and I put up 11 points over the first seven NHL games. Then things fell apart. Again I injured my knee; again I went to war with Brophy. But this time I wasn't in it on my own.

Over the summer there had been a few changes to the roster, as the coach wanted players with great physical presence. One of the new faces was Dave Semenko, a goon of the first rank who had been Wayne Gretzky's bodyguard with the Edmonton Oilers. He'd once boxed with Muhammad Ali in an exhibition. He may have looked like a mountain of flesh, but away from the ice he was a mild-mannered, witty, and intelligent guy. I liked him, and we got along well together.

As a player, he was very much Brophy's type. At least that's how it seemed at first.

Brophy had the idea that Semenko would thrash everyone who crossed his path. But Dave was a pretty good forward, and as he approached the end of his career, he wanted to play hockey. In Edmonton, he'd made good use of his muscles in defense of Gretzky; he didn't get into fights for no reason. Whenever Gretzky got fouled or roughed up, it was Semenko's job to make it clear to the culprit that he shouldn't try it again. He made space and kept things comfortable for the star. Now Brophy was demanding that Dave attack the opposition's best players, which went against the grain for him. It was okay to take revenge. It was okay to fight with another bruiser, provided it got the team fired up. But as he wasn't a thug, he refused to be a loose cannon at Brophy's behest.

It wasn't long before Dave was asking over a beer, "What kind of idiot is this coach, for God's sake?" In Edmonton, he'd been used to winning and an easygoing atmosphere; he found neither in Toronto. After another run-in with Brophy, Dave left the team and called it quits on his hockey career, before the end of the season.

McNamara realized the team couldn't stomach the coach and that everything was falling apart. He tried to make an emergency move in the middle of the season by forcing Brophy's firing. Better late than never.

But in the end, the one who got his marching orders from Ballard was McNamara.

———

We snuck into the playoffs in spring 1988, too. But this was nothing to brag about: in the overall rankings from the NHL regular season, we finished second from the bottom, with a measly 52 points. This made us the worst team in modern history to contest for the Stanley Cup.

Again, we faced the Detroit Red Wings in the opening round. I played in the first three games. Then John Brophy dropped me from the team. We went out in six. Game 4 in particular was a debacle that showed just how low this coach had brought us—we lost 8-0 at Maple Leaf Gardens. This was too much even for our loyal fans: they threw everything they found to hand on the ice. Sweaters, hats, pucks …

We'd reached rock bottom.

At that moment, I was absolutely convinced of one thing: there would be a notable absentee from the September training camp—either me or Brophy. Our dressing room couldn't contain both of us. At 29, I had no intention of wasting another season.

After the last game, I removed the nametag from my stall. "I'm taking this as a souvenir," I told the guys. Everyone sat up and took notice. Before long, the press got wind of the sensation that was about to happen. Okay; I'd kept quiet for long enough. Regardless of the consequences, I took a deep breath and launched into it.

I aired everything that had been getting me down for two seasons. All the frustration and disappointment. I told the media that Brophy hated the players and the players hated him. That he was unable to communicate with us. That in February the club had thrown out the wrong guy in general manager McNamara. That for the past two years

I'd awoken each morning sick at the prospect of facing Brophy at the arena. That it was either him or me.

As an example of the devastation wrought by Brophy on the Maple Leafs, I compared us to the Red Wings. In summer 1986, Brophy had come to us and Jacques Demers had gone to Detroit. In those two years, our performance had worsened by five points, and theirs had improved by 54! Largely thanks to the coach, it went without saying. Because I don't believe we were the weaker team.

Borje Salming joined me in laying into Brophy, although he did so more diplomatically. "If you can't get the players playing, then the coach has to take responsibility." And for the first time, he admitted that he might leave for another club. Other members of the team kept quiet or spoke to reporters on condition of anonymity. I understood why most of them did this, particularly the youngsters with their careers ahead of them. They didn't want to start out with the reputation of players who didn't respect the authority of the coach.

The fact that I had nothing to lose allowed me to criticize in a manner practically unheard of with the Maple Leafs. My comments caused such a stir that they put my name back in the headlines. And still I clung to the hope that Brophy would be forced out. After all, how could the owner persist with a coach who had managed just 52 points and was opposed by everyone in the dressing room? I couldn't believe Ballard would sacrifice me after twice blocking my trade to the Pittsburgh Penguins.

I was wrong. Harold Ballard declared that John Brophy was the best coach in the NHL and that he continued to trust him.

Well, I suppose the old man was a traditional Canadian in his views. The last time the Maple Leafs had won the Stanley Cup, in 1967, they had been coached by Punch Imlach, a man as hard as nails who gave his players short shrift and ruled with a firm hand. But this was two decades down the line. In the 1960s, hockey players were basically under bond. As there were only six clubs in the NHL, they had to keep their mouths shut if they wanted to keep their jobs. Anyone who fell out of favor with the general manager was traded to the worst club in the league or sent to the farm team, never to return. Our generation was different. We had greater self-confidence and more power, and there were things we wouldn't put up with. It was a while before Ballard realized this.

Brophy had won our little war, so I had to go. I still feel bitter, even though it happened 30 years ago. I saw the appeal of staying with the Maple Leafs for many years, as Borje had done, maybe even finishing my career there. I believed the team was capable of more and could succeed. I believed I was capable of more, too. Because of injury and Brophy, in the 1987-88 season I'd played in 38 games, but I'd contributed 32 points, which is a decent return. In the press, Brophy accused me of robbing the club of $400,000, claiming that in the two years under him my performances had counted for nothing. But the opposite was true. Brophy robbed me of two years of my hockey career.

I realize the pointlessness of playing "what if?" But I doubt I was a million miles away from staying in Toronto. Maybe a few more goals would have done it. In the last game of the regular season, against the Detroit Red Wings, we turned the scores around from 0-3 to 5-3, the last two goals coming from my assists. Had we lost, the Minnesota North Stars would have gone through to the playoffs in our place. It's unlikely Brophy would have recovered from such a grand failure. The Maple Leafs would then have gotten first pick in the draft, chosen Mike Modano, and the future of the famous club could have been completely different. My future too.

Instead, as expected, I was traded in June. When I received the call from Jacques Demers in Detroit, I was already at my parents' place in Germany. He told me that Wings defenseman Darren Veitch and I were switching teams, and that he was looking forward to working with me. It was a strange feeling—a mix of sorrow at the involuntary end of my time with Toronto and delight at renewing acquaintance with a coach who had made a great impression on me seven years earlier with the Fredericton Express.

Before the preseason training camp, I stopped by at Maple Leaf Gardens to collect my things. On my way to see the equipment managers, I happened to meet Brophy in the corridor. Our goodbyes were brief but candid.

"Fuck you!"

"Fuck you!"

18

Detroit, Edmonton, and Goodbye, NHL

AFTER SEVEN YEARS in hockey-mad Canada, I moved to the United States. But I didn't need to get used to a different world.

The Detroit Red Wings, too, are a traditional NHL club—a member of the Original Six. Many unforgettable stars had worn its jersey. But since the NHL expansion, the Wings had sunk even lower than the Maple Leafs; between 1967 and 1983, they had reached the playoffs only twice. Their miserable results were reflected in low attendance—this was certainly no pulsating "Hockeytown." The Red Wings became the "Dead Things." But then the club was purchased by pizza king Mike Ilitch, who appointed Jimmy Devellano as general manager, and things started to look up. Devellano chose Steve Yzerman in the 1983 draft, taking him fourth overall. A single step that achieved a rebirth.

When I arrived in 1988, I saw immediately that the Red Wings were on the right path. They are still on it today. The atmosphere was one of contentment, self-confidence, and ambition. Devellano had not only roused the club from its stupor but also laid the foundations for a unique hockey culture. Graduates of his Detroit Harvard are usually successful once their playing days are over. It's surely no coincidence that three of my teammates from that time (Steve Yzerman, Jim Nill and Mike O'Connell) went on to become general managers in the NHL, and four others (Paul MacLean, Gerard Gallant, Adam Oates and Glen Hanlon) became head coaches.

After a few days in Detroit, I felt myself re-energized. My Toronto blues were gone. Day and night, Heaven and Hell—these were the comparisons I chose in answer to journalists who wanted to hear my first impressions after my trade. And I joked that if Petr Klima could wear a number 85 jersey to commemorate the year he had fled from Czechoslovakia, in the new season I would wear a number 88 in celebration of my liberation from Brophy.

On second thought, I stuck with my number 14.

The main figure with the Red Wings was Jacques Demers, and everything revolved around him. Few could match his expertise on hockey. In each of the previous two seasons, he had won the Jack Adams Award for best NHL coach. No one had ever won it in consecutive years. Later, he would win the Stanley Cup with the Montreal Canadiens.

I admired most things about him, but what fascinated me above all was his eloquence. He was a brilliant motivator—to listen to him before a game was a real experience. He knew just how to put things. And he never closed up after a game. He could keep his company entertained all evening, and he always had something to say.

It came as no surprise to me when he went into politics and made it to the Canadian Senate.

But what did surprise me was the admission he made in his memoir a few years ago. He is functionally illiterate. None of us who played for him over 1,000-plus NHL games would ever have guessed. Evidently, Jacques was an outstanding actor. As far as I remember, he always carried a newspaper, and the desk in his office was often covered with paperwork. He played this game for years, to perfection. Some of his performances could have earned him an Oscar.

Looking back, I realize he never wrote our lineup on the board. He would simply tell us who the goaltender was and who would be playing on the individual lines, thus skating around the problem elegantly.

Perhaps the only thing he couldn't manage was sketching out his tactical strategies. When explaining his intentions at a team meeting, his hand was incapable of transferring what he had in mind to the board. He would make a few strokes, get tangled up in them, and end up with some Picasso-like scribble. "Everything clear?" he would ask us in closing. And we would nod obediently. No one could bring himself to admit the opposite. Because Demers was a kindly, decent man. And above all, he was a coach for whom it was a pleasure to play.

On my arrival in Detroit, Demers and I agreed that if I could stay fit, I was capable of scoring 30 goals a season. "I'll give you your chance, don't worry," he assured me. He never went back on his word.

"And when we travel, you'll room with Steve Yzerman," he added. "That way, you'll soon understand how things work around here."

Steve was still only 23, but this was his third season as captain. In many ways, he reminded me of Borje Salming. He wasn't one of those players who impose their authority by raising their voice or repeating empty phrases. If he felt there was a problem in the dressing room, he would say briefly and clearly what he thought should change. Everyone would listen attentively and respect his opinion. He was a quiet, gentlemanly type who led by example on the ice. He wanted to win, and he gave his all to the cause; he had everything straight in his head.

Steve and I could talk about hockey for hours on end. Hockey was his life—he thought about it all the time and made many sacrifices for it. He was a classic "hockey guy." I felt confident that sooner or later he would lead the Red Wings to the Stanley Cup—in the end, he managed it three times. Today, thanks to his intelligence and feeling for the game, he is a successful general manager. This is no more than I would have expected of him.

It was always good to spend time with Steve. With one exception. He and I didn't click on the same line: we both liked to nurse the puck and make the play. It had been the same with me and Ivan Hlinka. So the coach usually teamed me with Adam Oates and Dave Barr. That worked much better. Adam was an extraordinarily selfless center whose passes were inch-perfect. There were no frills in his play. He'd deke the opponent, then play the puck to me. A few seasons later, he would do the same with Brett Hull, who scored an amazing 86 goals in one season as a result. Dave was a classic workhorse who covered mile after mile, opening up space for us.

Although we were great in the preseason, we failed to carry our form into the regular season. The main cause of our downfall was an alcohol-related incident involving Petr Klima and Bob Probert at the end of training camp. After the media got wind of it, suddenly the Red Wings were no longer being written about as favorites for the title.

Both players were suspended, and the punishment continued when Petr was sent to the farm team and Bob to a rehab facility. In things like this, Jacques Demers would show a firm hand. Unfortunately, the team never recovered its composure.

Our regular season began with three games out west—in Los Angeles, Vancouver and Calgary—from which we squeezed out a single point. After our opening home game against the St. Louis Blues ended in an 8-8 tie, we realized the stress was getting to us. Two points in four games is no tragedy—I'd known worse runs of results in Toronto—but this was a club that had reached the Stanley Cup semifinals in successive seasons. Expectations were higher.

For me, the next game was an emotional affair. I returned to Maple Leaf Gardens for the first time as a player on the opposing team. I could never have imagined using the other dressing room, or changing into a red jersey, not a blue and white one. It all felt very strange.

Jacques Demers hadn't used me in our preseason game against the Maple Leafs: he knew John Brophy, he despised the man and his methods, and he didn't want anything to happen to me. "I'm not going to risk that idiot getting someone from his farm team to thrash you or target your knees," he said. Yet he had nothing against playing hard. The Red Wings' Bob Probert and Joey Kocur were much-feared bruisers, and Kris King wasn't far behind. But they fought with guys in their own weight class; you would never see them leaping over the boards with the intention of ending an opponent's season.

The game that faced me now was a tough situation. I wasn't expecting the warmest of welcomes from Toronto, which made me more nervous still. Brophy was popular with more traditionalist fans. And as I expected, my every contact with the puck was accompanied by booing from the stands.

Early in the final period, we were down 3-1. But fortunately for us, Adam Graves then scored his first NHL goal, and I tied it up 37 seconds later. I jumped for joy, about three feet into the air. In the end, we managed to turn the game around, coming out of it 5-3 winners.

We flew to Toronto for the second time on December 10. By then, the Maple Leafs were bogged down in another crisis, having lost five games in a row. It was being said that if they didn't improve by Christmas, John Brophy would be out. There would be no improvement. We swept them away 8-2, and I scored two of the goals. As I passed the Toronto bench after the final buzzer, I raised my middle finger to their coach.

As you can imagine, I felt enormous satisfaction.

That time, the mood that greeted me in the arena was different. A few fans even raised banners that thanked me for what I'd done for the Leafs.

I enjoyed being interviewed by the press afterward. "I hope Christmas comes early for him this year," I told them, referring to Harold Ballard's ultimatum. "Toronto is a great city and the people deserve a better coach behind the bench. Hopefully, I helped the people upstairs in the office at Maple Leafs Gardens reach a decision to fire Brophy. He deserves it and if I helped make it happen, good."

It was customary for a player who had scored against his former club to be moderate in his statements. He would limit himself to a few phrases about how hard it had been for him and how the two points were all that mattered. Nor would he overdo any celebrations. But I had no pity for Brophy. He'd had none for me. I never wished dismissal on anyone—we can't know what tomorrow will bring—but with Brophy, it was different. "He's the worst human being in the world I've ever met," I went on to tell the press. "And I knew a lot of communists in Czechoslovakia."

As I'd come to expect from him, Brophy retorted that he had no interest in the prattle of a commie.

By the time the week was out, the Leafs had given Brophy his pink slip. Twenty defeats in 33 games were too much even for Ballard, whose admiration for Brophy's old-school ways wasn't boundless after all. My joy at his firing was tempered by irritation—I'd left Toronto for the sake of a coach who had lasted two and a half months of the new season … What had been the point?

Brophy never worked in the NHL again. He went off to the East Coast Hockey League, where he probably belonged, and where his old-fashioned approach to hockey was far more appropriate. In 13 seasons there, he won the title three times and became a highly respected figure. Today, the trophy for the best ECHL coach bears his name.

———

With Brophy's dismissal, I was finally able to close the books on my time in Toronto. It was done with, once and for all. And now I had more important matters on my plate. Not least, my own future in hockey.

My promising start with the Red Wings began to crumble in a November game against the Philadelphia Flyers. With the score at 3-3 in the last minute, I came back to prevent speeding forward Murray Craven from shooting. The blade of my stick caught him on the shoulder before slipping behind his face shield and hitting him in the eye.

I'd cut Craven up good and proper. There was a lot of blood; it wasn't looking good. I glanced to my left and saw everyone on the Flyers bench leap onto the ice. When I looked right, I saw that my teammates, too, were up for the fight.

But the brawl was the least of it.

The NHL placed me under suspension, effective immediately, and I was summoned to a disciplinary hearing with the vice president of the league. Coach Jacques Demers and general manager Jimmy Devellano flew to New York with me, keen to assure me that I'd get off with a light punishment. "Two, three games at most, and maybe a fine on top," they said.

Way off the mark! The league dished out a 10-game ban. When the verdict was read out, I gasped—this was well in excess of what anyone had expected. Our arguments that I'd had no intention of striking an opponent's head, and that in seven years in the league I'd never before been disciplined, fell on deaf ears. Ten games was a real stretch. It was my bad luck to be maybe the fourth player that season to have caused trouble with his stick. My punishment was to make an example of me.

It couldn't have come at a worse time. I was rediscovering my mojo in Detroit, and now I'd be out of action for almost a month. Worse still, the team flew off on a 10-day road trip, so I couldn't even get on the ice. I had to keep in shape by running and playing tennis. My rhythm was broken; and once my suspension was served, I found I couldn't get it back.

I felt like I was on a broken carousel. I'd play well in one game and poorly in the next two. And so it went. Jacques Demers calmed me down by telling me to relax, I'd soon get over it. He gave me plenty of ice time; he didn't lose faith in me. But nothing helped. Probably the biggest mistake I made was wanting it too much. I longed to show that I was still good enough for the NHL, to convince people that my last two seasons had been poor only because of injury and John Brophy.

Maybe I'd have gotten through it if the whole team hadn't gone into a meltdown. We lost six of our last eight games of the calendar year. It was plain that changes were on the way: such an ambitious team couldn't get through a crisis by hoping for better tomorrows.

Management decided to let four players go—and I was among them. On January 3, 1989, the Red Wings placed me on waivers, which meant that for the next 24 hours, other clubs had the chance to take me for free. If no one chose me, I would have to join the farm team in Adirondack.

Jacques Demers invited me into his office. He was even sadder about all this than I was. As we sat opposite each other, neither of us felt like talking.

"I'm truly sorry, Mirko, but there's nothing I can do."

"I get it, I know how the business goes," I said, trying to make him feel better. "You've nothing to apologize for."

It was hard to say goodbye. I went to the dressing room to pack my things. Then I went home to await my fate.

I didn't believe another club would take me. My performances had been uneven; I'd struggled. Who would want me, and if so, why? I was reconciled to the idea of dropping down to the AHL. Maybe it would give me the kind of boost I'd gotten seven years earlier in Fredericton, I thought, trying to console myself. Maybe I'd rediscover my form in Adirondack, then give it a try elsewhere in the summer.

For the first time, it crossed my mind that I might return to Europe.

All that day, I sat by the phone, waiting for news. Would I be flying off somewhere tomorrow? If so, where to? The call came at five in the afternoon. The voice on the line belonged to Demers, and he sounded delighted. "We've traded you to the Edmonton Oilers! Good luck!"

I couldn't believe it. Moments earlier, I'd had one foot on the farm team. Now I was expected in the dressing room of the Stanley Cup champions! Depression turned to euphoria.

General manager and coach Glen Sather took me for a 10th-round pick in the entry draft—about the price of a pack of hockey sticks. But I knew he didn't want me just to make up the numbers on the roster. It was well known that he placed a lot of trust in Europeans. Two years earlier, the Oilers had obtained Kent Nilsson and Reijo Ruotsalainen, whose exploits in the playoffs had helped the team to the Stanley Cup. Now, I was to play the experienced European wild card.

I boarded a plane to Canada early the next morning. As I waited for my connecting flight, I bought a copy of the *Toronto Sun*, which contained an article about my trade, with a photo. It was the one taken three years earlier after the memorable shootout with Wayne Gretzky and co. This time, however, the four pucks in my hands bore not only the logo of the Toronto Maple Leafs but of all four clubs on my NHL CV—the Nordiques, the Leafs, the Red Wings and the Oilers.

The Albertan prairie welcomed me to the cold Canadian winter. The temperature in Edmonton was about minus 30. By the time I crossed the street from the hotel to the Northlands Coliseum, I was frozen solid. What's more, I was about to play my first game.

Glen Sather invited me into his office, where he wanted to know if my move had gone smoothly and everything was as it should be. I nodded. He said he was pleased to have taken me on and hoped I would enjoy my time in Edmonton. The usual polite formalities. I couldn't stop myself from asking about tactics and the role I would play that evening. He smiled and told me not to worry. "Just play hockey," he said.

He put me on a line with Mark Messier and Glenn Anderson. This was quite a leap. Two superstars and brilliant forwards who had been playing together for eight years. Naturally, I was keen not to spoil things for them. I thought it best to ask them about the offensive zone entry they expected of me, and how we would work the power plays. Messier's answer reminded me of Sather's from earlier: "Just skate and keep your stick on the ice."

This was classic Mark. Always keep things simple. As I soon found out, as well as being an outstanding player and leader, he was a great guy. Modest and true to himself—something most leading athletes have in common. They have nothing to prove to anyone; their behavior is normal and not showy. It's the people without talent who tend to put on airs for others. Later, in Europe, I would meet many mediocre Canadian players with more cockiness than Mark Messier and Steve Yzerman put together.

That evening we were due to play the Quebec Nordiques, my first NHL club. Although the team had changed a lot in the past seven years, Peter and Anton were still there. We wished each other the best of luck.

As I listened to the Canadian national anthem before the game, all kinds of thoughts rushed through my mind. I remembered my early days with the Nordiques. How long ago they seemed! I'd been a kid, fresh from my flight from Czechoslovakia, startled by everything. And now the newspapers wrote about me as a "veteran." I was wearing an Oilers jersey, having just been given maybe my last chance to achieve something big in the NHL. With a coach and great players who had won the Stanley Cup in four of the last five years. It occurred to me, too, that only yesterday I'd been sitting on my luggage in Detroit, and that I'd slept for barely four hours.

The tension soon fell away from me—thanks to the best of all medicines. I scored a goal. There was an element of luck involved—during a power play, I knocked the puck out of the air and it ended up in the net—but they all count. It was a good debut. We beat the Nordiques 4-2, and my optimism came flooding back.

This could be the perfect place for me, I thought.

Every player who gets traded to another team in the middle of the NHL season goes through some upheaval in his personal life. It's not enough to pack a shoulder bag, grab a hockey stick, take a taxi to the airport, and pitch a tent at your new place of work. A lot of things must be dealt with in a hurry—above all, moving yourself and your family, say, a thousand miles away.

Things dragged on in Edmonton. Because the moving truck with all our belongings froze up in the middle of Saskatchewan, I had to stay in a hotel longer than was pleasant for me. Another victory over technology for Canada's harsh winter. When our things arrived at last, we found a little house not far from Esa Tikkanen's place, and we started to settle in.

But I acclimatized rapidly to the Oilers. It was a great group of guys, and the mood was relaxed. There was a table-tennis table in the middle of the dressing room, and loud music would play up to 10 minutes before we went out on the ice. Glen Sather would switch off the cassette player before giving us a few words of encouragement: "Let's go get them!" He wasn't one for long motivational speeches. With a team filled with champions, maybe he had no need of them. He did his main job during practice and on the bench. Coaching was his strongest suit. He had a special feel for formations, and he was a great improviser; he knew precisely when to change the lineup or the tactics.

He put me on the penalty kill, too—an important sign of trust. I hadn't done many of those in Toronto. Glen was taking the European path; for him, penalty kills provided work for good skaters and skilled puckhandlers as well as dogged defensemen. He looked to Europe for all kinds of things. He was open to new ideas, not limited by what he'd learned 20 years earlier. For this reason, the gym in Edmonton was much better equipped than the one in Toronto, and great emphasis was placed on rehabilitation. The Oilers had their own masseurs and physios—player care was top-class. If a team wants to be a winner, it must get its injured players fully fit and back on the ice as soon as possible, Sather maintained.

My arrival in Edmonton came five months after the most famous trade in NHL history. In August 1988, Wayne Gretzky, Mike Krushelnyski and Marty McSorley were traded to the Los Angeles Kings for Jimmy Carson, Martin Gélinas, three first-round draft picks and $15 million. For Canada, this was like a lightning strike. The event of the decade. A lot was written about it. One of the prevalent views was that the Oilers were in for some hard times: the absence of number 99—the heart of the team—would leave a great, gaping hole, depriving the club of 80 percent of its success, and so on.

Such comments weren't really fair. As I looked around the team, I didn't have the feeling we were living in the post-Gretzky age. Yes, the greatest player in history had left, but the backbone of the successful team remained. On the roster, one great name followed another: Grant Fuhr still kept goal; the defense was still built around Kevin Lowe and Charlie Huddy; the goals still came from forwards like Mark Messier, Jari Kurri, Esa Tikkanen, Glenn Anderson and Craig Simpson. I saw how keen they were to prove that the Oilers hadn't been just "Gretzky and the others," and how desperate they were to win the Stanley Cup without him.

I would have a role to play in this, on a line with Messier and Anderson. Here I played my first game, and here I would remain. To play with these guys was an amazing experience. Both great players, today they are both members of the Hockey Hall of Fame. After years of "chase the puck," how I now enjoyed the rapid skating style and simple combination play of these guys! We were in constant motion, playing passes thick and fast. Three quick strokes and before you knew it, you were celebrating. Wonderful.

I was loving every minute of my hockey, and the mood on the team was brilliant. All was as it should it be. In Edmonton, I'd found my paradise.

Unfortunately, my happiness lasted just a month. Then came a game in Los Angeles where a body check sent me flying and landed me on my behind. An ordinary battle—there are dozens of them in every game. But this one had big consequences for my career. The pain was so excruciating, I knew right away that I had a big problem.

For a week, I gritted my teeth and tried to work through it. I played four games, but I couldn't manage a fifth. I couldn't skate properly—every step was misery.

Diagnosis: cracked tailbone. My injury curse had struck again! The bone I'd fractured was probably the most useless one in the body. But it hurt so much, I could hardly put one foot in front of the other.

The doctors and physios did what they could. They cared for me with incredible dedication. Under their supervision, I rode an exercise bike with a cushion under my behind, did weights, and jogged in the pool. There were times when I was incapable of getting out of bed; only after I called the doctors for a sedative injection and help with stretching did the pain become more bearable.

There was no quick road to recovery. Nothing would help me but rest and patience. The slight hope that I'd be back on the ice for the playoffs receded week by week, until it disappeared altogether. I was forced to accept that my season was over.

Although I found sitting uncomfortable, the fractured tailbone was more painful still when I was standing. As a result, I practically gave up going to games. Only once the playoffs started did I turn up to cheer on the guys. I wanted to experience—from a distance at least—what I'd missed out on in previous seasons. The quest for the Cup.

In the first round, we came up against the Los Angeles Kings, a series that attracted a lot of attention and excitement because of Wayne Gretzky. The guys got off to a great start. After we won three of the first four games, I was convinced we had one foot in the division final; an experienced team rarely surrendered such a lead.

But it can happen. In the dressing room before the next game, I remember someone saying: "Did you see Gretz? He's got that look of his." I didn't know what they were talking about. I knew Gretzky as an opponent, I'd played on the same team as him in the All-Star Game, we'd met in bars, but what was that look of his? It meant nothing to me. Only later did I understand. It was the look of a hunter. The look of a man with a great desire to win.

Suddenly, Wayne was all over the ice. It was mainly thanks to his amazing performance that the Kings turned the series around, winning it 4-3. And that was the end of my very strange season.

———

The Oilers had the option to keep me under contract for another year. I parted from Glen Sather after the playoff defeat knowing he was still counting on me. See you at training camp in September, he'd told me. But on the flight over to Germany, I began to wonder if I truly wished to return to the NHL. Did I really still want to work myself like a mule over the summer?

The body wasn't the problem. I'd rested up for a month, and my tailbone had healed. It was my head that was against the idea.

Each return from injury is harder than the last; every break from playing deals a blow to the psyche. And after the last one, something in me had broken. My frustration and bitterness from the past three seasons had come to a head and were about to boil over. I was mad at myself. Try as I might, I couldn't get my career back on track. I'd played just 104 times in the past three years, having been forced to sit out almost 60 percent of the games. For someone who could play hockey all day every day, this was close to torture. I'd been through two trades, several injuries, my own private war with John Brophy, a suspension for an unlucky infraction …

My disenchantment was stronger than my desire to continue. The NHL had once been my great dream. Now I felt that the flame within me was going out. There was nothing I wanted to keep going for.

Besides, over the summer a number of bids were made for me—from Germany, Switzerland and Italy. With 415 NHL games to my name, it wouldn't be difficult for me to get a contract in Europe. One of the offers was from Freiburg, where my father had coached the juniors, and where we had bought a house a few years earlier. It didn't take me long to decide to join up.

By then, I'd stopped thinking of myself as a National Hockey League player.

All I needed to do was arrange the termination of my contract with the Oilers. Sather wasn't keen to let me go. We spoke on the phone and sent faxes back and forth—I remained adamant in my choice. He urged me to get back on track and come to camp; as an experienced player, he still wanted me for when the going got tough. "I'm sorry, Glen, but I've simply had enough," I replied. "I won't be coming back. I forced myself to carry on for the past two years, and it came to nothing. I really don't think I can do it anymore."

Above all, it was clear to me that after a season in which I'd been mainly a spectator, my place on the team wasn't guaranteed. At the age of 30, and with a long career in the NHL behind me, I didn't want to fight for my place.

My discussions with Sather dragged on. Just a week before the start of the Bundesliga season, he gave me his consent, on condition that if I was in good shape when the German season ended, he would call on me for the playoffs. He'd tried this before, with Jaroslav Pouzar, and it had worked. And he really did call in spring 1990. Still I said no.

For a long time, I tried to persuade myself that I did the right thing in leaving for Freiburg. Now I know I was kidding myself. When deciding what to do next, I talked myself into believing that because I'd had a fine career in the NHL, playing alongside legends and making my mark, I should have no regrets; I just wasn't meant to carry on.

This was a lie. I should have given it another try. I should have bitten the bullet one last time by getting myself in shape that summer and returning to Canada—on my own, if need be—to fight for my place. Edmonton was worth it. But as it is with my mother, so it is with me—either/or. Having said goodbye to the NHL, I was going to stick with my decision.

Today it drives me crazy that I decided as I did. I have very few regrets in life: this is one of a handful of things I would change if I could. Those last seasons overseas are a blot on my CV as a hockey player, and I turned down the chance to keep my NHL career alive. The regret will stay with me always.

Not least as the Oilers ended that season by winning the Stanley Cup.

19

Old Men

THE NHL IS THE BEST hockey league in the world. *The Show*. With its fascinating history, legendary players, jam-packed arenas, and the enormous publicity and hype around it, it is in a league of its own. Once you leave it, you'll never find anything to compare. You'll forever be aware that you're playing at a lower level—whether in Sweden, Italy or wherever. And the longer you played in the NHL, the stronger this sense is.

I knew all this when I signed with EHC Freiburg. I wasn't there to fight for titles or individual awards, nor to prove what kind of player I was. I had a single aim—to enjoy playing hockey.

Freiburg was nothing new for me. Several times I'd trained with the team in summer, and I had friends in the city I played soccer and tennis with. Club president Hans-Georg Kouba was a friend of the family. Besides, my parents had applied for German citizenship, and I was thinking of settling in West Germany once my hockey-playing days were over. That's why I'd bought a house there for myself, too. In summer 1989, none of us had so much as an inkling that communism in Czechoslovakia had just a few months left to live.

There was another matter that made Freiburg an ideal fit for me: Ivan Hlinka had just become the club's coach. Our story had run the gamut—he'd been my idol, then my opponent, my teammate and my friend, and now he was going to be my coach.

Freiburg was Ivan's second post as head coach, after Litvinov, and he felt right at home among all the Czechs Kouba had brought in. Apart from me, there was Jiri Crha, Milan Chalupa, Slava Duris, Jiri Smicek and Tomas Dolak. Most of us were former teammates of Ivan's.

The composition of the team was less than perfect, however. We had a few good players, but the rest were pretty average. From the beginning, Ivan, being used to a higher standard, found this hard to deal with. He refused to accept the inability of Bundesliga players to control the puck and make sharp passes. Sometimes he would hit the roof in practice. "Get going, Frigo!" he would yell at me, and I'd skate down the right wing. The pass he played to me would make my arms vibrate. "That's how you do it!" he would shout, turning to the rest of the team. "Straight to the stick. Next!" A German kid would skate down the wing, and the ferocity of Ivan's pass would send the stick flying from his hands … Ivan would shake his head—it was hopeless.

Otherwise, though, I think Ivan liked it in Freiburg. In summer he'd play soccer with us, and sometimes we'd go for a beer together. As ever, his good mood was contagious. I enjoyed every day I spent in his company.

Sadly, there weren't many of them. EHC went from one defeat to the next. After 14 games, all we'd managed was two ties. After a 15-3 thrashing by EV Rosenheim in early November, Ivan resigned his position and went back to Litvinov.

I regret not having done more to help him. But I had no way to do so. I didn't play a single competitive game under him.

Maybe I really was cursed. In the last preseason game, against Krylya Sovetov, as I tried a deke, a Russian defenseman's knee struck my thigh. I limped off to the bench. Everyone assumed it was a classic charley horse and the pain would soon wear off. But the leg got worse and worse. After a few days, it was looking pretty black. At this point, Kouba, a surgeon by profession, got involved. He sent me to the clinic, where it was established that I had a burst blood vessel that required surgery. The doctors removed a large number of blood clots from my leg. A trivial injury I'd expected to keep me out for two weeks maximum turned into a two-month layoff.

Although EHC Freiburg was a professional club, it was amateurish in many ways. To start with, we didn't have a doctor of our own to take care of us on a day-to-day basis. Had we had one, I would have been spared this problem. We played games with hospital doctors in attendance; if someone got injured, Kouba would take him to his own doctor's office, or send him to a doctor friend of his. The club didn't even have a sport manager—Kouba covered this function, too. If need be, he even acted as coach. He was crazy about hockey. He took care of every side of the business, even pumping in his own money. If not for him, the club would have gone under.

After Ivan's departure, Kouba coached us for three games, all of which we lost. It was clear he would have to find a coach willing to take on the team at the bottom of the league—a team that had only two points in 17 games.

He made my father an offer. Now coach of the Freiburg youth teams, Dad had experience coaching the first team. But he wasn't keen on a return to the bench. I wasn't too excited by the idea either. This was very different from the situation we had found ourselves in at Vitkovice many years earlier. Even when I wasn't injured, it was clear to me that my best days were behind me. The club had high hopes for me, the newspapers wrote about me as a star of the NHL, but I knew I was a shadow of the player I'd been a few seasons back. And I didn't want Dad to sully the good name he had made for himself in German hockey because of my subpar performances.

For two days and two nights, Dad and I went over all the pros and cons. In the end, he agreed to take it. For one thing, he didn't want to let the club down; for another, he felt a debt of gratitude to Kouba, who had helped him a great deal in the months following his emigration.

He took charge of the team on November 26, 1989. I returned to the ice shortly afterward. I'd gained weight since September, and it took me three weeks to get back into shape. It was a while before I was happy with my game.

But the team remained at rock bottom. Anyone expecting things to improve after a few games with the new coach must have been very disappointed. There was nothing for us to draw on. The club didn't have the money for major reinforcements. And we players, experienced and holders of enviable CVs though some of us were, lacked the wherewithal to turn things around.

The fact of the matter was, we were simply past our hockey-playing prime. Crha was a good goalie, but at 40 he was more interested in his business than his duties on the ice. He thought nothing of flying off midseason to a business meeting in Canada … Dolak, Duris and Chalupa were all over 35, and I was no spring chicken either. We were old men, tired and battered from our many years as professional hockey players. Each of us marched to his own tune. Above all, our priorities weren't what they had been when we were younger.

Besides, the Bundesliga was a pretty good league. There was a strong Canadian influence—the hockey was fast and powerful. And there were some interesting sums of money in it. I ended up earning more than I did in the NHL—the figure in my contract was pretaxed. It was common for players from overseas to have their accommodation and car paid for. Players who in North America had peaked on a farm team or in the university league must have thought themselves in paradise. Murray Heatley, for instance, became a popular player in Germany; his son Dany, born in Freiburg, went on to become a 50-goal-a-season sharpshooter in the NHL. At home, Murray had scratched out a living in the minor leagues. In Germany, he became a title-winner and much-admired goal scorer, and he was chosen for the All-Star Team.

With our approach, we were no match for young Canadians with a big point to prove.

Dad's spell as coach ended two games before the end of the regular season. With us still in last place, the leadership decided that a new coach should take the team into the relegation round. They placed their trust in Canadian Mike Zettel. We saved ourselves by the skin of our teeth, five minutes before the end of the last game. We were fighting ESV Kaufbeuren for second place in the standing, and we needed to beat them. In the final period, we completed a glorious comeback from 4-1 behind. Thank God.

This indifferent season was far more stressful than I'd imagined it would be. But there was no reason for me to leave. I'd discovered that the Bundesliga suited me very well. As we played only two games a week, my body wasn't subject to the stresses and strains of the NHL. The distances we traveled weren't great, and the atmosphere was wonderful everywhere we went. Although the stadiums were smaller than in Canada, German fans kept the volume up for the full 60 minutes, as they were used to doing at soccer and handball games.

In my second season, I managed 18 goals and 23 assists in 33 games, making me the club's top scorer. We did a little better: we finished third from the bottom in the regular season, above Dynamo Berlin and Dynamo Weisswasser, teams from the East that had joined the Bundesliga before the unification of Germany. We didn't avoid the relegation round, but again we came through it successfully.

Freiburg had a strong Czech contingent when I arrived, and with the raising of the Iron Curtain, Czech practically became the official language of the dressing room. Kouba continued to rope in reinforcements from his former home. Because the number of foreigners was restricted, he was especially interested in players able to get a German passport quickly. Grandmothers and mothers-in-law from the former Sudetenland started going through their family trees. As a result, summer 1990 saw the arrival of Martin Reichel, Pavel Mann, Petr Gulda, Pavel Gross and Eduard Uvira. We joked that anyone who once had his photo taken with a German shepherd dog was eligible for citizenship.

My old pal from Toronto, Peter Ihnacak, transferred to us from Munich, plus there were two Poles on our team. Foreigners made up two-thirds of the roster, forcing the Germans into the corner of the dressing room. We were a strange eastern European mix, ranging in age from teens to 40s. Some of us were in the twilight of our career, for others Freiburg would be its pinnacle, for others it was a stepping stone to a better club.

For a while, we attracted a lot of interest. Newspapers exaggerated the case by referring to us as the Sparta Prague farm team. But it soon became clear that even this model was no guarantee of great results. Maybe there were just too many Czechs on the team, as would later be the case with the Pittsburgh Penguins and the Moskitos Essen. We think up all kinds of nonsense and get carried away.

But I can't say that we didn't have a good time away from the ice. After games, we'd go for a beer. Or more likely several beers. This didn't add to our popularity. Germans demand that foreigners are the team's stars; they have come for the money, so they should carry the team. Our coterie of Czechs didn't see things in these terms. As we were having a good time, we couldn't care less if someone saw us at midnight, ordering another round. We refused to adopt a mentality and set of standards different from ours. So when things went wrong, we took the flak. And Kouba took it with us. After a friendly game against HC Nitra, he announced that he had his eye on two 19-year-old forwards, Zigmund Palffy and Jozef Stumpel by name, and was considering a bid for them. The next day the press was full of it. This crackpot idea again? Were there so few Czechoslovaks on the team that he needed to buy more?

———

I didn't stay with Freiburg for a third season. My recent divorce, an unpleasant business, had cost me a lot of money and energy. I needed a change of scenery, I reasoned. My next port of call was Bruneck, a beautiful town in the German-speaking part of Italy.

It was love at first sight. Maybe I've become even more fond of South Tyrol than I am of Toronto. Its people are kind and easy to get along with, and there are wonderful views of the Alps from your window. The region is a precious coming-together of the best of each of Austria and Italy. The locals are very proud of being from *Südtirol*. It makes them different from other Italians, whom they imagine spending their days in idleness under the olive trees, while others (i.e., South Tyroleans) do the work for them.

The level of hockey in Serie A was lower than that of the Bundesliga, but I didn't mind. I'd come to Italy to finish my playing career, in the full knowledge that the ground beneath my feet was shifting.

I had no great ambitions for my time with EV Bruneck. Our squad was one of the weakest.

Although a few of our players had experience in Canadian hockey, we were no match for the richer clubs of the south. Media mogul and future prime minister Silvio Berlusconi was pouring money into the Milano Devils; a year before my arrival, he had found the sum needed to pay Jari Kurri. HC Varese and HC Milano, too, operated on big budgets. The Devils had Mark Napier; HC Milano had brought together my former teammates Bob Manno, Bill Stewart and John Chabot; and HC Varese had signed Tony McKegney and Jim Benning. I knew Benning very well from our time together in Toronto. (At the time of writing, he is general manager of the Vancouver Canucks.)

In Italy, these guys lived like kings. They earned more than they had in the NHL even though they played half the number of matches. And if, like Bob Manno and Frank Nigro, they took out dual citizenship, they became even bigger stars. Now they could play at the Olympics and the world championship.

The Italian season was special in that there were only 18 games in the regular season. We went on to play the same number of games in the newly established Alpenliga, in which we faced clubs from Italy, Austria and Slovenia. Our results were similar in both competitions. In Serie A, we were beaten heavily by the Milano Devils in the quarter-finals. In the Alpenliga, we finished ninth in our group.

Although I scored more than a few goals in Bruneck—28, to be precise—I played with gritted teeth the whole time. In the very second practice, I felt a pain in my back that would trouble me all season long. It was terrible. There were times I couldn't even get into my car, others when I'd spend an hour on the toilet because I couldn't lift myself from the seat until the cramp had subsided; my thighs would bear the blue imprints of my fingers, from all the trying and failing to stand up. There were even mornings when I couldn't get out of bed.

I was a shadow of the player who had been selected for the NHL All-Star Game and scored on the world's best goaltenders. To be able to play at least tolerably well, I had to stuff myself with pills and pain-killing suppositories. My behind was like a pincushion for injections— I'd be given the first shot before the opening period, another at each intermission, and the last as soon as the game ended. Without them, I'd have never made it onto the ice.

I knew I was done as a professional hockey player.

Once the season was over, I ended my time in Bruneck. In spring 1992, I returned to Germany—to Konigsbrunn near Augsburg, where Andrea, my second wife, came from. To keep myself occupied, I arranged to ply my trade for the local club in the third league. I managed no more than a few friendly games.

My back problems persisted, even though I now trained less. I sought expert opinions in Germany, Switzerland and Canada, but no one could give me an exact diagnosis, let alone rid me of the pain. In the end, a doctor in Stuttgart discovered in my lower back a crack of about 2.5 millimeters by 3.5 millimeters. It wasn't the result of a single blow but wear and tear sustained over a long period. If you keep bending an aluminum spoon, sooner or later it will break was how he explained it to me.

This small area bore eloquent witness to all the blows, falls, cross-checks to the back, and crashes into the boards I'd sustained over my career, plus all the tough games and practices I'd been through. Having started out as a professional hockey player at 16, I'd remained one for 16 years. Now I was being told that one more check could put me in a wheelchair.

The doctor suggested I undergo surgery. The crack could be filled with bone marrow and fused with bolts. I wanted to know if it offered any guarantee that the pain would go away once and for all. He shook his head. I decided the stakes were too high. Any procedure in the spinal area is risky and its outcome uncertain. I refused to take the chance.

So the story that had begun in the ice rink in Zagreb came to an end in a doctor's office in Germany. It was over. For good.

20

Coach

A HOCKEY PLAYER who can freely decide when to end his career is a privileged one indeed. One day he simply tells himself his time has come; he has nothing more to give or prove, and he has reached an age when he would like to try something else. He plays his last game before circling the rink and waving goodbye to the fans. If he has a medal around his neck or has just drunk champagne from a trophy, all the better.

This is the kind of departure I dreamed of. Ideally at Maple Leaf Gardens.

Unfortunately, my farewell was of a very different kind.

There's a huge difference between wanting to quit playing hockey and having to. Aged 33, it was hard for me to accept that my career was over—it was terribly early. I had no idea what I would do next. I felt empty.

A player must come to terms with the end of his career in his own way. Some miss the glory and adulation, and they end up playing in celebrity golf tournaments and doing well-paid autograph sessions. Living off their names, they continue to bask in the limelight. Such things never appealed to me. As a player, I considered spectators to be essential to my work. I was a gladiator whose job was to entertain; there was no hiding place for me in the crowd. Neither when I left the NHL nor when I stopped playing for good did I shed any tears over the fact that people had stopped patting me on the back.

The story of Dave Keon, who was recently named the best player in the history of the Maple Leafs, is a strange one. After his career ended, he moved to Florida, where he totally vanished from the scene and went into real estate; he refused to have anything to do with hockey for many years. Nor was this the way for me to go. Other players opened bars or invested in the stock market—neither of these were for me. I'm no barkeeper, and I have no head for business.

I often imagined that after my last game, I would put my feet up, light a cigarette, and from then a lead a life of leisure. But it's not that simple. Having been on the hockey-playing carousel from early childhood, you find out very quickly that you're going to miss it. Hockey is under your skin. I didn't miss the applause from the stands, the practices, travel and stress; I didn't even miss the adrenaline of playing. But I did miss the focus and fun of the dressing room.

I didn't wish to cut myself off from that world.

A few months into my retirement, my wife and I decided to move to Toronto, where a friend had offered me a job at his hockey school. I traveled from rink to rink, teaching kids how to skate, deke and pass. It was great. I know I wouldn't be able to coach youngsters at club level, day after day, season after season, because I lack the patience for it. But I enjoyed spending two hours a day on the ice. The work was undemanding, and I earned a little, too.

After a year and a half in Canada, my wife began to miss Europe. For a while we shuttled between continents. But when Mike was born, we had to make a choice. In his first 10 months of life, I reckon he flew over the ocean four times. We decided on Germany.

We were all packed up when the phone rang. My old friend Frantisek Cernik was on the line, wanting to know what I was doing now, and what my plans were. I told him we were returning to Europe. Did I fancy trying my hand as coach? he asked. HC Havirov was looking for a new one.

At first, I had my doubts. It was a pretty big leap from a kids' hockey school to the second Czech league. I talked the offer through with my father. He encouraged me to take it. "What do you have to lose?" he said. "The worst that can happen is you'll find out that coaching's not for you, and that'll be that."

On flying to Europe, I met with the Havirov management, and we discussed our ideas. Then we shook hands.

I became a coach in June 1994.

For my first practices, I referred to my father's old diaries, adding just a few drills of my own. Dad came along to the first sessions and watched carefully. Then we analyzed them together. What had I done well and what should I change? We had similar discussions after games. Dad's observations were as important to me then as 25 years earlier, when I was starting out as a player. One of his first pieces of advice was: "Never make a decision right after a game, when emotions are high. Sleep on it and deal with it the next day."

Havirov was pretty much the ideal place for my first coaching post. I was fortunate to have a great group of players, none of whom were playing in the second league because they were incapable of better. A few of the guys on the squad had played in the top league, and the younger ones were keen to get there. They were ambitious, and when they saw that I knew what I was talking about, they followed my instructions, gave their all, and put their bodies on the line. We played an exciting attacking game—we had the highest attendance in the league. And we were flying high in the standing. Not bad for starters.

As you know from earlier chapters, I wasn't the kind of player coaches loved unconditionally. I had a mind of my own. Told to turn right, I would turn left first. Some may have thought I was the last person who should be teaching discipline, responsibility and tactics. But I managed to adapt to my new role. If I'd lorded it over the others, I'd have fizzled out in a year, never to be heard of again. But I didn't flop—in fact, I took to coaching like a duck to water.

Perhaps my greatest advantage was my wealth of experience. I'd encountered many interesting coaches, and I'd learned a lot from them. In Czechoslovakia, I'd played under Ludek Bukac and Pavel Wohl—both experts and outstanding psychologists who were ahead of their time. In the NHL, I'd learned the most from Jacques Demers and Glen Sather. I thought often about these gentlemen, because a coach spends more time behind a desk than he does on the bench or leading practice. There he sits, at home or in the office, thinking up new drills, tinkering with the lineup, plotting tactics on a whiteboard. At such moments, I would be forever asking myself questions like "How the hell did Glen work his power plays?" and "What did Jacques used to say before a game?"

My experience of playing under John Brophy worked in my favor, too. Thanks to him, I had clear idea of the kind of coach I *didn't* want to be.

Unlike Brophy, I never humiliate players or psych them out; I never attack their dignity. I try to be positive and ensure the team keeps calm. It's my belief that if things are right in the dressing room, they are right on the ice, too. I prefer to take a friendly approach, and in this I take my inspiration from Ivan Hlinka. But players must know where the boundaries lie, of course. If they don't, things can go badly wrong. I've also learned to thump the desk and yell a bit, so they don't get the impression I'm nothing but a kindly uncle, and this is good for the group, too.

I don't do things that got on my nerves as a player. I always hated long speeches during intermission. Back in the dressing room, players need to drink, get their breath back, and exchange a few words before the next period, not listen to a coach give a sermon on the system. Long speeches at this time are counterproductive—players can listen for five minutes max before their brains stop taking in even the most well-reasoned words. Also in the dressing room, I never berate a player in front of the others. I prefer to speak in general terms, but in such a way that the player in question knows I mean him. Failing this, I take him to one side and vent my grievance in his company only.

I don't doubt that I made a lot of mistakes at Havirov. But they helped me progress as a coach: I learned what it takes to do the job while I was doing it. For the first time, I had more than just myself to worry about. Now I was responsible for 20 others, each with his own ego and temperament. To create a well-oiled team, I needed to learn psychology.

I had to discover within myself a tact and sensitivity for many things above and beyond the game—what Germans call *Fingerspitzengefühl.*

In the early days, I found it difficult to let a player go. In the past, my decisions had affected me only, and now I was required to tell a young man he had no place on my team. I thought back to my time in the NHL, and how the general managers had done this at the training camps—with tact, so that feelings weren't hurt. So I explained to the young man that he was basically one of the best players, but he needed more room to breathe; for his continued development, a season in the third league would be ideal. Work hard on yourself and your time will come, I told him.

I know I'm no Scotty Bowman. But I'll venture to say that most players I have coached appreciated my humane approach and my fairness. I'm still in touch with many of them—from Czechia and elsewhere; I have become friends with some of them. In my eyes, such a distinction is worth as much as a winner's medal.

———

I was extremely happy at Havirov. I liked the way that everything ran smoothly, and I learned many new things. Yet I lasted only 15 games. Because at the beginning of November I received an offer I couldn't refuse.

From Vitkovice.

The club leadership had just dismissed Alois Hadamczik and promoted Vladimir Stransky from the juniors in his place. I knew Stransky well—he was a former teammate of mine and a member of 1981 Czechoslovak championship-winning side. I was offered a place alongside him. As Vladimir had an A coaching license, he was officially the head coach, although I had the main responsibility for the team from the start; I led practice, and I coached from the bench.

I was returning to Vitkovice and the top league after an absence of 13 years, but I didn't need many weeks to feel myself to be in familiar surroundings. Hockey still had the same people in it, albeit in some cases in different positions; former teammates and opponents were now coaches and managers.

I paid more attention to other things that had changed. Above all, there was the money. The communists had poured vast sums into the sport—I can't deny them that, no matter how much I despise them. We'd often taken a plane to games in Kosice or Prague, money being no object. But now, every expense was anxiously scrutinized. The behavior of the players was a far more pleasant change. The new generation wasn't backward in coming forward, and I liked this self-confidence. I've never had much time for the type you put in the corner only to find them still there a week later. I preferred the kind of son of a bitch I'd once been myself.

The first games at Vitkovice were great. In 1994, the NHL announced a lockout, so many guys returned home from overseas, immediately raising the level of competition. We were strengthened by the arrival of Richard Smehlik from the Buffalo Sabres and Vladimir Vujtek Jr. from the Edmonton Oilers. Our game against Jaromir Jagr's HC Kladno was a sellout. It was amazing.

But before long, I became disenchanted with the Czech Extraliga. The group at Vitkovice wasn't as tight as the one at Havirov. Besides, my suspicion that there was something rotten in Czech hockey became ever stronger. Not every result was decided on the ice, it seemed to me. A player would score and not celebrate the goal, if you know what I mean. Anyone who has been in the game for a quarter of a century knows when a team is playing at full throttle, just as he knows when what he sees is bad theater. Unfortunately, I can say no more about this even 20 years later. I have no proof, just a firm conviction.

After a few games like this, I'd had enough. I wasn't prepared to stand powerless by the bench and have others make a fool of me; I wasn't so attached to the position of Extraliga coach. Fortunately, back in the HC Havirov had heard of my disquiet, and in January the owners of that club asked me if I'd like to come back. They would sort something out with Vitkovice. I was happy to agree.

At Havirov, things took a turn for the better for me. Having reached the playoffs no problem, we advanced to the semifinals, in which we played a tense series against Kometa Brno in the hope of promotion to the Extraliga. Although we fell to them 3-0, I was satisfied with my first season as a coach.

We approached the next season with the same ambition. But the idyll of the previous year was over. I would turn up for practice to learn that since yesterday I'd lost one player and gained two. This was because Havirov had made agreements with a number of Extraliga clubs to take players on loan who needed game practice, sometimes as part of their comeback from injury. One of those who appeared at Havirov in this way was Petr Cajanek, then 20 years old, who would become an outstanding player, a world champion and a mainstay of the St. Louis Blues. But we had him for just three games before he went back to AC Zlin. What was the point? This was happening more and more. All the comings and goings were a major distraction in my work.

We couldn't repeat the feat of reaching the semis. In fact, we went out in the very first round, against HC Pisek—mainly thanks to their Ales Kratoska, an outstanding forward who scored six goals and one assist in the deciding game. This 9-3 quarterfinals defeat marked the end of my first contract as a head coach.

———

In the years leading up to this, I'd vacationed in Bruneck at every opportunity. During the time I was a player there, I'd made a lot of friends, and I remained as enchanted by South Tyrol as ever. To my surprise, in summer 1996 I was given a chance to spend a second year there.

The club was looking for a new coach, and they made me an offer. No sooner was the question asked than I accepted the job. I didn't need to think twice. I jumped into my first coaching contract abroad with both feet, so beginning my travel around non-traditional hockey countries.

The team was led by a really nice guy who didn't interfere with my work. Every coach's dream. "I don't understand hockey, so I employ people who do," he would say. We succeeded in putting together a good team, from mainly local players. Some of these guys I had played with, plus I promoted a few good youngsters from the juniors. We finished fifth, missing advancement to the semifinals by a single point. For a club the size of ours, this had to be considered a success.

The next year things started to go wrong, unfortunately. The management changed, and with it the atmosphere at the club. When at season's end I was offered the chance to coach HC Merano, I was glad to change my place of employment without having to leave South Tyrol.

After we shook hands on my new deal, I left for a vacation in the Czech Republic.

But in the middle of the summer, I received a call from the club president. Merano had had a change of heart—their new coach would be some Canadian guy, not me. I found out later that someone from the old management of EV Bruneck had blackened my name. No, not because of the alcohol. It was no secret that I liked a drink after a game. *Frycer ist ein guter Trainer, aber er trinkt*, was the word on the street. A drinker but a good coach nonetheless. There must have been something else that bothered them.

I was out of work and that was that. I decided to take a little break.

A month later, the club president called back. The Canadian had turned out to be a real bust—he'd wanted the players to write poems at home about why they liked hockey. After the dressing room turned against him, Merano decided to get back to me. Could we let bygones be bygones? I had no problem with that. Business is business. I got into my car in Ostrava and hurried down to Italy.

If my time at Havirov could be considered my high school graduation, those first months at Merano were like studying at university.

The Canadian had left quite a mess behind. On top of this, for the 1998-99 season the quota of foreign players had risen to 12, so I was up to my eyes in work. First and foremost, I needed to craft a team of disparate parts into a functioning organism. It was a Babylon of seven nations: we had Karel Metelka (son of a former coach of mine at Vitkovice), Italians from different regions of the country who didn't always get on, a Finn, a Swede, two Americans, two Russians, plus anglophone and francophone Canadians who weren't bosom buddies either.

But I managed to make them into a team where every player worked for the others. We'd go out together after games for pizza, and the cliques gradually disappeared.

I succeeded in convincing them that on the subject of hockey, I knew what I was talking about. Canadians who play in Europe don't have the best reputation, but I had to give these guys one thing: when they realized what kind of career I'd had, they treated me with respect. Whereas several of them had failed to make it beyond the farm team, I'd played eight seasons in the NHL. This made my work a lot easier.

The only one I had any real trouble with was a kid called Ryan Duthie. He was a good player—the Calgary Flames had taken him in the fourth round of the entry draft, he'd played in Finland, and he'd represented the Canadian national team. But he sometimes lost his judgment. On the ice, he did as he pleased, believing himself to be the best. Once he made me so mad that I threw him out of the dressing room and dropped him from the team for the next game. "Once you realize how you're supposed to play, you can come down from the stands," I told him.

He was mad at me for several days. He refused to greet me, looked daggers at me; given the chance, he might have killed me. But sometimes a coach must make a stand. In this case, I was making it clear that if our top player was behaving like a prima donna, I was prepared to drop him for the sake of the team.

Having left Duthie to stew for a while, I put him back on the team for a league game. It was very plain how keen he was to prove himself the best. He put in a brilliant, problem-free performance.

Although we went through to the playoffs in second place, no one gave us much of a chance. HC Bolzano and SG Cortina were the favorites. We met the latter in the semifinals. What a battle it was! As there were problems with Cortina's stadium, we played the deciding game in Milan. And we came out winners. Åke Lilljebjorn made a number of brilliant saves. A good goaltender is crucial in every playoff game, regardless of whether it's the Stanley Cup or the Italian league. Without a good goalie, you don't stand a chance. And Åke wasn't just any old goalie. With the Swedish national team, he'd won a world championship in 1987 as well as played in the Canada Cup; indeed, he'd had a good career altogether. He may have been 37 by then, but he still had it.

The trip home from Milan was unforgettable. At every gas station we stopped, our escort of fans bought us wine, salami and sandwiches. No one would have believed how crazy the Italians could be about hockey. They celebrated our victory to the full. When we got back to Merano, half of the team practically fell out of the bus. Fortunately, there was enough time for them to shake off their hangovers—the final was in four days' time.

We would be battling Bolzano—Merano's greatest rival—for the title. South Tyrolean rivalries are always spicy, especially in the playoffs. Having brought in some more Canadians at the last moment, Bolzano fancied their chances against us. But we were all over them, winning the series 3-0. The cup was ours! It was an incredible feeling. We'd lost just one game in the playoffs; otherwise we'd always been on top. Luck played a part, too, of course. We'd turned a few games around in the closing stages, and we'd been helped by the odd fortuitous goal. The last game of the final series was decided by Jari Torkki in overtime. But even the greatest champions need a slice of luck.

As the final buzzer sounded, I could still hardly believe we'd done it. This was my first title as a coach, and only the second of my hockey career. It had been a long wait—18 years. My six-year-old son, Mike, joined our celebrations on the ice in Bolzano. He was wearing a Maple Leafs jersey, which made me happier still.

A champion's euphoria is a beautiful thing in every town, in every country. And those Merano celebrations were quite something! We were drowning in liquor for maybe two weeks. Then the son of the club's owner got married, and we just carried on.

Little did I know this would be the last time I toasted a hockey triumph with alcohol.

21

Free Fall

IN THE EARLY '90s, when I first went to Bruneck, one of the main lessons the locals taught me was that the real Italy begins south of Lake Garda. It's easy to tell. In South Tyrol, if you order a glass of wine with your lunch, they bring you a small one. In the south, you get a large carafe.

On my first visit to Milan, my eyes popped out of my head when the waiter brought me about a liter of red wine. But I soon got used to it. Everyone drank wine with their meals. Even players. No one thought it strange. "It's good for the digestion," I was told.

I was happy to adapt. I'd learned to drink wine in Canada: Canadian beers are so fizzy, it's difficult to drink one after another. In Italy, for years I drank from bottles from the very best vineyards. It would have been a sin not to try them. When we went for pizza after a game, fans would compete for the right to buy us a drink, especially if we'd won.

I liked drinking wine, and I drank a lot of it. Sometimes I couldn't remember how I'd made it home from the pizzeria. This is how my free fall started.

After winning the title with Merano, I returned to the Czech Republic. Alone. Things hadn't worked out with my wife, and we'd gone our separate ways—she was in Germany, I was in Italy and Ostrava. Which freed me up to go from one party to the next. Every day that summer, I found a cause for celebration. And with each passing day, I felt worse and worse. I was losing control of myself.

Ales Pavlik, my friend and former charge at Havirov, took one look at me before telling me to visit to his bride-to-be. She was studying to be a doctor, and her mother was the senior consultant at a hospital department of internal medicine. I didn't want to go at all, but I allowed myself to be persuaded.

The results of my examination were terrible. The doctor discovered I had severe renal impairment. I should stop drinking alcohol immediately and undergo a course of treatment. There was little room for doubt in this prognosis, but I didn't take the warning seriously. I knew what I could manage, didn't I?

But I was too far down the road. I was vain enough to consider myself immortal—so I could do as I chose. Instead of taking care of my health, I continued along that road at the same speed.

My condition got worse after I returned to Merano. As my skin turned yellower, I started to feel really, really bad. After a friendly game before the start of the season, we went out for pizza as usual. I barely touched my food and had only a little wine to drink. I was feeling terrible again. I was heading into the unknown, I realized.

The date was September 10. I'm in no doubt about that. Because when I got home, I wrote this on a piece of paper: SEPT 10 1999 NO MORE DRINKING.

But it was too late. My decline could no longer be arrested simply by abstinence and a change in lifestyle.

Neither my liver nor my bowels were working properly. Whatever I ate or drank, the result was the same: diarrhea, cramps, vomiting and a bleeding stomach. Then my kidneys went on strike, and my body started to swell. My legs were like tree trunks—I couldn't even force my feet into my skates. Whenever I moved, I could feel the water sloshing about inside me. It was like shaking a plastic beverage bottle.

After practice one day, I was approached by manager Giulio Pallaver. He told me I looked so dreadful that I should go to the doctor's office immediately. Then club president Hansjorg Brunner got involved by sending me to the office of a doctor friend of his. As soon as this doctor saw me, he called for an ambulance.

I was shocked. What was going on? Why the sudden panic?

The ambulance took me to the hospital in Merano, where my condition was stabilized. I lay there for five days, taking pills to drain my body. The pills didn't work for me very well. The first two nights were the worst. I was going cold turkey, and I could neither sleep nor eat. All I did was lie there and wait for what would come next.

As he was discharging me, the doctor told me there was no more help he could give me, and that I would have to go to a clinic in Innsbruck. "But I'm afraid your liver is so badly damaged, it's very unlikely it'll be saved," he said.

That was my next dose of shock therapy. Only then did I fully realize how serious the situation was. It was a matter of life and death.

But I didn't fall into depression. I'm not in the habit of feeling sorry for myself. I knew I was simply paying the price for how I'd lived to this point. I would just have to accept it and hope for a happy ending.

Back at the stadium, I went to see Frantisek Kalivoda, who oversaw the HC Merano juniors. I asked him to take over the first team until I was fit to return. Then I set off for Innsbruck.

The first thing they did at the clinic was drain the surplus fluid from my body. At this point, I weighed almost a hundred kilos, 220-odd pounds. They fitted me with a tube that fed into a 10-liter barrel next to my bed. I filled this barrel almost three times over. Suddenly, my weight had dropped to 72 kilos. Now I was nothing but skin and bone.

The doctor pulled no punches with me. "A transplant is our only hope," he declared, before handing me some pills. "These will last you three months," he said. "You must hope that we find you a donor in the meantime. But even a donor is no guarantee that we'll save you. I'd put your chances of survival at about 20 percent."

This news hit me hard. After someone tells you that not only are you very sick but there's a strong likelihood you won't even be here in a few months' time, the drive home is a tough one. Before I was discharged, they took me down to the basement to photograph me. They also do this before a transplant—and after, if the patient survives it.

The drive to Merano was very difficult. Not just because I was thinking hard about what was ahead of me. Because of all the fluid I'd lost, I got terrible cramps. I had to stop a few times because I couldn't grip the steering wheel. The cramps were so strong that the memory of them still lurks in the back of my mind. Whenever I feel a twitch in my calf at night, for instance, I remember the horror and panic of that time as if it were yesterday.

Over the next few weeks, on top of the cramps, I had problems with my blood. It was so thin that it wouldn't clot. One scratch from a fingernail would cause a flow of blood I couldn't stop. Once, I had to call Karel Metelka for help. Before he drove me to the hospital, he packed so many towels and sheets around me that I looked like a citizen of ancient Rome. At the hospital, my tiny wound received two stitches. Then I was sent home.

The wait for a donor was stressful. I had to carry my cellphone always, even when I was on the bench or directing practice on the ice. Every time I got a call from an unknown number, I started shaking. But still the call from the clinic in Innsbruck didn't come. And my pills were running out. October came and went, then November. Still nothing. By the time December arrived, I was feeling terribly anxious and insecure.

What kept me going were the times I spent with my son. My wife would sometimes bring him from Konigsbrunn to see me. Hockey was good for me, too—it kept my mind busy and drove out grim thoughts. I drew up my game plans and prepared my training drills well in advance, to keep me from sitting at home, staring helplessly at the wall. I enjoyed every game and every practice because I knew each could be my last.

The players were amazing. Since we won the title, the squad had changed quite a lot, mainly because the Italian league had decided to reduce the number of foreign players from 12 to two. But the vital core remained. Everyone knew about my situation. The guys worked even harder than before, and no one ever sounded off in practice. I sensed that the extra effort was for my sake. The two summer arrivals from Canada looked on without understanding what was going on.

I spent Christmas with my wife and Mike. As soon as I returned to Merano, the period of uncertainty ended. I received the message I'd spent three months waiting for. I set off for Innsbruck, for my second birth.

———

I spent the first days of the new millennium in the intensive care unit, wired up to beeping machines. I could see great shows of fireworks beyond the window. I was transferred to the ward a week after my surgery. It was like an automobile repair shop in there. Every patient was learning to live with a new body part. Mine was a liver; others had a new heart or a new kidney.

For the first two weeks, no one was allowed to approach me without a face mask. The only person from outside let in to see me was my wife. Apart from the club president, who paid me a short visit thanks to his connections with the senior consultant. He delivered some gifts for me from the players—a jersey with all their signatures and (as a joke) a little yellow toy figure, because that was how I'd looked before I started my treatment.

As I lay in my hospital bed, I had plenty of time to think. I knew my new life would be very different from the old. I was determined not to let the second chance I'd been granted slip through my fingers. I went through my address book very thoroughly, sorting the true friends from the fair-weather ones. I have lots of friends still, but now I know I can count my true friends on the fingers of one hand.

I was discharged from the hospital three weeks after the transplant. I still tell myself this was a miracle. Professor Margreiter and his team of doctors did excellent work, and I will always be grateful to them for saving my life. And I thank my lucky stars for the incredible advances modern medicine has made. Who knows whether I would have survived this a few years earlier.

Before I left the hospital, I was asked if I wanted to know the name of my donor. I was emphatic in saying no. I know my life was saved by another, but I said no and that was an end to it.

It's difficult to explain this refusal to anyone who hasn't been through something similar. But the moment the hospital gates closed behind me, I began my new life. From zero; from the starting line. I didn't want to look back. I didn't want to think about the fact that I had an organ from a dead person in my body, and that it was the reason I was alive.

This was something else I'd learned in Canada. Not to fret about what has been; not to waste time thinking about things I can't change. I remember a game against the St. Louis Blues when I'd given up the puck to Joe Mullen, who then scored the goal that beat us. A bad situation, I'm sure you'll agree. But what was the point in going over it again and again? I couldn't take back what I'd done. And there would be another game tomorrow. There's nothing older than yesterday's game. Or yesterday's anything.

Perhaps this attitude, too, explains why I survived my health problems.

My homecoming in Merano was a moving occasion. The players had a cake ready for me, and the dressing room was filled with balloons. I got a hug from everyone. Many of us were close to tears, I think. Me more than anyone, especially when I found out how the boys had spent the night of my operation. After their game against Varese, they had stayed on at the stadium, where families who knew me came to join them. They kept calling the hospital and tearfully praying for my life to be spared. My knowledge of this gave me goosebumps.

Before long, though, the teasing began. I would need to pay a fine for missing 20 practices, the boys claimed. Soon it was the same old dressing room, with the jokes bouncing off the walls. But on the ice, everyone was attentive to and careful with me. They could see how much weaker I was. If I stumbled on a groove, three kids would skate over to check that I was all right.

A month after my transplant, I was back on the bench. Another minor miracle, another moment of high emotion. We beat our rivals

Bolzano in the game. This time, though, the result was the last thing on my mind.

Yes, I was definitely back.

———

"It won't hurt you to have the occasional small glass of red wine or beer," the doctors told me before I left the clinic in Innsbruck.

I haven't had either yet. And I never will, I'm absolutely sure of that. I had a different liver, but my brain was the same. I really did have my last taste of alcohol on September 10, 1999—and I've kept the piece of paper with my pledge on it.

When my mother and mother-in-law are doing their Christmas baking, they make special rum balls for me with no rum in them. Even the smell of alcohol bothers me. I won't put anything in my mouth that has that smell. To be on the safe side.

My drinking days are behind me, and I don't miss them at all. But this doesn't mean I have no social life. I enjoy spending time with friends. At a dance, for instance, I can have fun till the early hours, then drive everyone home. By four in the morning, the mineral water and coffee will be coming out of my ears, but I don't mind. I've replaced alcohol with a new addiction. My metabolism has changed completely, and now I can't get enough of sweet things. I can eat any amount of these at any time of day, yet I never put on weight. In the past, to pile on the pounds I just needed to look at food. These days, I have no problem maintaining my weight of 82 kilos (180 pounds).

Some people who have had a drinking problem are embarrassed to talk about it. I talk of mine without shame. If what I have to say puts just one person off drinking, it will have been worth it. I talk about alcohol with children, my friends and the players in the dressing room. When someone I know appears to be heading for a problem, I warn him. "Give it a rest," I'll say. "You're your own worst enemy."

I want others to realize how easy it is to find yourself on that slippery slope. Not every story ends as happily as mine. And as the doctors told me, I was anything but a typical alcoholic. Although I had a problem with alcohol, I wasn't addicted to it. There was no risk of my drinking us out of house and home and ending up on the street or in rehab. Otherwise I was in control. I turned up at practice and for games on time; I wasn't ruining my life. Yes, I filled cola bottles with red wine, which I would sip at break times, but that was all. I would drink myself silly only after games, at the pizzeria. Plus, part of my condition was a congenital liver defect, which my lifestyle made so much worse that a transplant became unavoidable.

Since the transplant, my instinct for self-preservation has served me well. There were six of us with a new liver on that ward in Innsbruck. The other five all became jaundiced again. I asked my doctor how it was that I was the exception. "When we take your blood, it's absolutely clean. Theirs isn't," he explained. "They've have a deciliter of wine, and another. They get to thinking they can manage four, or even six. Before long, they've fallen back into it. Sad to say, they've blown their second chance, and the Man Upstairs won't give them a third."

I've been living in my own personal overtime for more than 18 years. I know the end can come at any time. I'm reconciled to the fact that I won't live to see 80, like a normal, healthy guy. At least I don't think I will. Although I've always been an optimistic realist, my doctors have told me from the start that the pills that help my transplanted liver will harm my other organs. My kidneys, for instance, have been troubling me for the past year or so …

About two thirds of patients survive 15 years with a new liver. After that, with each passing year the survival rate gradually decreases. I'm becoming something of a rarity. When I go to the center of transplant surgery in Brno for a checkup, the nurse will say to me with a smile, "You're quite the veteran, aren't you? There's no need for me to tell you how things work here."

It's easy to forget how long it's been. These have been beautiful years. Not least because I've succeeded in feeling grateful for every new day, for every new hour.

22

Returns

I SAID GOODBYE TO MERANO in spring 2001, having coached the team for two seasons after my transplant. We didn't succeed in capturing the title again. Both times we fell in the quarterfinals in the deciding fifth game, to HC Alleghe and WSV Sterzing Broncos, respectively. We were especially disappointed the first time, as we'd gone into the series as favorites.

I left the club on good terms. As we shook hands, I thanked the club management for everything they had done for me. I will never forget my time in Merano.

But I'd stayed there more than long enough. In my opinion, a coach shouldn't lead the same team for longer than three or four years. The novelty wears off, and after a while there's nothing he can do to surprise the team, and this is usually reflected in the results. There are exceptions, like Lindy Ruff of the Buffalo Sabres, but there are very few of them.

I didn't leave Italy straightaway—the next season, I coached SV Ritten—but the time had come for me to take a step forward. This step would take me to the DEL, Germany's premier hockey league. I was also attracted to Germany for family reasons. After my surgery, my wife and I tried to rebuild our marriage, not least for Mike's sake. We discovered we were able to live alongside each other, albeit no longer together. I abandoned thoughts of a return to Canada, wanting to be as close as possible to my son.

I received an offer to become coach and sports manager of the Schwenninger Wild Wings. A great opportunity, it seemed. A few years earlier, I would have accepted it eagerly, but now I took my time before eventually turning it down. The DEL had suddenly lost its attraction for me. I realized that Mike needed me more. He was nine now, and I didn't want to pass up the chance to spend more time with him. If I'd jumped back onto the hockey merry-go-round, I would have seen little of the boy. The only practices I was interested in now concerned him. He played soccer and was good at it. As a good dad should, I wanted to drive him from school to the playing field, and to cheer him on during games. This was the most important thing to me now.

I decided to take a break from coaching. This break would stretch on for four years.

Not long after I made this decision, I was approached by Daniel Lammel, a native Czech whom I'd known since I played for Freiburg. He was setting up a players' agency and wanted me as his partner. *Why not?* I thought. It would mean sticking with hockey, but in a different, less demanding role.

The company, which was registered in Germany, represented players from that country, Austria, Switzerland and Italy. For me, this was an interesting new world. But before I could fully immerse myself in the business, something happened to change my plans. In 2003, Dad died. I couldn't leave my mother on her own: I went back to Ostrava.

HC Vitkovice gave me work as a scout. I traveled to the occasional game to watch players tapped by the general manager as possible reinforcements. This alone probably wouldn't have been enough for me, so I decided to run my own agency in the Czech Republic. I had confidence in my ability to help players and pass on my experience to them. Unlike other agents, I knew professional hockey from the inside, not just from the stands. There had been many critical moments in my career, I knew what it was like to start out abroad at a young age, and I had contacts in Europe and overseas.

I attracted a fair amount of interest. The boys who got in touch with me either had no agent or one who didn't bother with them much. They included Zbynek Irgl, Petr Hubacek and Bedrich Kohler.

"There's a new nuisance on our patch," claimed Jaromir Henys, one of Czech hockey's most influential agents and the right-hand man of Ritch Winter from Edmonton, shortly after my return to the Czech game.

It's true that I tried to do things differently, in my own way. Money wasn't as important to me as it was to some others. I'm not a workaholic, and I didn't want to have more clients than anyone else. But I wanted to care for the clients I did have to the best of my abilities—regardless of whether they were 30 or at the beginning of their careers, like my later clients Ondrej Palat and Petr Mrazek. I bought sticks, skates and gloves for all my young players, and I negotiated the best contracts for them. I made it clear to them from the beginning that if they weren't satisfied with my services, I would make no fuss about ending our relationship. "If you think someone else could take better care of you, go to him," I would tell all my boys. "We can dissolve our contract without argument. No need for the courts to get involved."

I enjoyed working as an agent. I loved the feeling of helping someone make his hockey-playing dreams come true, or improve his conditions at the very least. It didn't take me long to realize how corrupt the business was. It was a hive of intrigue, envy and low blows. I was amazed by how many crooks there were. For the sake of their commission, some were willing to promise young players and their families the moon.

When I was an agent, I didn't make many friends in the hockey world.

One of my biggest conflicts flared up in November 2005. It was with Milos Holan Jr., who had played for the Philadelphia Flyers and the Mighty Ducks of Anaheim and was now the assistant coach at Vitkovice responsible for defense. He took a strange approach. Although he was just starting out as a coach, he behaved like an arrogant know-it-all. So be it—his behavior wasn't my concern. But it was my concern when he arranged for young Michal Gulasi, whom I represented, to be dropped from the lineup.

The problem had nothing to do with hockey. Michal happened to be a friend of forward Patrik Valcak, who was living with Holan's ex-wife. I represented Valcak, too. On one occasion, Holan had a go at me. He wanted to know how I could be the agent of his enemy. Anyway, Michal didn't make the lineup after Holan saw my two clients together at the stadium. Yet in the summer, Vitkovice had recalled Michal from the Lethbridge Hurricanes in the WHL, insisting they were keen on him and would give him a chance. Now he was sitting in the stands because of a problem in his coach's private life. The war of words between Holan and me in front of the dressing room was widely reported in the press.

The following summer, Holan was promoted to head coach. It didn't go well. After a run of only 39 goals in 21 games, the team was one place from the bottom of the standing. In November 2006, I was offered the chance to take Holan's place. I was glad to accept.

On the very day I signed the contract, I handed the agency over to my partners. I had flicked a switch and become a coach again. But the transition didn't go smoothly. Because of my past as an agent, I was attacked from all sides. Not just for a week or two, but for the whole time I oversaw the Vitkovice team. The problem was that the roster included plenty of my players, and there was talk of a conflict of interest. My loudest critic was Jaroslav Holik, 1972 world champion and later a successful coach of the national junior side. This made me laugh—Holik's son-in-law Frank Musil combined jobs as a scout for the Edmonton Oilers and an assistant with the national team, something Holik failed to mention.

I made even more of a stir when I replaced some injured players with kids from the youth team. One of them happened to be 16-year-old Adam Sedlak, son of my current wife, Lenka. The press wrote in ironic tones of "Frycer's nursery," nepotism, the high profile kept by my clients before the NHL draft, and other such nonsense. I was well aware of which way the wind was blowing, just as I knew the identities of those unnamed agents quoted in articles critical of team selection at Vitkovice. After a few years in Czech hockey, none of this came as any surprise to me.

My critics must have believed I was born yesterday. I hadn't gone back into coaching as a sideline, and our results really mattered to me.

If I'd believed the kids weren't up to it, I would never have put them on the first team—I'd have harmed myself as well as wrecking their careers! But they played well, making few mistakes and conceding very few goals. And anyway, a few games later, once the injured players had recovered, the youngsters returned to the youth team.

The most ridiculous aspect of this tempest in a teacup resided in the fact that hockey experts had been moaning for years about how youngsters weren't being given a chance in the Extraliga, resulting in their flight to Canada. I was giving them this chance (by force of circumstance, admittedly), and I was being lambasted for it. It wasn't as if I was the first coach to try such a thing! Far from it. I'd broken into the Vitkovice first team aged 16 myself. The later, golden generation of Dominik Hasek, Jaromir Jagr, Robert Reichel, Pavel Kubina, Petr Sykora, David Vyborny and Milan Hejduk had started out among professional stars at the same age.

Fortunately, squabbles in the media don't last long. What happened on the ice was far more interesting. The team was gaining in self-confidence and momentum. I believe our hockey was a pleasure to watch. We moved up to 10th place, missing out on the playoffs by just one point. In our last home game, we beat Slavia Prague, a feat Vitkovice hadn't managed in six years. We were nipped at the line by Znojmo, who had gotten the win they needed at Karlovy Vary. A pity. If we hadn't stumbled a few times after starting a game well, the season might have ended all smiles.

We didn't get off to a good start the next season. Zbynek Irgl had moved to Russia in the summer, and his 25 goals were proving hard to replace. Viktor Ujcik, who had come from Karpat Oulu in Finland, was tasked with getting them, but for a long time he struggled to score. I sympathized with him. Every forward goes through spells like this, as I know better than anyone. When the press began to complain that our expensive new signing wasn't working out, I told him to keep his cool and not overthink what he was doing on the ice. The goals would come. His run of bad luck finally ended in the ninth game, when he converted a penalty shot against Karlovy Vary.

After his struggles in the first quarter of the season, Viktor's performance began to improve and his self-confidence to rise. Unfortunately, I came to bear the brunt of this. Suddenly, he was coming up with all kinds of ideas and tips about how I should lead the team. My tactical preparation should be more thorough, he claimed, and he would like me to use video analysis, which he was used to.

I have no problem with someone presenting an opinion that differs from mine. If he can convince me his view is better, I can reappraise my own. But Ujcik didn't succeed in doing this. His main argument was that they did things differently in Finland … He became ever more demanding, and he really began to get on my nerves. I appreciate what he did for Czech hockey—a three-time world champion, he was a shooter par excellence—but at Vitkovice he overplayed his hand. Not only did he interfere with my work, he failed to keep his opinions to himself. Willing listeners can always be found. In this instance, coaches who thought that they, not I, should have replaced Milos Holan a year earlier.

Our results failed to improve. Before long, there was a strange atmosphere around the club. Even the fans turned against me. Maybe I'm not an ideal coach for this time in this country. I'm interested in the game and the result; I'm interested in my team. Unlike some others, I don't know how to deal with stuff that goes on around me. I'm not a savvy media operator who presents himself in his best light in public, nor do I enjoy a chat with sponsors with the purpose of consolidating my position. I don't know how to sell myself, and I have no interest in personal PR. I'm a straightforward kind of guy. And in this country, straightforwardness can work against you. In this regard, I'll never change. Nor would I wish to.

Also, I'm not used to doing things I don't enjoy. Life's too short for that. That November, I reached the conclusion that I wasn't enjoying my work at Vitkovice. I didn't want to lose time and energy arguing with Ujcik or listening to slurs on my name from within the club; I considered myself above all that. I decided to quit. Besides, I'd received an offer from SG Cortina, and a return to Italy seemed the ideal solution.

I informed the club management and the three players to whom I was closest that in one week I'd be leaving for a country where I'd be happy. We lost my final game, against Kladno, 4-3. I would have left even if we'd put 10 past them.

Two days later, I appeared on the bench in Cortina. On leaving Vitkovice, I'd made a resolution never to return to the Czech Extraliga. So far, I've had no trouble keeping it.

———

Mike played a big part in my other plans for 2008. Now 15, he could decide which of his parents he wanted to live with. Because soccer coach Verner Licka had told him he'd like him to play for the FC Banik juniors, he chose me. When he started attending a sports school in Ostrava, I was free to return to Italy.

But no matter where I live and work, I continue to visit Toronto once in a while. I have lots of friends there, and I'm attached to the city by many beautiful memories. I've never lost touch with the club and my former teammates. I'm a proud member of the Toronto Maple Leafs Alumni Association. Once, I was even honored by an invitation to drop the puck at a game against the Canadiens commemorating play-ers of the 1980s. But the day before this game, I was offered a three-year contract by SHC Fassa; if I accepted, I would have to fly to Italy immediately. It wasn't much of a dilemma. Which would I prefer, five minutes of fame at the Air Canada Centre or three years under an azure sky in the Dolomites?

I opted for the latter and headed straight for the airport.

They were three beautiful seasons. In the last, however, we failed to reach the playoffs, and the club's direction, leadership and finances were all up in the air. Fortunately for me, I received an offer from

Merano as soon as the season ended. A nostalgic return to old stomping grounds was very appealing; I was happy to accept.

But this comeback didn't last long either. A lot had changed in Merano in 11 years. The club had been relegated to Serie B and joined the Inter-National League, a competition for second-tier teams from Italy, Austria and Slovenia. Unfortunately, after a month, management realized the financial demands of such a demanding season were too great. The team was poorly provided for on its travels; conditions were very amateurish. What's more, the INL didn't draw the fans—we found ourselves playing to near-empty stands. I wasn't enjoying myself. I had no desire to keep coaching there, not least as I was working for nothing. In November, I decided to leave.

Again, I wondered what to do next. The first offer I received was from KH Sanok in Poland. I didn't accept it. I didn't think much of Polish hockey, nor was I attracted by the idea of moving east. I decided to wait for something to turn up in Italy. Till then, I'd take a break.

But the Poles wouldn't take no for an answer. I turned them down again. They called me a third time in January 2014.

They were obviously so keen to have me that my wife and I decided to give it a try. I had nothing to lose. I sat down at my computer and googled Sanok—I had no idea where it was. According to the map, it was a town close to the Ukrainian border, about four hours' drive from Ostrava.

I don't regret taking the job. It was a great experience.

I was surprised by the level of Polish hockey. It was better than I'd expected. Poles are tenacious and really put their hearts into the play. In addition, I had six good Czech players on my team. Toward the end of the season, I recruited a few Canadians, something new for Poland.

One of these was Mike Danton, a guy with more than a few demons. While his NHL career with the St. Louis Blues was in full swing, he attempted to hire a hitman to kill his agent, who, he believed, was prepared to tell Blues management about his problems with alcohol and drugs. Although the plan wasn't carried out, Danton ended up spending five and half years in jail. After his release, he roamed the world—before arriving in Sanok, he played in Australia, Sweden, Znojmo in the Czech Republic, Slovakia, Kazakhstan and Hungary. He was a pretty good player. He knew how to wind up an opponent, provoking and then withdrawing so that the opponent picked up the penalty. A player like that sometimes comes in handy.

We finished the regular season in second place, going through to the playoffs. Sanok went so crazy, reminding me of Vitkovice's Kotas Arena. People stood in line for tickets from early morning. In the evening, we were cheered on by a full stadium. Full buses of our fans traveled to away games. League hockey was a big deal to them; apart from volleyball in Rzeszow, there was no other top-level sport in the region.

In the final, we came up against GKS Tychy, the favorites. They were coached by Jiri Sejba, who scored a hat trick for Czechoslovakia in the 1985 world championship final against a Canadian team containing a young Mario Lemieux, Ron Francis and Steve Yzerman. We won the final series 4-2. The title was ours. A job well done. I was as euphoric as I had been 15 years earlier in Merano. This was confirmation that my coaching style still worked.

In the summer, the club offered to extend my contract. But I chose not to go back. It's best to end on a high. It had been a great four months topped off with a title win, but I wanted to try something else.

In the next season, Sanok stumbled from one defeat to the next. My former boss called to explain that the club needed me and the Czech and Polish players had been asking for me. He persuaded me to go back. I wish he hadn't.

Many things had changed. The title win had served to convince Mike Danton that he should be running the show. He demanded the captaincy and the right to be involved in every power play, plus he was urging management to appoint a Canadian coach. On learning that I would be returning, he was pretty annoyed: he knew that I would give his suggestions short shrift. He went out of his way to make trouble for me. The unrest in the dressing room was apparent on the ice.

Then, in midseason, the manager brought in Zenon Konopka, another Canadian. Konopka had played 346 games for seven different clubs in the NHL, and he was a well-known goon. But as a hockey player, he wasn't even good enough for the Polish league. All he was interested in was booze. The first time he appeared at practice, the others were incredulous. "Where did you find *him*?" forward Martin Vozdecky asked me. "In a league for trade unionists?"

Because Konopka's father was a Pole, club management considered his signing a marketing coup, and it was important that he should play. He admitted to me later that his career was over because of back pain—Sanok had persuaded him to come out of retirement. Not for free, of course. "I can't even bend properly for the face-off," he complained.

Three or four times I considered packing it in and going home. What was the point? But the Czech boys persuaded me to stay. In the end, it was mainly for them that I did. Had I left, they would have gotten a Canadian coach to make the rest of the season hell for them.

Even so, we made it to the semifinals, where Tychy was waiting for us. They had learned from our encounter of the previous year and were leaving nothing to chance. They had so much money, they would go through regardless of their performance. We went up 2-0 in the series. But they had the officials on their side, which proved our undoing.

I'm not in the habit of complaining about officials or yelling at them during games, as certain other coaches do. It changes nothing, helps no one, and messes with the mind. I do my best to keep my players calm, so that questionable decisions don't unsettle them. But this was too much even for me. We had two weekend games in Tychy, and we were up against it from the first. We were shorthanded for eight of the opening 11 minutes. It was worse still on the Sunday. The fact that the game was broadcast on national television made no difference to the officials. We were given one penalty after another. I had more players in the box than next to me on the bench.

When we were down 4-0, I found I could take no more of it. I've been in hockey long enough to recognize when the officials are simply having a bad day at the office. That wasn't the case here. These guys were definitely out to get us.

After two more of our guys were dismissed, I blew a gasket. I pulled our goaltender, John Murray, from the ice for an extra attacker. The goalie was confused. Was I kidding? I assured him that I knew what I was doing. It took him a while to catch on. Other players came over to join him. For the whole time that we played as a four without a goaltender against a five with a goaltender, our nonactive players banged their sticks against the boards. It was hilarious—not least as it took Tychy about two and a half minutes to get an empty-net goal.

I intended to provoke, of course. I wanted the authorities to realize what was going on in this playoff series.

The excitement of the game spilled over into the press conference. Again unable to keep myself in check, I gave my Polish an airing. "The officials are a bunch of clowns and idiots," I declared, getting myself disciplined for my trouble.

The club leadership reckoned I would be given a one-game ban. How wrong they were! I was hit with a six-month suspension and a fine of 8,000 zloty. The six months were on paper only: it was March, and the new season began in September. But thanks to my punishment, my playoffs were over. As was my time at Sanok.

I was still around for the next game, though. I stood some distance from the bench, sending instructions to the players through the trainer. But I didn't bother turning up for the sixth game, in Tychy. There was no point. Not even the Pittsburgh Penguins could come away from Tychy with a win.

When I started out as a coach 24 years ago, it was never my dream to make it big by leading a national team or establishing myself in the NHL. I don't have the right character for it. I'm no diplomat, nor am I sharp-elbowed. I'm not sorry for this. I found what I was looking for elsewhere. I enjoy coaching in countries like Italy, Poland and France.

I realize that many people look down their noses at jobs like this. There's no doubt these leagues can't match the Czech Extraliga for quality, but that doesn't mean it's any easier to win a title in Italy or Poland. Far from it. It's every bit as difficult, but you must go about it by different means—especially if you're coaching at a club that isn't one of the richest.

In many respects, coaching in Czechia is a comfortable job. The facilities are great, and you've got a well-stocked roster. If a few players get injured or go into a slump, you can bring others in from the juniors or the farm team. Coaching abroad uses more adrenaline. In Italy, once I turned up for practice to find that four of my players were missing. One was looking after his kids while his wife was at the gym, another had taken his dog to the vet, and the other two hadn't made it back from the ski slopes because of a broken cable car. When this happened, my preparations went out the window. On the spot, I had to come up with training exercises of the right import and intensity, regardless of the fact that I was missing four key players. Such work makes far greater demands on your skills of improvisation and feel for good coaching. But therein lies its magic for me.

On the other hand, the coach isn't under as much pressure as his counterparts in countries where hockey is part of the culture. Coaches are rarely fired for losing five games in a row. In Italy, unless you behave like a halfwit, you can expect to keep your job till the end of the season, even if your results are poor.

In a land where soccer, basketball and volleyball are hugely popular, hockey is like the baby brother. It appeals more to frequenters of ski resorts than to big business. It is played in small arenas, to 2,000 to 3,000 spectators. But homegrown players really value the chance to play in the league. Most of them have jobs or run their own businesses; their hockey must be fitted around their other commitments.

Italians may be limited in terms of talent, but I love the way they approach the sport. I've never come across anyone slacking or scowling because he isn't enjoying practice. I never have to yell at anyone. But they yell at each other, to work harder. It's great to work in such an environment. And how good it feels to watch them improve, knowing I'm giving them something! I won't turn them into NHL players—or even internationals in most cases—but if I can help them move a few rungs up the ladder, that's enough for me.

Most teams have one good group of five, with the rest of the team made up of with weaker players. This, too, offers a challenge to the coach. He must be able to improvise during the game to ensure that his every lineup is as well balanced and competitive as possible—modest circumstances permitting. Back in the dressing room, there's no big whiteboard and video technology; the coach doesn't have three assistants to call on.

Nearly all teams contain foreign players—in most cases, Canadians. I've had to learn to work with them. The humbler ones rarely grumble; all they want to know is which net to shoot at. Others have more complicated egos. I realize it wasn't their childhood dream to represent SHC Fassa or HC Merano. But I tell them to give their all in every game, as every good performance has the power to take them higher. If they do well in Italy, maybe they will attract interest from Switzerland or Germany. If they make a name for themselves, they will earn more money. And they may continue to move up the ladder.

Many of these players didn't even reach the farm teams in their homelands. Rather than toiling away in the ECHL for $500 a week, they prefer to move to Italy, Hungary or Austria, where their starting salary is 3,000 euros a month. On top of that, however, they usually get free accommodations, a car to drive, and the chance to live in a beautiful European setting. "How lucky you are to be playing here!" I tell them often. "People pay crazy money for a vacation in the Dolomites. The club pays *you* for living here for eight months and playing two games a week."

By coming to Europe to play hockey, these men can set themselves up for life. They can gather contacts and experience for later use in a business, coaching or management career. Plus, they get to know a different part of the world, which is never a bad thing. And they learn fast. Given a few days off in Italy, the boys on my team would hop over to Venice, Rome or Florence. Or they would get on a plane and fly off to Prague or Berlin. The season over, their parents would visit from Canada, and they would tour Europe together.

This world of hockey is a special one. I've enjoyed traveling around it since 1996, when I started out as a coach at Bruneck. Some of my gigs have been brilliant, others not so much. But all of them have given me a great deal, as a coach and otherwise.

I wouldn't mind going back to try for a third title. That would give me my coaching hat trick.

23

Hockey for Life

TORONTO PEARSON INTERNATIONAL AIRPORT, summer 2013. Before boarding the plane, I must go through a security check. At last, I reach the front of the line. Before I can even take my papers from my pocket, the uniformed guy of about 50 uses my name. "Let me tell you something, Mr. Frycer," he says. "If you'd put a little more into your game, with your talent, you could have scored 50 goals a season. But you were fun to watch. You gave us some great memories."

I answer him with a smile. Lenka, who is standing next to me, shakes her head in amazement.

It's a paradoxical truth about me that I'm better known in Canada than at home. I may have left the Maple Leafs 30 years ago, but people still remember me. I don't exactly get mobbed when I walk along Yonge Street, but if I chose to open a hockey school in Toronto, there would be no shortage of interest. If I'm visiting any ice rink in the Toronto area, people always stop me to tell me about how much they enjoyed watching me play. I often get photographed with someone's grandson. The little boy has no idea who the man standing next to him is, but it makes Grandpa happy. Not long ago, a package from Canada arrived at my mother's place in Ostrava. Inside was a child's-size blue and white jersey with the number 14 and the name FRYCER on the back. There was also a touching letter from a fan, asking me to sign the jersey for his newborn son.

As I was telling you, the Maple Leafs have the best fans in the world.

In hockey, it's great to win trophies and individual awards. I respect every winner of the Stanley Cup, even if he was just a slogger on the fourth line. The closest I ever got to it was by walking past the Hall of Fame. In 1980s Toronto, this was the best we could do. Trophies are evidence of success in particular seasons. But people's respect and admiration years after the event please me more than any award would. They remind me that I made my mark in the NHL. I had great fun playing hockey, and I succeeded in entertaining others. Their appreciation means a lot to me.

But the security guy was wrong about one thing. I wasn't the kind of player with the potential to score 50 NHL goals a season, even though with five hat tricks in my first season I may have given people this impression. I wasn't a sniper who shot at the net from any position. I enjoyed my time with the puck.

But on one thing, the security guy and I agree: I could have achieved more. My career could have burned brighter and lasted longer; like Mike Gartner, I could have scored over 30 goals every year. I didn't use up every drop of my talent. One reason for this was my approach, another my bad luck with injuries. Dad used to say that an athlete's career was one great mosaic, in which all the pieces should fit together perfectly. In my case, a few of these pieces didn't quite fit right, while others were missing altogether. The final picture isn't as complete as it might have been.

I'm proud of my career nonetheless. I think of that little kid swiping at a tennis ball with a hockey stick in a Karvina street and how he went on to play in the Olympics and the All-Star Game and amass 330 points in the NHL, and I'd say he did well.

I made my dreams come true, and that's the best thing that can happen to anyone. I was honored to play with and against legends of Czechoslovak and world hockey. I played in the NHL in what may be the most interesting decade in its history. I have no cause for complaint. Masses of Canadian boys long to play for the Toronto Maple Leafs, if only for one game. I spent six years with them—and what's more, they paid me for the privilege. I remain the 44th most productive player in the history of the club, a true badge of honor.

Yet in my homeland, hardly anyone knows my story. Under the communist regime in Czechoslovakia, no one who didn't listen to Voice of America radio and Radio Free Europe would have heard of the successes and hiccups of my career. By the time the Iron Curtain came down, in 1989, and athletes who had defected could be mentioned in the press, I was playing in the German league, which was of little interest. Fortunately, I'm not the kind of guy who is troubled by such things.

The decision to flee to Canada is the best I've ever made. I haven't regretted it for a second. It may have lost me a little fame among Czech fans, but it gained me eight years of life in freedom. I've seen quite a lot of the world. Today, I can get by in five languages, and I've got friends and acquaintances all over the planet.

If I'd stayed at home, I would have played for Vitkovice until I was 30. After that, I may have been rewarded with a trade to EV Landshut. Maybe I'd have played alongside my former U20 teammates on the Czechoslovakian team that won the world championship in 1985. But I wouldn't have traveled all over Canada and the United States; I wouldn't have gotten to know Steve Yzerman, Borje Salming, Mark Messier and Jacques Demers; I wouldn't have played against Wayne Gretzky and Guy Lafleur; and I wouldn't have had all those great times in the company of Harold Ballard.

I didn't win many trophies in my career, and I no longer have much of the money hockey earned me. In the end, though, my memories are the main thing. Most of them are wonderful. They are stored on the hard disk of my brain; no one can take them from me. In addition to my memories, hockey has given me self-confidence, maturity and an ability to deal with the negative things that come my way. I have much to be grateful to this great game for.

All it deprived me of was time with my children. We were together less often than I would have liked. My alcoholic escapades were to blame for this, too. To my regret. There are things one can never get back …

Hockey has made its mark on my health. My body shows signs of heavy wear and tear. Long before my 60th birthday, I had to accept pain as part and parcel of my daily life. When the weather is about to change, I feel it in my hips. My right hip is ripe for replacement— I can't get around without crutches. Shoulder pain, too, is a regular thing with me: in our day, the boards were more like walls, and the Plexiglas wasn't as impact-friendly as it is today. My knees and back are just as bad. And when my fingers twitch with cramps, the sensation is far from pleasant.

It's not going to get any better. It used to be better than it is. That's a statement of fact, not a complaint. It's a tax I have to pay, something I've come to terms with. Professional sport is about more than success, glory and money. Damaged health is a full part of it. It's just that fans don't often read about it in the newspapers.

Lada Svozil, Frantisek Cernik and I sometimes meet up at the stadium. You should see us. It's a rare occasion when we don't mention the Vitkovice title in '81, because that's something exceptional that will stay with us for the rest of our lives. A few years ago, we would talk of our younger years, when women would make a play for us, or we'd tell each other stories from the Salajka bar. These days, our conversations follow a different path. Instead of hockey, we talk about ailments and weight gain.

"What are those pills of yours for?"

"High blood pressure."

"Really? My doctor's prescribed me a different sort."

"And what's in that box?"

We make a joke of it. There's no other way.

The last time I played hockey was in 2004. At that year's world championship in Ostrava, there was a veterans' game between the Czech Republic and Slovakia, and I was talked into playing in it. They wanted a reunion of the Frycer-Svozil-Cernik line. I prepared by putting in four or five training sessions with Frantisek and his pals—it was a proper game after all, albeit a fun one. I got through that game somehow, and two days later I played in an old men's game for Karvina against Vitkovice. That was as much as I could manage. I may have been the same age as Jaromir Jagr when he scored 46 points in an NHL season, but I knew I'd never don a uniform again. I've no desire to show off my old man's belly, and I must think of my health.

On returning to Ostrava from a spell coaching the French team HC Morzine-Avoriaz-Les Gets in 2016, I was convinced my career as a coach was over too. I received a few offers, but I turned them all down. I felt my story was at an end. The thought of the bench and a cold stadium no longer appealed to me.

For the next two years, I spent time with my family and watched over my health. Plus, I worked on this book, the Czech edition of which was published in September 2017.

I became an observer of the hockey scene rather than an actor in it. I stopped running an agency long ago. If one of my friends needs my help, I'm happy to give it—I'll pass on a contact, or make a call to someone I know abroad. But I no longer make a living out of it. Enough was enough.

I seldom attended a hockey game. Whenever I turned up at Vitkovice, people were forever engaging me in conversation, wanting to know my opinion on this, that or the other. I didn't enjoy this. I'd have preferred to go up into the stands and watch the game in peace, leaving my wife to cheer the boys on with the rest of them. Besides, I don't have much time for the Czech league. If I was at home at five in the afternoon, I'd sometimes fire up my laptop, but if the game turned out not to be worth watching, I'd close the device down after the first period and do something more useful.

In January 2018, I got another offer. From an old friend of mine who's the sports manager of HC Orli Znojmo (otherwise known as the Znojmo Eagles), a team from southern Moravia that plays in the EBEL, an Austrian league supplemented with one team from each of

Czechia, Italy, Croatia and Hungary. I declined the offer immediately, explaining that I was currently laid up with flu and that these days I walked with the aid of crutches. On top of that, my doctors were telling me to expect a kidney transplant in the summer—and one can never be sure how that will work out …

I declined once. Twice. A third time. But in the end, I allowed myself to be talked around. It's hard to say no to friends.

The EBEL isn't a bad league. It's strongly influenced by the Canadian model, and I know something about Canadian hockey, wouldn't you say? So, at the beginning of February, I made my way to Znojmo in a determined mood. We'd agreed that I would lead the team for the last seven games of the season; after that, if everything, including my health, was working well, we would extend our agreement by another year.

I was a little worried that things wouldn't work out. My comeback would either spark me into life or it would kill me, I told myself. Fortunately, the first proved to be the case. After 10 minutes of my first practice, I was truly back in the flow. It was like getting back behind the wheel after two years away. For the first few moments you're unsure, but then you pick up speed and go through the gears.

I'm extremely comfortable in Znojmo. We live in a lovely house with a view of Austria. I tell myself that if the communists should return to power in my homeland, I can be in Vienna in a flash. I have a disabled parking spot right next to the stadium. My assistants lead most training sessions, so I'm required to get my skates on only rarely. My pals joke that I manage everything from afar, in the manner of Scotty Bowman. I've begun to enjoy games immensely. Once I've squeezed myself onto the bench and pushed my crutches into a corner among the sticks, I'm in my element. My head is in a 200 percent better place than when I decided to take a break from hockey.

I'm in no doubt that Znojmo will be my last coaching job. This is my farewell tour—around many important places in my life. We'll play games in Zagreb, where I first picked up a hockey stick and learned to skate. We'll play in Bolzano, at the stadium where I won my first title as a coach, with HC Merano. And we'll appear in Innsbruck, where I was given a new liver and so was born again.

As soon as I feel my time as a coach is up, I'll leave the bench for good. I wouldn't wish to overstay my welcome by a single day; I would hate it if others forced me to quit. And I'll have no regrets. I can imagine my life very well without coaching. And why not indeed? I'm not dependent on hockey for my living. I'm no spendthrift, so I'll always have enough for coffee, Marlboros and a nice vacation.

When my coaching days are over, maybe my wife and I will move to the seaside. If we do, we'll be very happy there. There was a time when people prophesied that our relationship wouldn't last; certain envious types accused Lenka of being with me only because I was coaching her son. But as you see, we've been together for over 10 years and we're still very happy together. We have three grown-up children—Terezka, Adam and Mike—and we enjoy our life together.

Who knows, maybe we'll settle in our beloved Sardinia and open a small café there. As a hobby, not a business. Just a small counter with two tables out front. We'd serve coffee, prosecco and panini to passers-by. I'd love to do that. Occasionally, I'd glance at my cell to see how Vitkovice or the Maple Leafs were doing, but for the rest of the day I'd be interested in nothing but the sun, the beach and the sea.

Yes, I'm looking forward to that.

Acknowledgments

My greatest thanks go to Mr. Miroslav Frycer. In April 2016, when I approached him to ask if I could write his life story, he must have thought I was mad. Here was a person he'd never heard of telling him over coffee that he was determined to put this story together in a book he would publish himself—because he was convinced that it would interest more than two or three hundred people. Fortunately, he took my word for it. As a result, I got to know a man who talks about hockey as no one else can—objectively yet with passion, and with a special sense of humor. A man who told me without embarrassment the kind of things most people are reluctant to open their hearts about.

Whenever we met in Ostrava, as if by magic I was returned to the 1980s. I would have the feeling that I'd been present at those NHL games, and experienced first-hand what had gone on backstage. I will always treasure the memory of those several dozen hours.

But for Kvetoslav Simek, *Můj divoký hokejový život* (the original, Czech edition of *My Wild Hockey Life*) would never have come into being: the whole thing was his idea. I wish to thank outstanding graphic designer Pavla Vesela for the cover and Petr Schimon for finding flaws in the Czech manuscript.

I'm indebted to Martina Musteen and Davor Vecerin for acting as my consultants on trickier points of the English language. We sent a bunch of emails over the ocean, didn't we? I thank Barbora Kubinova for her help with Quebec French. And many other things besides.

Without Andrew Oakland, *My Wild Hockey Life* would have remained in the land of diffident dreams. Although he is used to working with leading lights of Czech literature, he had nothing against translating the work of the two of us into English. I'm also thankful to Patricia MacDonald for her diligence in the final round of editing.

I wish to thank everyone who kept their fingers crossed for us. Plus, of course, all our readers, past and future, without whom none of this would have any point.

My final words are for my parents. When I was at elementary school, Mom wrote my homework compositions, ensuring that my end-of-term report wasn't spoiled by a poor grade in Czech. Dad taught me to love sport, and I know that he would like this book. Thank you.

Lubos Brabec,
co-author and publisher

About the Authors

MIRO FRYCER is a former hockey player. Over his eight seasons in the NHL, he played for the Quebec Nordiques, Toronto Maple Leafs, Detroit Red Wings and Edmonton Oilers. He was the first Czech player to ever appear in an NHL All-Star Game and scored 147 goals and added 183 assists for 330 points in 415 career NHL regular season games. He was the highest-scoring Maple Leaf in the 1985-86 season, as the first European in the club history.

As a member of the Czechoslovak national team, Frycer won a silver medal in the world championship in 1979 and a bronze medal in 1981. He also played on the 1980 Olympic team.

He is currently the head coach of the HC Orli Znojmo in the Austrian Hockey League (EBEL). Previously, he won championships in Italy with the HC Merano (1999) and in Poland with the Ciarko PBS Bank KH Sanok (2014).

LUBOS BRABEC is a Czech sports writer. He is the author of successful books *Maraton a jiné pošetilosti* (*Marathon and Other Foolishness,* 2013) and *Můj dlouhý běh* (*My Long Run,* 2014, with ultramarathoner Daniel Oralek).

Manufactured by Amazon.ca
Bolton, ON

10507133R00157